/22

FREEDOM FROM VIOLENCE AND LIES

FREEDOM FROM VIOLENCE AND LIES

ANTON CHEKHOV'S LIFE AND WRITINGS

MICHAEL C. FINKE

REAKTION BOOKS

*To the Chekhov-scholar friends who have made studying
the life and writings of Anton Chekhov a delight*

Published by
Reaktion Books Ltd
Unit 32, Waterside
44–48 Wharf Road
London N1 7UX, UK
www.reaktionbooks.co.uk

First published 2021
Copyright © Michael C. Finke 2021

Printed and bound in Great Britain by TJ Books Ltd, Padstow, Cornwall

A catalogue record for this book is available from the British Library

ISBN 978 1 78914 430 7

CONTENTS

NOTE ON TRANSLITERATION, CITATIONS, ABBREVIATIONS AND CALENDAR

BIBLIOGRAPHIC INFORMATION in footnotes referring to Russian originals and the original Russian titles of works provided in the body of my text are transliterated per the Library of Congress method; elsewhere in the body of the text, however, I use common renderings of Russian names and terms and intuitive, pronunciation-friendly transliterations oriented towards the reader in English.

All references to Chekhov's writings translated by me from Russian are keyed to the fullest scholarly edition, A. P. Chekhov, *Polnoe sobranie sochinenii i pisem* (Complete Writings and Letters), ed. N. F. Bel'chikov et al., 30 vols (Moscow, 1974–83). The eighteen volumes of writings and the twelve volumes of letters were numbered separately by the publisher, with each subset of the thirty-volume collection beginning with one. I have tried to rely on translations readily available to this book's reader as much as possible, however.

As a rule, letters are cited by date, so as to facilitate searching them out in translated sources; this suffices to locate them in the *Pis'ma* (Letters) as well. If no other source is indicated, then the translations are mine and *Pis'ma* is the source. I have cited many translated letters from the excellent selection by Michael Henry Heim and Simon Karlinsky.

Chekhov used ellipses prolifically. In order to distinguish between his ellipses and those indicating omissions from cited text, all of my ellipses indicating material omitted from the original will be enclosed by square brackets; ellipses that are not enclosed by brackets are Chekhov's own (or, once or twice, those of another cited author), reproduced as they are in his text.

I have relied very heavily on the two variants of the wonderful *Letopis' zhizni i tvorchestva A. P. Chekhova* (Chronicle of the Life and Works of Anton Chekhov), the first a single volume from 1955 and the second an as-yet-unfinished, multiple-volume edition that has been published since 2000. Items directly cited from these sources are noted with page references, but my debt to these scholarly sources far exceeds what those notes indicate. Since both works have the same title, the later, multi-volume edition will be indicated by the presence of a volume number in the reference.

Citations from sources most frequently referred to will be provided in the text by references to the following editions:

Letopis'	N. I. Gitovich, ed., *Letopis' zhizni i tvorchestva A. P. Chekhova* (Moscow, 1955)
Letopis' I	L. D. Gromova-Opul'skaia and N. I. Gitovich, eds, *Letopis' zhizni i tvorchestva A. P. Chekhova*, vol. I: *1860–1888* (Moscow, 2000)
Letopis' II	I. Iu. Tverdokhlebov and N. I. Gitovich, eds, *Letopis' zhizni i tvorchestva A. P. Chekhova*, vol. II: *1889–1891* (Moscow, 2004)
Letopis' III	M. A. Sokolova and I. E. Gitovich, eds, *Letopis' zhizni i tvorchestva A. P. Chekhova*, vol. III: *1891–1894* (Moscow, 2009)
Letopis' IV.1	A. P. Kuzicheva, ed., *Letopis' zhizni i tvorchestva A. P. Chekhova*, vol. IV.1: *1895–1896* (Moscow, 2016)
Letopis' IV.2	A. P. Kuzicheva, ed., *Letopis' zhizni i tvorchestva A. P. Chekhova*, vol. IV.2: *1897–September 1898* (Moscow, 2016)
Letters	Anton Chekhov, *Anton Chekhov's Life and Thought: Selected Letters and Commentary*, trans. Michael Henry Heim, ed. and commentary Simon Karlinsky (Berkeley, CA, 1975)
Novels	Anton Chekhov, *The Complete Short Novels*, trans. Richard Pevear and Larissa Volokhonsky (New York, 2004)
P	Anton P. Chekhov, *Polnoe sobranie sochinenii i pisem*, 30 vols, *Pis'ma* [Letters] (12 vols), ed. N. F. Bel'chikov et al. (Moscow, 1974–83)
Plays	Anton Chekhov, *The Essential Plays*, trans. Michael Henry Heim (New York, 2003)

S	Anton P. Chekhov, *Polnoe sobranie sochinenii i pisem*, 30 vols, *Sochineniia* [Writings] (18 vols), ed. N. F. Bel'chikov et al. (Moscow, 1974–1983)
Stories	Anton Chekhov, *Stories*, trans. Richard Pevear and Larissa Volokhonsky (New York, 2000)

The Julian calendar was still in use in Russia throughout Chekhov's lifetime, and it is observed in the 'old style' handling of dates in this book. In the nineteenth century the Julian calendar lagged the Gregorian by twelve days; early in the twentieth century this increased to thirteen.

Chekhov, November 1891, photograph by Alexander Chekhov.

Introduction

ANTON CHEKHOV remains one of the most widely known, accessible, influential and imitated authors of the Russian literary canon, both in Russia and in translation in the West and Asia. His works, including the non-fictional *Sakhalin Island* (*Ostrov Sakhalin*), encompass a social reality arguably broader and more varied than those of any other major Russian writer;[1] they do so with a keen realist's eye that has led them to be taken as primary materials in historical, sociological and psychological studies.[2] Somewhat contradictorily, study of Chekhov's prose also reveals a modernist's self-reflexive emphasis on stylistics and profound symbolic depths, which have been truly appreciated only in the past three or four decades.[3]

The same is true of his drama. Moscow Art Theatre co-founder Vladimir Nemirovich-Danchenko speaks of the

> sad everyday realities of Chekhov. Nothing extravagant in the costumes; no violent make-up; a complete absence of crowd scenes; no cascade of external tints – in a word, nothing with which the actor might protect himself against revealing his individuality to the point of nakedness.

In his plays, 'Life unfolded in such frank simplicity that the auditors seemed almost embarrassed to be present; it was as if they eavesdropped behind a door or peeped through a window.'[4] This is Chekhov's distinctive realism. And yet his mature drama, like his major prose, actually hangs together by virtue of hidden, larger networks of meaning. Actions, images and utterances that appear disconnected from the whole, that are part of the accidental *thereness* of Chekhov's represented world, resound in meaningfulness when integrated into satisfying readings and stagings that attend to symbolic undercurrents. Utterances by characters do not directly verbalize coherent thoughts that might then elicit dialogic response from other characters or incite action. They instead function lyrically and, to the extent that they characterize their speaker, in some sense synecdochically and symptomatically, pointing to larger hidden complexes. The brilliant actor and director Vsevolod Meyerhold wrote rather polemically of Chekhov's 'drama of mood', 'hidden in the rhythm of his language'.[5] In Chekhov's drama, as in his prose, coherence and sources of dramatic tension may arise less through exterior action than via a somewhat ineffable dynamic of impressions – what he called the musical aspect. Chekhov bridges the world and values (including aesthetic ones) of the great Russian nineteenth-century realists with the avant-garde and revolutionary first decades of the twentieth century.

What definitely set Chekhov apart from the great Russian realistic tradition as represented by the expansive narratives of Tolstoy and Dostoevsky, though, was his gravitation to the short form. It is commonly held that, during the last two decades of the nineteenth century, the novel was in decline and small forms ascendant; in retrospect it is clear that truly creative, new and long-lasting writing was to be found in poetry and short fiction, but the contemporary view was different. Indeed, for many years Chekhov believed what others and the canon told him: to secure a place in the Russian literary world he needed success with a major novel. But the long form just was not right for him; as Nabokov put it, 'he was a sprinter, not a stayer.'[6] The novel he did work on, and which he abandoned in the late 1880s, was tellingly conceived as a cycle of short stories, as indicated by its prospective title, 'Stories from the Lives of My Friends' ('Rasskazy iz zhizni moikh druzei'). In any case, he lacked both the time and the financial breathing space to work on a novel until he no longer had the physical stamina or length of life remaining to do it.

In the end, investing himself in the short form did not, as he feared, mean publishing with invisible ink. Now universally acknowledged not only as a master of the modern short story but as an innovative playwright, for a century Chekhov and his works have served as a school for budding authors of fiction and drama. He features heavily in theatre training as well, in particular as a component of the lasting impact of the Moscow Art Theatre and the Stanislavsky method. Even many of his early short humorous stories have been adapted to the stage, a procedure he initiated.[7]

Further, in spite of his own sceptical remarks about the appeal of his works outside Russia or in the future – he could not understand how his stories would work in translation, and he famously predicted to Ivan Bunin that he would be read for no more than seven years beyond his death[8] – his plays and short stories have proved eminently translatable, and we certainly read and stage him still today. Translations vary in quality, but some of his best translators of recent years have declared him to be comparatively easy to translate. For D. S. Mirsky this quality betrayed a language 'devoid of all raciness and nerve', which is 'colorless and lacks individuality', an evaluation far from predominant.[9] True, Chekhov's accessible prose often appears in intermediate-level Russian language courses; nevertheless, his stylistic nuances and palpable depths reward close attention by sophisticated readers as well. And though his drama is known chiefly through a mere four major works, this sufficed to earn him a role in launching a new era in European theatre. He remains second only to Shakespeare in the frequency of his staging in the American theatre, and it is not uncommon to find him referred to as the 'Shakespeare of the twentieth century'. For contemporary short story writers, to be called the American Chekhov (or the Canadian, British, Indian, Japanese and so on) remains high praise. In short, if you read to gain insight into the lives of other human beings, read Chekhov; if you read because you want to learn how to write, read Chekhov!

Chekhov's person also continues to attract us, as evidenced by the regularity with which new biographies appear. For Westerners his life may resonate more than those of the landed gentry authors he succeeded: it was a hard-scrabble, middle-class life that dipped into the lower depths but eventually found a toehold in the nouveau riche cultural elite. Chekhov's father, Pavel, had been born a serf but came to own a retail business in Taganrog and entertained pretentions to town fatherhood before being crushed by bankruptcy and fleeing to Moscow. Soon thereafter Anton became the family's main authority and source of support. By the late 1880s the family had regained considerable stability, and in the next decade Chekhov acquired a small estate south of Moscow. Scholars, writers and fans make pilgrimages to his various home-museums and often write about them quite penetratingly: the home he rented in the late 1880s on the Sadovaya-Kudrinskaya in Moscow; the estate at Melikhovo where he lived for most of the 1890s; the house he built outside Yalta as an invalid at the turn of the century; the nearby seaside cottage he acquired at Gurzuf; and his childhood home in Taganrog.[10] For educated Russians, Chekhov remains an unquestionable model of *intelligentnost'*: educated, considerate, well mannered, and of a generally liberal and humanist world view. The Soviet émigré writer Sergei Dovlatov declared, 'You can delight in Tolstoy's mind, Pushkin's refinement, and Dostoevsky's deep psychological penetration, but the one you can wish to be *like* is Chekhov.'[11] The fictional historian in Vasily Grossman's *Life and Fate* calls Chekhov 'the bearer of the greatest banner that has been raised in the thousand years of Russian history – the banner of a true, humane, Russian democracy, of Russian freedom, of the dignity of the Russian man. [...] Chekhov said: let's put God – and all these grand progressive ideas – to one side. [...] Let's begin with respect, compassion, and love for the individual – or we'll never get anywhere.'[12]

Chekhov was an admirable overachiever when it came to good works. He served and he gave quite out of proportion to his resources. His social engagement was absent of dogmatism or, indeed, conventional ideological commitment of any kind; while this may recommend him well to many readers, in his own highly politicized setting he was often criticized for his putative lack of position. In the mid-1880s, when Chekhov was first becoming known, the important critic A. M. Skabichevsky of the *Northern Herald* (*Severnyi vestnik*) asserted that the young writer's lack of clear ideological grounding and mission would have him 'die completely forgotten in a ditch'; Chekhov always remembered this.[13] Even as late as 1890, just a few weeks before he was to leave on his journey to the prison island of Sakhalin, Chekhov was listed among the 'priests of unprincipled writing' in the important journal *Russian Thought* (*Russkaia mysl'*). In retrospect such rebukes seem unfathomable: anyone familiar with Chekhov's biography marvels at his evident drive to make an impact, whether through mentoring others with literary aspirations, building schools and a church belltower, stocking public libraries on Sakhalin and in his hometown of Taganrog, providing healthcare to the poor, or landscaping. Chekhov was always planting trees, even when in very temporary locations, and for memoirists and biographers this activity reflects his unselfish wish to make better a future he was unlikely to inhabit. Tubercular the last two decades of his life, Chekhov could expect his years to be shortened by an infection that had plagued his family; the courage with which he faced the certainty of an early death can appear as denial or a psychological enigma, but it facilitated an impactful life.

Outside view of the house where Chekhov was born, Taganrog, 2016.

Chekhov's intimate relations with illness and death derived also from his training and practice as a physician. At the apex of his literary success, Chekhov was still prone to remarks like the one he made to Stanislavsky by way of comparing himself to Gerhart Hauptmann: 'Listen, I'm not a playwright at all, I'm a doctor.' As biographer Mikhail Gromov put it, 'Chekhov would never have said: "I'm a good writer." But he said many times: "I'm a good doctor."'[14] Physicians in turn have always responded to Chekhov. During his lifetime, while the 1902 Pirogov Medical Congress was under way in Moscow, the Moscow Art Theatre staged a special performance of Chekhov's play *Uncle Vanya* (*Diadia Vania*), which features a physician character. Attendants celebrated Chekhov with a procession featuring a life-sized reproduction of his portrait by Osip Braz, and Chekhov was bombarded with appreciative telegrams from his medical colleagues. There are many articles and books on Chekhov by admiring physicians who have been moved to try their hands at literary scholarship, and his works often feature in courses of medical humanities in medical schools.[15] Memoirists who knew Chekhov and scholars of his work since have often associated Chekhov's powers of observation with his training as a physician.[16]

Chekhov's dual career was made possible by a remarkable capacity for work. The most comprehensive academic edition of Chekhov's writings includes more than 580 published works that might be classified as prose fiction, though scholars vary in just what they count. A short fake letter to the editor or a letter of denunciation? (I do count these as discrete works.) The caption to a cartoon drawn by his brother Nikolai or another graphics artist? (These I do not count.) Moreover, some items that occur once in that edition's table of contents were published multiple times in different variants, whereas other items were recast and retitled and therefore appear multiple times.[17]

However you count, Chekhov's production, especially in the first half of his writing career, was astounding. Add to that his practice as a physician and other good works; his travels and prolific letter-writing; and his ill health in later years, when he also mentored many aspiring writers and reread and revised (or rejected) for the collected works everything he had himself previously published. Chekhov's mind-boggling level of activity poses quite a challenge to the biographer. This brief account of his life will dwell on key points in his literary career and offer analysis of select, representative works so as to flesh out the most distinctive features of his writing and to model approaches that will pay off in tackling others of his texts.

I

Family Background
and Early Years

ANTON CHEKHOV was born on 17 January 1860 in what was then the rather cosmopolitan port city of Taganrog, on the Sea of Azov. He was the third son of Pavel and Evgenia Chekhov; his mother's merchant family name was Morozova. The other siblings in his remarkably close-knit and talented family were Alexander (b. 1855, while Taganrog was besieged by the British fleet during the Crimean War), Nikolai (b. 1858), Ivan (b. 1861), Maria (b. 1863) and Mikhail (b. 1865). Another sister, Evgenia, much cared for by Chekhov, was born in 1869 and would die two years later.

Chekhov's grandfather Yegor had been an enterprising serf who managed to purchase his family's freedom in 1841, two decades before emancipation in Russia, when Chekhov's father Pavel was a teenager. He became the manager of a grand estate, which he ruled tyrannically and explosively. He also quite forcefully determined the lives and prospects of his sons, apprenticing Pavel to an important Taganrog merchant as a means of starting him on his own socioeconomic ascent. Chekhov's eldest brother published recollections of childhood visits to his grandfather. The man, whom locals called the 'viper', left contradictory imprints in his grandchildren's memories: he was a brutal authoritarian, but he was also a family culture hero; what family would not pay homage to the ancestor who had freed them all from bondage? If one can trace back to Yegor the family strain of ignorant self-assurance, pomposity and explosive anger so prominent in Chekhov's father (and stringently expunged in Chekhov himself) – Russian offers the wonderful term *samodurstvo* for such petty tyranny – then so too with the family's brilliance and ambition. The family patriarch was still stepping in to render judgment and assist financially when the Chekhov family suffered bankruptcy and, in stages, fled Taganrog in the mid-1870s. It is no surprise that Chekhov's writings betray a kind of obsession with both the name Yegor and serpents, as a leading Chekhov scholar has revealed.[1]

By the time Anton Chekhov came into the world, his father Pavel was an independent merchant in Taganrog, the owner of a small general store and an upstanding member of the city's religious community. Chekhov was born on Politseiskaia (Police) Street, which at one end led to a high cliff at the seashore and at the other a muddy square; indeed, Taganrog was famous for its mud, as well as abundant stray dogs and the absence of running water.[2] Nevertheless, it was a cosmopolitan, multilingual city, and in the mid-1860s, though Odessa now surpassed it in goods trafficked, you could still walk along its shore and observe many English, French, Belgian, Greek, Italian, Norwegian and Turkish ships, among others. The city had a large and wealthy Greek population, so Pavel put his sons Nikolai and Anton in a Greek school, but only for a year: an embarrassing impromptu demonstration of his sons' linguistic competence in Greek, instead of impressing shop customers, revealed that they had learned nothing.

By Chekhov's high school days, the city was in sharp decline, and so too were Pavel's fortunes. The private tutors who had taught his older brothers French, and Nikolai the violin, were financially impossible by the time Anton reached equivalent age. Perhaps because of the hours he was compelled to work in his father's shop, Anton by no means shone as a pupil, twice repeating academic levels (his third and fifth classes).[3] It cannot have helped that for a couple of years he was sent to study tailoring and cobbling as well: with his academic prospects looking doubtful, his father wanted him to have a trade.

In 1873, while the economic climate in Taganrog worsened, Pavel, by all signs a poor businessman, overextended himself in building a home for the family. To add insult to injury, he was cheated by the contractor. If his trade fell off catastrophically, one telling anecdote suggests why: when a drowned rat was found in a barrel of cooking oil, Pavel had the oil 'cleansed' and rehabilitated for sale by means of a priest's prayer. In April 1876, with creditors closing in, he fled Taganrog for Moscow, where he joined his eldest sons Alexander and Nikolai, now students there. He still faced the possibility of extradition back to Taganrog and debtors' prison, though, and had to lie low. In this period Alexander was making his own way as a successful university student and tutor, but the rest of the family,

Chekhov family, 1874, Taganrog. Back row, from left: Mikhail (sitting), Ivan, Anton, Nikolai, Alexander and uncle Mitrofan; front row, from left: Maria, Pavel (father), Evgenia (mother), aunt Liudmila and cousin Georgy.

whether in Moscow or in Taganrog, underwent crushing financial strain. Back in Taganrog, the inability to pay fees got the Chekhov children remaining there banned from attending school.

That July, Chekhov's mother, his youngest brother, Mikhail, and his sister, Maria, joined the others in Moscow. Anton and Ivan were left to continue their schooling in Taganrog and sell or send to Moscow those possessions that had been hidden from creditors. Chekhov's efforts were not always appreciated: when he sold the wall clock, his father rebuked him for not having given it to Chekhov's uncle Mitrofan, also a small-time shopkeeper in Taganrog; when Chekhov sent upbeat, joking letters, his mother answered that they had only four kopecks for bread and he ought to send money instead; when Chekhov sent twelve rubles rather than the twenty his mother had been hoping for, his father informed him that she 'burst into floods of bitter tears'.[4] Ivan lived with relatives and after a year moved to Moscow, while Chekhov exchanged tutoring services for room and board with a bank functionary who had himself previously boarded with the Chekhovs, Gabriel Selivanov. Selivanov had forestalled legal action against them by purchasing the foreclosed property for much less than was owed on it; while the initial plan may have been for the Chekhovs to buy the house back from him, Selivanov eventually took full possession and was joined by young relations from the country who came to Taganrog for schooling.

Chekhov improved as a student once freed of his family: his overall record was less stellar than Alexander's, who had won a silver medal, but when Chekhov graduated in 1879 his exit exams earned him one of ten town scholarships for higher education, worth 25 rubles per month. Meanwhile, during his last three years of secondary schooling he tutored other children and managed to send most of his earnings beyond room and board north to his family. So it was that the high school pupil who had been left behind by his family initiated the pattern by which he would assume the role of family patriarch.

Somehow Chekhov also found time to read extensively. He subscribed to the new Taganrog public library, which had opened shortly after Pavel fled the city, and began with travel accounts, an early sign of the wanderlust that would characterize his mature years. During the 1877 spring break, Alexander financed a visit by Anton to Moscow, where he had a chance to taste the semi-independent, precariously bohemian life Alexander and Nikolai were carving out for themselves. Back in Taganrog, tutoring Selivanov's relations brought opportunities for summer visits to country properties belonging to members of that family, some of whom were quite wild. Chekhov enjoyed considerable freedom and, if his own elliptical accounts can be credited, early erotic experiences. He also suffered grave illness during one of these summer visits: a case of peritonitis that may have signalled the tubercular infection that would eventually kill him, and which some conjecture to have influenced his decision to study medicine.

Sometime in this period, too, Chekhov began to write. In 1873–4 he tried adapting Nikolai Gogol's historical novel *Taras Bulba* (1835) for the stage. Among other juvenilia, now lost: a hand-written magazine called *The Little Hare*; skits for family entertainment; a short comic play titled *It's Not for Nothing the Hen was Singing*; two full-length plays; and some poetry. Chekhov sent certain pieces to Alexander, who had developed contacts and begun publishing in the so-called 'small press', lowbrow venues serving a newly literate and expanding lower-middle-class urban population. It is likely that some poetry, signed with the pseudonym

'Nettles', was rejected in March 1877 (*Letopis'* 1, p. 42). We know of such early efforts largely from Alexander's responses and family memoirs published after Chekhov died. Several pseudonymously published and rejected items from this period that might be Chekhov's cannot be proven so, because the manuscripts, like almost all of Chekhov's own letters from this period, were lost. We thus lack material basis for study of the earliest stages of Chekhov's creative development.

Still, one cannot help asking: where did Chekhov's particular forms of creativity come from? And from where derived the ambition, self-discipline and sheer capacity for work that enabled him to realize his enormous talent – talent that went utterly to waste in his artist brother Nikolai and was, at best, less than fully realized in the brilliant Alexander?

Chekhov himself generously affirmed, 'We got our talent from our father, and our soul from our mother's side.'[5] Pavel's considerable ambition was interwoven with pretention and a concern for status long on self-righteousness and short on genuine labour and achievement: the grandiosity of a petty and ignorant man. He did however pass real musical talent on to some of his children. Nikolai was a gifted, intuitive violinist and pianist, and Chekhov is supposed to have had a beautiful tenor voice. Pavel's icon painting perhaps also translated into Nikolai's painterly brilliance and Maria's serious engagement with the art. Chekhov's correspondence with his brother Alexander, which contains much mimicry of their father's speech, suggests that coming to terms with that voice helped develop their literary talents.

What is most surprising, though, is the miracle by which the dysfunctional aspects of family life, which turned his elder brothers into alcoholics and, in Nikolai's case, a morphine addict, somehow drove Chekhov to inimitable productivity. So many hereditary negatives were turned into positives. Whereas the abusive patriarchal behaviour that characterized grandfather Yegor and father Pavel was replicated in his eldest brother, and at times also in his younger brother Ivan, Chekhov deliberately struggled to discipline this trait out of himself, developing an ethical stance that programmatically respected the integrity and autonomy of other human beings. As children, Chekhov and his elder brothers were subjected to endless liturgical readings and religious harangues, and they were forced to practise long hours and sing in their pedantic father's church chorus. Chekhov would write in a letter to Ivan Leontyev (Shcheglov) that 'when I and my two brothers would sing in a trio in the middle of the church "Let My Prayer Arise" [*Da ispravitsia*] or "The

Archangel's Voice" [*Arkhangel'skii glas*], everybody looked on us kindly and envied my parents, while we were simultaneously feeling like little convicts' (9 March 1892); and yet he later made abundant literary use of his thorough knowledge of holy texts and the liturgy and had a life-long love of church music and bells. The father who had beaten him and whom he had mimicked and mocked in letters Chekhov nevertheless sheltered in his own homes until Pavel died in 1897, allowing him to play the grand signior at the estate he purchased after returning from Sakhalin. How was it that he came to credit his father as the source of his talent?

To be sure, Chekhov was scarred. Among distinctive bodily features noted in his passport was a scar over his brow – he had struck a rock when diving into the Taganrog bay – but that was the least of it. Chekhov once wrote to his friend and publisher Alexei Suvorin that he believed in progress because of the dramatic difference between when he was beaten and then when such treatment ceased (27 March 1894). For the rest of the family, that moment came later than it had for Chekhov. In the family's close Moscow quarters, the hullabaloo Pavel raised in attacking Ivan provoked intervention by the Chekhovs' landlords. Alexander, who was living independently, wrote to Chekhov about a list of domestic duties which 'Father of the Family Pavel Chekhov' had attached to the bed-room wall; the schedule began at 5 a.m., listed Nikolai, Ivan, Mikhail and Maria (and their ages), and ended with the warning that howling during punishment for infractions was forbidden (*Letopis'* 1, p. 48). All changed soon thereafter, though, when Pavel, now able to register as residing in Moscow without fear of arrest and extradition for his debts, found employment at a merchant's warehouse on the other side of the city (where Chekhov's cousin Mikhail worked) that paid 30 rubles per month and provided food and lodging. He now became largely a visitor to his family, and the last vestiges of his authority were displaced when Chekhov arrived at the end of summer 1879.

The family's financial catastrophe must also have marked Chekhov. It certainly created any number of humiliating situations: his school friend A. Drossi recollected Chekhov's embarrassment at his torn and muddy shoes, which he would take pains to hide under the table during lessons (*Letopis'* 1, p. 40). Achieving a level of personal dignity was a chal-lenge. Who were his models? His father never lacked the self-assurance of a resolutely self-centred individual blind to his own failings. He was right and deserved what he wanted regardless of the situation. He loved uniforms, coveted banal official positions and awards of any sort and medals, and Chekhov never saw him with dirty underclothing or an unstarched shirt.

Chekhov, himself a careful dresser, no doubt learned something from that sort of dignity, but his was a different path. In what is perhaps his most famous letter, he wrote to Suvorin in 1889 about his personal struggle to achieve self-respect as a human being and an author of fiction. He is glad, he says, that he did not write a novel when all were urging him to do so a few years ago. 'There are other things no less necessary than talent and an abundance of material. Maturity, to begin with. Then, *a sense of personal freedom* is also quite indispensable. And this sense didn't begin growing inside me until very recently.' He continues, in a revealing statement to which we will return,

> What aristocratic writers take from nature gratis, the less privileged must pay for with their youth. Try and write a story about a young man – the son of a serf [...] raised on respect for rank [...] receiving frequent whippings, making the rounds as a tutor without galoshes [...] needlessly hypocritical before God and man merely to acknowledge his own insignificance – write about how this young man squeezes the slave out of himself drop by drop and how, on waking up one fine morning, he finds that the blood coursing through his veins is no longer the blood of a slave, but that of a real human being. (7 January 1889; *Letters*, p. 85)

The bulk of this process seems to have taken place before Chekhov left Taganrog. It was liberating for Chekhov to be on his own, and the burdens that his father's collapse shifted to his shoulders sparked a preternatural maturation.[6] Missives from his father continued to proselytize humility and submission to authority; in congratulating him on his *gymnasium* exit exams, he wrote: 'don't rely on your abilities and also never ever take pride in your knowledge [...] what's absolutely necessary is humility (*Letopis'* 1, p. 61). In contrast, Chekhov's fatherly letter to his youngest brother Mikhail encouraged dignity and self-respect:

> Why do you refer to yourself as my 'worthless, insignificant little brother'? So you are aware of your worthlessness, are you? [...]
> Do you know where you should be aware of your worthlessness? Before God, perhaps, or before human intelligence, before beauty

or nature. But not before people [...] respect yourself for being a good honest fellow. (6–8 April 1879; *Letters*, p. 36)

Many memoirists comment on Chekhov's vain streak or *amour propre*. That trait likely reflects a traumatized child's struggle for dignity that was never fully resolved for the self-aware Chekhov. Modulating the sense of self was a lifetime project that involved great sensitivity to both abuse and praise. This psychological dynamic is also one of the grand overarching themes of Chekhov's fiction and drama and, in the early works, often a source of comedy.

However plausible the story biographers tell, the gaps in our knowledge of how Chekhov became Chekhov exceed the body of available facts, as is always the case with the lives of others. Documentation of Chekhov's early history, and that of his family before him, is particularly thin.[7] Moreover, the memoirs of Chekhov's siblings differ in fundamental ways.

Most famously, Chekhov's sister Maria and youngest brother Mikhail contested the grim picture drawn by the eldest brother Alexander, asserting that, because he was ill with alcoholism, his word could often not be trusted. But Maria (d. 1956) and Mikhail (d. 1936), between them keepers of Chekhov's legacy well into the 1950s, were sufficiently younger than their brothers to have quite different views of the family's life. Fewer demands had been placed on them as children: they did not participate in running their father's shop or sing in his church choir, and the parents could not take the same active interest in their schooling as they had with the older boys. Also, they far outlived their siblings and therefore became invested in shaping the Chekhov legend, as is apparent in their censorious editing of Chekhov's letters and careful crafting of his memory. While it is certainly true that Alexander's memoirs express bitterness towards his father, they do not involve the strain of egocentrism to be found in the writings of Mikhail and Maria, who proved eager to insert themselves into Chekhov's story as centrally as possible.

Chekhov's letters substantiate the view left by Alexander: the beatings and 'convict labour' of working in the shop and singing in the choir are confirmed by Chekhov's own remarks.[8] 'In my childhood,' he famously stated, 'there was no childhood.'[9] It is clear from Chekhov's correspondence with Alexander that the two shared something that neither did with Maria or Mikhail. There is a constant reference to shared life experiences, a sense of two witty, thoughtful men on the same wavelength, that you do not find in his correspondence with Maria or Mikhail, or anyone else for that matter. Indeed, only Chekhov's very different correspondence with his wife, Olga Knipper, manifests the intimacy to be found in the letters between him and his brother Alexander. Letters to Suvorin approach it at times, but their communication does not rely on an unspoken, shared background, and in any case we have only the Chekhov half of that correspondence.

Among the mysteries of Chekhov's early years is just when or why he decided to study medicine. Letters from both his father and his mother urged him to become a physician; they were thinking of both earning potential and social status, and they had their own interests in mind more than Chekhov's. At the end of 1877 Pavel tells Chekhov, 'When you finish studying in the Taganrog gymnasium, apply to the medical faculty without fail'; he writes that Chekhov's brother Alexander, by contrast – who had been a brilliant student in school and started Moscow University in the department of mathematics but transferred to the department of natural sciences (both within the faculty of physics-mathematics)[10] – 'chose thoughtlessly, against our will' (*Letopis'* 1, p. 50). Six months later, Pavel tells Chekhov that he has done well to ask his parents for advice in the matter, again contrasting him with Alexander, and that 'the medical faculty is practical and modern, and you can acquire means more quickly, which is indispensable for us all right now' (*Letopis'* 1, p. 54). His mother wrote, 'Please go to the medical faculty. The best thing. Please, respect me' (*Letopis'* 1, p. 55).

If Chekhov respected his parents' wishes, he also never earned his or his family's keep through medicine. An educated young man of Chekhov's generation had other motivations for becoming a doctor. In his last year of gymnasium Chekhov participated in a *zemstvo* doctors' club, together with others who went on to study medicine. *Zemstvo* medicine was rural public health service for the poorest of the poor, and interest in it reflected idealism and altruistic social commitment. So too did Chekhov's lifelong practice of medicine, which included *zemstvo* employment for which he never took a salary.

All along, however, Chekhov was also aiming towards an academic career in medicine. We know of three doctoral research projects that Chekhov conceived, worked on, and in one case completed, with the possibility of an academic career in mind. The first, 'A History of Sexual Dominance', was a Darwin-inspired project, laid out in an April 1883 letter to his brother Alexander, to research the socio-historical causes of putative developmental inferiorities in women and propose remediating initiatives. The prospectus's wrongheaded theoretical suppositions reflected the science of the day, but the project also demonstrates Chekhov's social commitment and progressive sentiment. The second was a history of doctoring in Russia, towards which Chekhov collected considerable materials. The third was the book Chekhov published after his 1890 research trip to the prison island of Sakhalin.

2

From Novice to Fame

C hekhov's first significant literary efforts accompanied his steps towards a medical career. He wrote a play, still extant but missing its title page and published in 1923 as *An Unpublished Play of A. P. Chekhov* (*Neizdannaia p'esa A. P. Chekhova*); it has been translated as *Platonov* (after its non-heroic hero).[1] The manuscript only came to light long after Chekhov's death, when Bolshevik authorities confiscated Maria Chekhova's safe deposit box. There remains some debate as to whether this is the play referred to in letters to his brother Alexander and in his brother Mikhail's memoirs as 'Fatherlessness' (*Bezottsovshchina*), which Chekhov wrote in Tagangrog, sent to Alexander in Moscow and then – according to Mikhail – tore to pieces when he moved there himself. Most scholars consider it a reworked version of that play, though biographer Donald Rayfield makes a strong argument that these are two entirely different works.[2] Chekhov had shown the surviving manuscript to the famous actress Maria Yermolova during his second year in Moscow and then continued working on it after her rejection. Our discussion will refer to the play as *Fatherlessness*, less to take a definitive one-play position – the question remains undecided – than to highlight its theme of the absent father, which resounds quite broadly in Chekhov.

The play is jam-packed with characters and frenetic action and runs roughly three times the length of Chekhov's mature full-length plays. In other words, it was unstageable, though Chekhov's cachet has resulted in adaptations for both stage and screen since the 1920s. Unsurprisingly, it also contains many nuclei for characters and plots of the mature Chekhov. *Fatherlessness* reflects Chekhov's sense, as an avid provincial theatregoer, of what it took to be successful on the stage at a time when melodrama dominated the scene. But it also distorts the genre's key features in ways that prefigure the pathbreaking modern dramatist Chekhov was to become. It repeatedly boils over with emotional excess, as one expects of melodrama,[3] while the Chekhov-to-be is visible in abrupt deflationary twists where characters flip from passion to cynicism or simply grow exhausted.

The play's central character is a burnt-out local wunderkind and seducer, Mikhail Platonov, and the plot involves multiple romantic entanglements overlaid by financial intrigues, an impending bankruptcy, and plans by certain characters to maim or murder others. The field of action is starkly polarized from a moral point of view, but, in a departure from formulaic melodrama, virtue does not win out. By the end of the play only Platonov's victimized wife remains innocent; all others are compromised, and none more so than Platonov. As he puts it shortly before he is killed: 'They all love me. When I get better, I'll seduce you. I used to help prostitutes, now I help to recruit them.' And: 'Now I understand Oedipus putting out his eyes. How low I've fallen and how well I know it.'[4]

Because Platonov's interiority is on display in the play, and because other characters remain largely sympathetic to him, he elicits an ambivalent response. And while all the play's characters scheme against and abuse one another, they nevertheless remain tied by affect: it's all in the family, so to speak.

Once a brilliant, radical university student, Platonov has settled down to a humdrum marriage and pedestrian schoolmaster's career. As a middle-class, provincial offshoot of the self-critical 'superfluous man', a character type established decades earlier by Pushkin, Lermontov and Turgenev, he lashes out at others in proportion to his dissatisfaction with himself. But Platonov acts largely at the instigation of others and drink; in constructing a character who is intoxicated and complaining of illness for much of the play, Chekhov medicalizes his bad deeds, another twist on convention.

Among Platonov's lovers is a young, easy-going, widowed landowner, Anna Voinitseva, whose estate faces bankruptcy and sale at auction. In Act Four, the play's manifold entanglements are exposed through a series of confrontations in the study of Anna's late husband, the absent father of the play's title. A deranged Platonov takes a revolver from the dead man's arsenal and places its muzzle against his temple, referring to Hamlet in his monologue, but then puts the weapon down. An old flame enters and declares herself in love with Platonov, and for a moment he is impassioned; deflation and the melodramatic last lines cited above follow, after which his current paramour enters the scene, observes her betrayal and shoots Platonov. The denouement of *Fatherlessness* concludes with the fatherless Platonov, having ravaged the fatherless home of the Voinitsevs, alluding to the two literary cornerstones of Freud's Oedipal complex (two decades prior to its elaboration): Hamlet and Oedipus.

Platonov's death is but one of a thickly orchestrated series of culminating events from side-plots too numerous to summarize here. Oodles of love, money, and an on-stage murder at the end – this is not the Chekhov of whom so many say that nothing happens in his works. Still, we shall see that much of the later Chekhov has its roots in this melodramatic work and its theme of the absent father. Though his mature poetics of fiction and drama rejected the principles organizing *Fatherlessness*, he nevertheless returned again and again to its character types and plot situations, especially in his plays. The titular character of his first successful play, *Ivanov* (1887, 1889), is like Platonov a washed-up, cynical former idealist who claims to have overstressed himself; the bankrupt estate owner of his last, *Cherry Orchard* (*Vishnevyi sad*, 1904), is prefigured in Anna Voinitseva, the loose widow who tells Platonov, 'Smoke me like a cigarette, press me out, smash me, be a man.'[5] Much that is on the surface of *Fatherlessness* remains as deep structures in the mature work. A horse thief whom Platonov overtly associates with the Devil represents a criminal underworld that, together with references to mineral wealth underlying Voinitseva's estate, bespeaks a theme of hero's descent and hellish visions that will pervade Chekhov's writings.[6] There is also Chekhov's career-long involvement with Shakespeare; as one Russian critic put it, 'Shakespeare is mentioned so often in the stories and plays of Chekhov that one could call him one of Chekhov's heroes.'[7] Platonov's *Hamlet* will rank first among such allusions. In later works, too, Chekhov's invocations of the Danish prince are connected with references to the figure of Oedipus and seem to be part of a pre-Freudian contemplation of what Freud would call the Oedipal complex. This is most notable in *The Seagull* (*Chaika*, 1896), where the young writer Treplev laces his speech with citations from *Hamlet* and contests an established author for both the affection of his mother and recognition as an author; meanwhile, Treplev's uncle, Sorin, refers to the riddle of the Sphinx.[8] In *Fatherlessness*, Platonov is an Oedipal victor who berates and punishes himself relentlessly for that, while at the same time failing to be a father to his own child (who never appears onstage). Hostility towards women, all of whom he might seduce and pimp, as he puts it at the end of the play, results from the success of this little Oedipus, for whom every innocent is in fact a whore. This Madonna-Whore theme, like much that is on the melodramatic surface of *Fatherlessness*, subtly pervades the later Chekhov.[9]

The same may be said of the play's overreaching wittiness. Dosto-evskian gut-spilling alternates with extreme irony and cynicism in the work of a youngster eager to show himself older and wiser than his years. This melodramatic deployment of wit and aphoristic wisdom would transform into the submerged, pervasive irony that, for most, is the hallmark of the mature Chekhov, and Chekhov's famous understatement should perhaps be understood as a negation of the overstatement everywhere palpable in *Fatherlessness*. In just what is being stated, however, there are striking continuities. The depths of emotion, verbalized and acted out in the early melodramatic play, are submerged in the later works; tempestuous, rollicking waves become undercurrents.

'Fatherlessness' could have been the title of *Cherry Orchard*, and it is the keynote of *Three Sisters* (1901). True, *Fatherlessness* is so packed with characters and subplots that its function as a reservoir for Chekhov's later works is not so very surprising. Those looking to Chekhov's first two decades can also find details drawn from his life, insofar as we know it. Rayfield's revisionist biography created a Don Juanish image of the author that accords in many respects with Platonov's. A Greek girl with whom Chekhov had a romance in his last years in Taganrog may be reflected in the character of Mary Grekova, Platonov's former lover who returns during the action of the play, at first fails to even recognize Platonov, and then proposes resuming their relations just before Platonov is killed by Voinitsev's wife Sonya. The diverse, multicultural milieu of the play is reminiscent of cosmopolitan Taganrog (without the sea): old gentry, rich Jews, merchants, peasants, a horse thief, student, a teacher, a doctor and a bluestocking all come together and interact in the drawing room of a bankrupt estate somewhere in the south of Russia. And with the bankrupt family home that will be sold at auction, Chekhov made use of his own family's financial failure shortly after that trauma.

Chekhov learned from the failure of *Fatherlessness*: spending it all did not work, whereas holding back would make Chekhov the author we now appreciate. Self-restraint – to which there is a certain cost, no doubt – becomes a dominant personality trait in Chekhov. You can see it in his growing reticence to talk about his works in his letters, as well as in his decreasing literary production and greater care with creative ideas, traceable in what we have by way of notebooks documenting his creative process. Those notebooks begin in 1891 and show a Chekhov husbanding his resources: bits of dialogue, microplots and other details would be banked until a worthy vehicle for their deployment was in the works. An analogous pattern stands out in Chekhov's revisions of the early works he included in the collected works that was published in the last years of his life: his edits always involved cutting, toning down, introducing greater subtlety.

Nevertheless, one has to register the strikingly keen observation behind the aphorisms and witticisms of the adolescent *Fatherlessness*. The precocious young writer eager to show what he knew was indeed wise beyond his years. As the Yale scholar Robert Louis Jackson once put it, 'At twenty Chekhov was forty or fifty.'[10] Chekhov's first published pseudonym may have been 'Young Old Man' (*Iunyi starets*), under which appeared a few pieces likely attributable to Chekhov while he was still in Taganrog (*Letopis'* I, pp. 54, 55, 56). In the years after *Fatherlessness*, Chekhov developed better ways to make artistic use of his wisdom.

The family's finances improved as soon as Chekhov arrived in Moscow: in his first year of university, Chekhov brought more income to the family than did his father's employment. To supplement his scholarship, Chekhov pursued tutoring opportunities and recruited two of his schoolmates from the Taganrog *zemstvo* doctors' club as boarders. Obtaining his monthly 25 rubles involved difficulties, though: the funds were transferred through the university, which had to certify Chekhov's enrolment; and since the family had pulled up stakes in Taganrog, Chekhov had to return there from time to time to maintain his status as a son of the city. Soon his writing turned profitable as well: with connections facilitated by his two older brothers, he was quickly off and running, earning five kopecks a line for very short pieces that, at the start, added 150–200 rubles in income a year.

Chekhov debuted with short sketches infused with the spirit of parody and play. The first published work that can be attributed to him with certainty was 'Letter of the Don Landowner Stepan Vladimirovich N to the Scholarly Neighbor Dr Fridrikh' ('Pis'mo donskogo pomeshchika Stepana Vladimirovicha N k uchenomu sosedu d-ru Fridrikhu'), which appeared under a pseudonym comprising only the last letter of his family name (V) in the journal *Dragonfly* (*Strekoza*) in March 1880.[11]

The fictional missive combines ignorance and assertiveness in advancing absurd, pseudoscientific arguments – for instance, against evolutionary theory – while demonstrating low but pretentious literacy in a way that calls to mind the Chekhov family patriarchs.

A second piece soon followed, 'Elements Most Often Found in Novels, Short Stories, Etc.' ('Chto chashche vsego vstrechaetsia v romanakh, povestiakh i t. p.'). Little more than a list of devices that mocks melodramatic and implausible plots, it is almost short enough to cite in full; instead, here are the first and last lines:

> A count, a countess still showing traces of a once great beauty,
> a neighboring baron, a liberal man of letters, an impoverished
> nobleman, a foreign musician, slow-witted manservants, nurses,
> governesses, a German bailiff, a squire, and an heir from America.

> More often than not, no ending.
> Seven deadly sins at the beginning and a wedding at the end.
> The end.[12]

Soon Chekhov was publishing regularly in the 'small press', into which his brothers had ushered him: anecdotes, stylized letters, dialogues, spoofs on authors of romance and adventure, captions to accompany the humorous illustrations of his brother Nikolai and other graphic artists, and odd and incongruous lists like 'Elements Most Often Found'. In addition to appearing in *Dragonfly*, his works were featured in *Alarm Clock* (*Budil'nik*), *Spectator* (*Zritel'*), *Russian News* (*Russkie vedomosti*), *Moscow* and *Worldly Chatter* (*Mirskoi tolk*). Chekhov published under pseudonyms, the most famous and frequently utilized of which was 'Antosha Chekhonte', and such variations as 'Chekhonte' and 'A. Chekhonte', based on the nickname coined by his teacher of religion at the gymnasium in Taganrog. By the time of his death, Chekhov had used more than fifty such monikers, if one counts all variations. Some notable others were 'Brother of My Brother' (*Brat moego brata*), 'Doctor without Patients' (*Vrach bez patsientov*), and 'Man without a Spleen' (*Chelovek bez selezenki*).

What was at stake in hiding behind pseudonyms? On the one hand, Chekhov was far from anonymous in the milieu of the small press; indeed, his publishing activities created a wide network of personal associations that lasted the rest of his life. Moreover, operating under pseudonyms was conventional in that world, and distributing them among various venues allowed Chekhov to market a degree of exclusivity to multiple publishers: some did not want to see him appear with competitors under a name he was also using in their periodical. Also, if one aspired to higher literary status, then – as Chekhov warned one of his protégés, Yelena Shavrova, two decades later – pseudonyms might protect the mature, serious author of the future from embarrassment on account of juvenile works that had appeared in lowbrow journals.[13] At the start, however, Chekhov hardly anticipated a serious literary career; rather, he was saving his family name for the scientific work he hoped someday to publish, beginning with a dissertation in medicine.

On the other hand, Chekhov certainly had deeper reasons for sticking with pseudonyms. A complicated dialectic between self-exposure and hiding pervades both his life and his works, where the vicissitudes of seeing and being seen comprise a ubiquitous theme. He told the writer Yeronim Yasinsky that writing under a pseudonym was 'just like walking naked with a large mask on and showing oneself like that to the public'.[14] Fame would become difficult for Chekhov, for whom it mattered very much whether and how the public saw him. Writing for the theatre became a particularly risky endeavour for him precisely because it involved a heightened visibility to the public. Wholly attributing Chekhov's use of pseudonyms in the early part of his career to conventions of the field would be facile.[15]

Soon after Chekhov's arrival with the boarders the Chekhov family began a series of migrations from the cramped, damp, basement location in the red light district where they started to ever more comfortable rentals.[16] Then, in August 1880, Chekhov's younger brother Ivan took a position as director of a parochial school in Voskresensk, near Istra and the New Jerusalem Monastery northwest of Moscow; the following year, Chekhov's mother, Maria and Mikhail summered with Ivan, and though Chekhov was too busy with his publishing activities to join them, he visited. This started a tradition of summer family holidays outside Moscow, and it also shaped Chekhov's future medical career: he met the director of the nearby *zemstvo* hospital in Chikino, Dr P. A. Arkhangelsky, and when in 1882 and 1883 Chekhov did spend some of the summer in Voskresensk, he saw patients with the hospital's doctors and gained practical experience. He would return after finishing his course of study in 1884 and, for his first authentic medical job, serve two weeks as a locum in nearby Zvenigorod hospital while its director, Dr Uspensky, was on holiday.

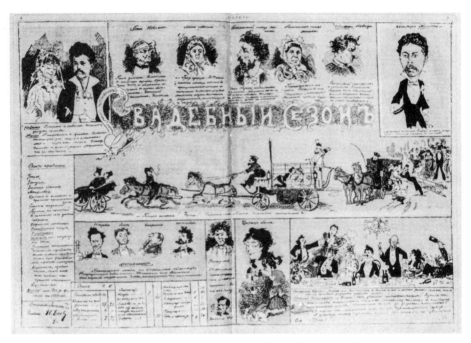

'The Wedding Season', 1881, with graphics by Nikolai Chekhov and text by Anton Chekhov.

In the summer of 1881, Chekhov and his brother Nikolai returned to Taganrog to serve as best men at the wedding of a cousin from a wealthy family on their mother's side. The result was a lampoon, 'The Wedding Season' ('Svadebnyi sezon'), for which Nikolai provided graphics and Chekhov the captions. Family and friends were angry to find themselves caricatured when the piece came out in *Spectator*; a year later Alexander, who had moved to Taganrog for work as a customs official, still recommended against their returning anytime soon (*Letopis'* 1, pp. 87–8, 96). Over the years Chekhov would periodically anger, and sometimes flatter, friends and associates through such allusions. Their propensity to read themselves into his works could reach unbelievable extremes; nevertheless, Chekhov's own denial of any connection would usually ring false. The person Chekhov and his brothers probably made fun of most often was their sententious, self-centred father. The siblings' letters often mimic their father's turns of speech. How can you not laugh at a family patriarch who tells his sons (without irony) that they need to give him money so that he can pay his rent, because 'It's not appropriate for a man of my age to blush before the landlord – I am a man of character, a staid man' (*Letopis'* 1, p. 105). Although Pavel's language made it into

Chekhov's fiction, this caused no scandal: he seems not to have read his sons' writings or seen Chekhov's plays, in spite of demanding respect as the father of famous sons.

By the end of 1881 the Chekhov family home had regained a degree of bourgeois comfort and stability. The poet Liodor Palmin, who was scheming to introduce Chekhov to Nikolai Leikin, publisher of the St Petersburg humour magazine *Fragments* (*Oskolki*), wrote to Leikin: 'Amidst their family wafts something warm, artistic, civilized, European. By the way, they have a piano, violin, and Nikolai has the soul of a true artist' (*Letopis'* I, p. 88). A few years earlier he might have witnessed a beating and the howling of a patriarchal scandal scene, but with Chekhov in charge those days were over; so too was Chekhov's deference to his older brothers, in particular Alexander. Whereas prior correspondence had included much fatherly advice from Alexander on matters of life and literature, now it was Chekhov identifying faults in his elder brother's writing and personal conduct.[17]

In autumn 1882 Palmin succeeded in connecting Chekhov and Leikin, and by the end of November Chekhov was publishing in *Fragments*. This was a major break: Leikin quickly became the early Chekhov's most important publisher, and he would help pave the way for the following steps in Chekhov's career, and introduce Chekhov to Petersburg publishers. Leikin was the leading master of the genre of the 'little scene' (*stsenka*); he had found a winning formula with *Fragments* and stuck to it. Chekhov's works were cut or rejected if they ran beyond the word limit, lacked the required comic dimension, were out of season or late in addressing news of the day. At times Leikin would take pieces and hold them in reserve for better timing: a cartoon about a fire that was ready too long after the newsworthy event that had prompted it could await the next catastrophe, since fires were reliable givens of Russian life. A belated Christmas story might be transformed into a New Year's piece, or it might appear the following year. Chekhov the craftsman produced according to his buyer's specifications; Chekhov the artist bristled under the restrictions, and he had to turn to other venues for longer works lacking the *Fragments* style of humour, as with an 1883 piece about a hunting addict, 'He Understood! (A Sketch)' ('On ponial (Etiud)').[18]

Throughout the 1880s Chekhov showed a mind-boggling capacity for work. His university grades indicate a better student than he had been in Taganrog. Meanwhile he produced a prodigious quantity of short stories and sketches: 42 between March 1880 and November 1882;

Chekhov with his brother Nikolai, early 1880s.

an astounding 224 over the next two and a half years; 106 between May 1885 and February 1886; and 156 between the latter date and March 1888.[19] Virtually all the works from the first five years appeared under pseudonyms. Chekhov also enjoyed Moscow's musical and theatrical scene, which he could turn to profit by publishing reviews, and he led a very active social life, developing ever more contacts in the arts world.

Chekhov as a student, 1882.

Still, Chekhov was a committed student who expected medicine to be his chief profession and who had ambitions for higher degrees and an academic career. His coursework and grades are a matter of record, and student colleagues who left memoirs describe him as diligent and responsible in attending lectures and completing assignments. In a time of frequent student political activity, he held himself somewhat apart – if he attended a gathering, it was as an observer, not a participant.

Well before finishing his studies he was providing medical care for family and friends. He was particularly proud of his diagnostic abilities, and after the death of a friend he had been attending, the writer Fyodor Popudoglo, he crowed that he alone 'among 20 doctors' figured out what was ailing him while he was still alive: 'He died from alcohol and good friends' (*Letopis'* I, p. 137).

Nevertheless, autumn 1883 brought a small sign of Chekhov's increasing investment in his literary activities. For the first time, the signature 'A. Chekhov', rather than one of the many pseudonyms he had been using, appeared with the story 'At Sea' ('V more'), in *Worldly Chatter*; earlier that month he had likewise sent in 'He Understood!' under his own name, and some months before that the longish parody of a detective story, 'The Swedish Match' ('Shvedskaia spichka'), for publication in a *Dragonfly* almanac. These first deliberate public exposures of himself as an author were toes in the water that did not cause him to plunge in. On the contrary, he was upset when *News of the Day* (*Novosti dnia*) published one of his trifles ('The Exam', or 'Ekzamen') around the same time under his name, though he had provided a pseudonym with it; and he also attempted, too late, to withdraw the salacious 'At Sea' from publication, perhaps as anxious about the signature as its content: a sailor and his father win the right to stand at peepholes carved into the wall of a steamer's bridal suite. In a letter to Leikin, who had complained about Chekhov's appearances among his competitors – though *Fragments* would never have published those pieces – Chekhov averred that he was ready to start using his name (25 December 1883), but it would be a few more years before he took that step, and then only after prodding from an important new publisher.[20]

With Chekhov's writing career launched, this seems a good moment to linger over an exemplary story from the period, generalize on Chekhov's early comic tales, and outline key features of his poetics of prose. Doing so will flesh out implicit principles guiding the brief and unavoidably fragmentary interpretations that are scattered through the book, and it will also contest the frequently dismissive scholarly attitude towards Chekhov's early work.

'The Death of a Clerk (An Incident)' ('Smert' chinovnika (Sluchai)'), published in *Fragments* in 1883 and signed with the pseudonym A. Chekhonte, was rated highly enough by Chekhov to be placed (with minimal changes) in the collected works he prepared towards the end of his life. It has since been frequently anthologized and adapted for the stage, including by Neil Simon.[21] Like much of the early comic Chekhov, the brief tale flaunts Gogolian features: a digression-prone narrator, the motif of noses and theme of rank-consciousness, and a denouement where a petty official dies after a dressing down by a high superior all recall Gogol's 'The Overcoat' ('Shinel'', 1842). But Chekhov avoids any pathos-laden evocations of sympathy for his victim, or the grotesque and fantastic elements that so surprise Gogol's readers, to say nothing of the new psychological depth and genuine empathy that characterized Dostoevsky's development of the so-called 'little man' character in his early works.

Chekhov's minor civil servant sneezes in a theatre, splattering a general from another branch of service seated in front of him. The general's dismissive attitude towards the civil servant's apologies leaves the latter anxious: unconvinced that his efforts in the theatre have been registered, he compulsively and repeatedly visits the general in his office. He makes such a nuisance of himself that the general finally grows enraged and kicks him out, whereupon 'Something in Cherviakov's stomach snapped. Seeing nothing, hearing nothing, he backed his way to the door, went out, and plodded off… Reaching home mechanically, without taking off his uniform, he lay down on the sofa and… died' (*Stories*, p. 3).

The comic effect of this anecdotal tale relies in large measure on three obvious features. First, there is the machine-like repetition of apologizing, which recalls Henri Bergson's assertion that 'The attitudes, gestures and movements of the human body are laughable in exact proportion as that body reminds us of a mere machine.'[22] Repetition is reduplicated on the stylistic level of the story as well, beginning with the very first sentence: 'One fine evening the no less fine office manager Ivan Dmitrich was sitting in the second row of the stalls, watching *The Bells of Corneville* through opera glasses. He watched […]' (*Stories*, p. 1). Second is an odd disjunction between the transgression comprising the plot's complication (a sneeze) and the outcome or denouement (death). The third feature, another disjunction of sorts, is the incongruent location of the *psychic* trauma that results in death in the *belly* of Cherviakov, where 'something snapped'.

And yet, however caricaturish and unreal this tale may be, it exhibits principles of plot construction and psychological themes that pervade Chekhov's writings and characterize the mature Chekhov at his most profound. As is often the case in Chekhov's early works, what is extraordinarily subtle and often unspoken in the late Chekhov appears right there on the table for us to see. To begin with, there is the handling of plot. In the mature Chekhov's prose and drama, traditional conventions of plot construction are famously eschewed. Now, this story could hardly be called plotless; indeed, the reverse is signalled by the opening metaliterary digression on the frequency of the phrase, 'but suddenly…' (*Stories*, p. 1). Nevertheless, canonical aspects of Chekhov's later handling of plot already appear here. Where is the dramatic conflict? The sneeze that crosses from row two to row one to splatter the bald pate of the general may transgress rules of audience comportment and social-hierarchal boundaries, but all consequences from this action issue from the sneezer's own worries about the sneeze, right up to the point where that anatomically absurd 'something' snaps in Cherviakov's gut. This projection of plot inwards – into the mind (or belly) of one individual, rather than as emerging from the actions, reactions and interactions of a set of characters – is utterly characteristic of the later Chekhov and will also become a defining feature of his drama, as is implicit in Meyerhold's description of the mature Chekhov's 'theatre of mood'.[23]

Unsubtle and overt aspects of this story's humour persist in modulated and nuanced ways in the mature Chekhov. Thus the talking name of the sneezer, Cherviakov, alludes to the Russian for 'worm' (*cherv'*). This detail fits into the story's psychological theme of self-esteem, the drive of the small to be seen by the great and the dependency of selfhood on the acknowledgement of others. It also connects with the temptation to exhibitionism, grandiosity and vanity that tickles Cherviakov's nose; after all, sneezing at a concert or theatrical event means drawing attention to oneself and, however momentarily, away from what all in the audience have come to see: it involves a kind of unsuccessfully suppressed exhibitionism. Exhibitionism, hiding and peeping, construed in the widest possible sense, together comprise a pervasive theme in Chekhov, one that is most often handled overtly to comic effect in the early works, but much more subtly in the later ones. It creates a node between Chekhov's literary works, his professional career as a physician, and his thinking about professional identity in general, fame, and his personal life as well.[24]

The official positions of the two main characters in this story evoke an irony that pervades Chekhov, but without the subtlety of later works. The name of the department of transportation in which the general serves, *putei soobshcheniia*, translates literally as 'ways (or means) of communication'. Failure of communication has long been recognized as one of Chekhov's arch themes, and it is the general's refusal to communicate with Cherviakov (beyond a dismissive wave of the hand) that incites the latter to ever more desperate means. Cherviakov's own position is as *ekzekutor*, that is, the official charged with overseeing the order and proper functioning of an office or department; this makes his nasal breach of etiquette also a disruption of his own positional or professional identity. This cartoonish story thus lays out thematic concerns that will persist through Chekhov's mature career.

By the end of spring 1884, Chekhov had passed his final exams at the faculty of medicine. Official certification would wait until the autumn, but in the meantime he asked that his credentials be sent to the town of Voskresensk in preparation for his medical work there that summer.

A critical next step in his literary career was also under way: Chekhov had arranged for six of his stories to be printed in a volume titled *Tales of Melpomene* (*Skazki Mel'pomeny*), under the signature of A. Chekhonte. In a vanity publishing venture, the Moscow print shop of A. A. Levenson produced 1,200 copies on credit, giving Chekhov four months to come up with 200 rubles (*Letopis'* 1, pp. 156–7). Alexander distributed them to Moscow bookshops, since Chekhov was now working in Voskresensk and nearby Zvenigorod, where in addition to hospital duties he performed as coroner and forensic pathologist for the district. He somehow managed to write, too, and also enjoy a bit of fishing, mushrooming and hunting.

On a quick trip back to Moscow in July, Chekhov submitted his only full-length novel for publication in *News of the Day*. A detective parody, *The Shooting Party* (*Drama na okhote (Istinnoe proisshestvie)*), was serialized from August to April 1884; Mikhail was sent weekly to collect Chekhov's meagre pay for it. Chekhov came to dislike this newspaper intensely, nicknaming it 'Trash' or 'Dirty Tricks' (*pakosti* instead of *novosti*) of the Day. The novel, which Chekhov later excluded from his collected works, involves a remarkable experiment in the handling of narrative point of view, a hallmark of Chekhov's stylistics: only at the end do we learn that its narrator, a detective investigating the murder of a young woman, was both her lover and her killer. Agatha Christie would borrow the device in *The Murder of Roger Ackroyd* (1926).

In September, back in Moscow, Chekhov had the sign 'Doctor A. P. Chekhov' attached to the door of his home. This legally obliged him to see any patients who might visit, though his practice mostly served acquaintances and their families, especially those without means from the lower echelons of the world of arts. Chekhov never showed any inclination to turn his medical work to profit, though that autumn he did apply to work at the Moscow Children's Hospital (*Letopis'* 1, p. 175). Doctoring met the obligation to serve that had been implicit in his education, and it reflected an altruistic social commitment. Given Chekhov's many undertakings, this new chapter in his life might have taken the title of one of his *Entertainment* (*Razvlechenie*) stories from September, 'Out of the Frying Pan and into the Fire' ('Iz ognia da v polymia'). Leikin visited Moscow and, seeking to draw Chekhov closer to himself and away from Moscow journals, offered to help him find a doctor's position in St Petersburg (*Letopis'* 1, pp. 167–8, 192), but Chekhov had become a confirmed Muscovite and family tied him down. Besides, most other journals paid more than *Fragments* and would publish works that did not fit the *Fragments* template. Above all, these days 'I absolutely cannot earn less than 150–180 rubles a month,' he wrote to Leikin (17 November 1884), and that was far more than he could draw from *Fragments*. Leikin was particularly upset when Chekhov appeared elsewhere during the annual subscription period and blamed him for circulation declines. Eventually Chekhov offered *Fragments* exclusivity for certain pseudonyms, but by this time he was already moving on.

The year 1884 was a portentous one in other ways as well. In the late autumn, while covering the court case resulting from a scandalous bank collapse for the *Petersburg Gazette* (*Peterburgskaia gazeta*) under the pseudonym of Ruver, Chekhov suffered his first serious bout of blood spitting, which lasted several days. He was now on notice that his life would likely be short. In this instance he sought medical assistance from his old friend Dr Savelyev, and he even considered seeking financial help to travel abroad for his health. But he would soon adopt a policy of underplaying signs of tubercular infection, avoiding all medical attention and dismissing any thoughts of organizing his life around his health needs, until a massive haemorrhage defeated that strategy in 1897. Also on the sick list by now was Chekhov's best-known pseudonym: Chekhonte had been outed in an article, 'A Dictionary of the Pseudonyms and Initials of Russian Writers' ('Slovar' psevdonimov i initsialov russkikh pisatelei'; *Letopis'* 1, p. 179). Although Chekhov would continue to use pseudonyms in the 'small press' for several years, he was approaching a fundamental change in this aspect of his literary practice.

In St Petersburg, Leikin could not quite figure out how to handle his star. He threatened to denounce Chekhov as unreliable to other journals while also boasting about having 'discovered a new Shchedrin' – high recommendation indeed. In May, Chekhov's fiction started appearing under the pseudonym of A. Chekhonte in the *Petersburg Gazette*, where he had previously published as Ruver. This gave him a venue for longer and more serious works (*Letopis'* 1, pp. 186, 189, 191).

In 1885 Chekhov once again took his family to summer in the appealing Voskresensk area, this time renting a dacha at Babkino, the gentry estate of the distinguished but declining Kiselev family, with whom the Chekhovs would grow quite close. Maria Kiseleva was a children's author, and her father, V. P. Begichev, was director of Moscow theatres (a government position). Chekhov took Dr Arkhangelsky's place at Chikino for a few days, which included performing an autopsy on a peasant who had died suddenly. At summer's end he told Leikin that he had seen several hundred patients and earned all of one ruble (14 September 1885); he had also found time for outdoor recreation and writing.

Chekhov's friend Palmin had recently lamented that the talented Chekhov 'stoops to the writing of petty little scenes in this pitiful contemporary, bourgeois puppet-theatre, spirit' (*Letopis'* 1, p. 194). This sentiment was soon echoed by a pedigreed literary figure. 'The Huntsman' ('Eger''), a bitingly ironic short sketch with clever handling of narrative point of view, poetic nature description and poignant dialogue between a peasant husband and wife, caught the attention of Dmitry Grigorovich, an old-timer best known for his peasant characters. Grigorovich had been Dostoevsky's roommate when the latter wrote *Poor Folk* (*Bednye liudi*, 1846) and played a supporting role in making Dostoevsky an instant literary star. Now he took two steps that were fateful for Chekhov: he showed Chekhov's piece to Alexei Suvorin, publisher of Russia's biggest daily newspaper, *New Times* (*Novoe vremia*); and the following March he wrote to Chekhov, praising the tale's verity and warning Chekhov that he would commit a 'great moral sin' if he did not take himself seriously and realize his talent (*Letopis'* 1, pp. 198, 236). Chekhov's response was self-abasing: the letter, he said, 'struck me like a thunderbolt'. He blamed his low status on the Moscow literary milieu, where 'I can't remember even one of them ever reading my things or considering me an artist', and also his medical profession: 'I am a doctor and up to my ears in medicine. The saying about chasing two hares at once has never robbed anybody of more sleep than it has me.' He had never been able to put more than a day into a story, and 'The Huntsman' was written while out swimming (28 March 1886; *Letters*, p. 58). Over the years Chekhov would often deploy the saying about chasing two hares, almost always negating it to assert that his dual career benefited both medicine and literature; now, however, he sought an excuse.

In explaining why he wished his pseudonym to appear over a volume of his stories in the works, *Motley Tales of A. Chekhonte* (*Pestrye rasskazy A. Chekhonte*), Chekhov had written to Viktor Bilibin at *Fragments* that he was saving his family name for medicine, and that 'sooner or later he would have to part with literature' (14 February 1886); then, after receiving Grigorovich's letter, Chekhov asked that 'An. P. Chekhov' be placed in parentheses after his pseudonym (*Letopis'* 1, pp. 238, 279). As we shall see, Chekhov had decided to publish under his own name – in the appropriate venue – even before Grigorovich's intervention.

Grigorovich would claim to have discovered Chekhov, a matching bookend for his exploit with Dostoevsky early in his career. But in fact Chekhov had already begun taking himself quite seriously as a writer. In mid-December 1885 Leikin had finally succeeded in bringing Chekhov to St Petersburg, where he proudly squired his protégé about, introducing him to key figures of the capital's literary scene. Chekhov professed shock at discovering that he was known. In his New Year's letter to Alexander, now serving in Novorossiysk, he tried to share this pleasure and its promise:

> But the main thing: as much as possible, watch out, take notice and strain yourself, rewriting everything five times, cutting, and so on, remembering, that all of Petersburg is following the work of the brothers Chekhov. I was astonished by the reception given me by the Petersburgers. Suvorin, Grigorovich, Burenin... invitations and praises everywhere... and I became horrified at how carelessly I had been writing, not bothering to roll up my sleeves. If I had known that they were reading me, I wouldn't have written that way, to order... Remember: they're reading you. (4 January 1886)

Soon Chekhov was publishing under his own name in *New Times*. He sent his first story, 'The Requiem' ('Panikhida'), in February 1886 under the pseudonym Antosha Chekhonte, but readily agreed when asked to use the Chekhov family name, which then became his regular practice with that paper; this was before Grigorovich's letter. Fittingly, the paternal name is a significant motif in 'The Requiem', where a pedantically religious tradesman very reminiscent of Chekhov's father cannot understand why the priest rebukes him for offering communion bread 'For the departed servant of God, the harlot Maria' (*Stories*, p. 22); he is ashamed of his daughter Maria, who became a famous actress but died young.

Suvorin grew very close to Chekhov over the next decade. A travelling companion and Chekhov's most important interlocutor on matters of aesthetics, politics and philosophy, he kept a room for Chekhov at his St Petersburg mansion. Still, there was a downside to publishing with Suvorin that, fifteen years later, would drive Chekhov from the orbits of both the journal and the person. Suvorin's social background was much like Chekhov's, and in his early years as a journalist he had been a progressive. No more: *New Times* was now a bullhorn for reactionary ideology,

Isaac Ilyich Levitan,
Anton Chekhov (study),
1885–6, oil on paper.

and Suvorin's financial empire owed much to a government-controlled monopoly on book and newspaper sales at train stations. Collaborating with *New Times* put Chekhov at odds with most of the literary elite, and especially those in control of the most important publishing venues, the so-called 'thick journals', which tended to be liberal in outlook. Chekhov relished not toeing the ideological line, though there can be no doubts regarding his critical stance towards the tsarist regime. Above all, he prized independence of thought, rejecting groupthink and reflexively correct positions. As an author of fiction he put aesthetics before politics. He knew the association with Suvorin could hurt him: when Bilibin urged him to become more ambitious and write something major, Chekhov agreed, but asked for help finding a place to publish a long work, since the thick journals would be unlikely to let him in after his debut in *New Times* (28 February 1886). Fuel was added to the fire when, in October 1886, *New Times* published Chekhov's story 'Mire' ('Tina'), with its overtly antisemitic theme (mouthed by the story's Jewish female seducer). Vukol Lavrov, editor of the weighty, liberal *Russian Thought* (*Russkaia mysl'*), asserted that the story could only have appeared in *New Times* (*Letopis'* I, p. 269).

Leikin struggled to maintain control of his star. He encouraged Chekhov to send pieces to the *Petersburg Gazette* that were inappropriate or dangerous for *Fragments*, on which the censors were severe, but he was jealous all the same. He cut *Petersburg Gazette* out of the deal to publish Chekhov's next collection of stories, *Motley Tales*; he offered Chekhov 600 rubles a year if he would desist from further publication with *Alarm Clock*, his Moscow competitor; he tried to stipulate how much and with which other venues Chekhov might publish; he told Chekhov that his long pieces were inferior to the short comic stories he wrote for *Fragments*; he advised Chekhov to hold out for higher royalties from *Petersburg Gazette*, which happily paid a higher rate than *Fragments*; and he even raised *Fragments'* pay to eight kopecks per line (*Letopis'* I, pp. 222, 216, 230, 267, 268).

Suvorin paid twelve kopecks per line, which the *Petersburg Gazette* offered to match starting in 1887, whereas Leikin would not. Above all, with *New Times* Chekhov enjoyed flexibility of genre, length and timetable – no more nagging deadlines! Leikin badgered and, in ungenerous responses to what Chekhov sent to *Fragments*, often tried to cut Chekhov down a notch while keeping him tethered. Outwardly polite, Chekhov mistrusted Leikin and spoke of him with hostility to Alexander and others even while trying to help them publish in *Fragments* (and elsewhere, if he could). His letters to Leikin still contain surprising intimacies – for instance, about his blood spitting and fear of being sounded, lest he be diagnosed as tubercular (6 April 1886) – but with Leikin references to his bad health also served the pragmatic function of warding off deadlines and demands for new stories. On the same day that he confided about his health to Leikin, to Alexander he boasted, 'Leikin has gone out of fashion. His place is now taken by me. In Petersburg now I'm very much in fashion' (6 April 1886). Though their business relationship withered, Chekhov did maintain contact with Leikin, who in later years repeatedly proposed travels together, from which Chekhov always begged off. They shared a passion for dogs, and Leikin would regularly supply Chekhov with animals bred on his estate, including, in 1892, the famous dachshunds that Chekhov named Bromide and Quinine.

For now, Chekhov continued placing pseudonymous works in *Fragments*, *Petersburg Gazette* and other 'small press' venues, though soon he would be receiving invitations to collaborate with top-rank journals and banking energy and material for longer, more ambitious efforts. He had to produce and sell, as expenses steadily rose and funds were always in short supply: in January 1886 he could only attend his friend Dr Rozanov's wedding as best man by borrowing clothing and cash (*Letopis'* 1, p. 218).

By mid-May 1886 Chekhov had returned for the summer to Babkino, where his friend and Nikolai's colleague, the landscape artist Isaac Levitan, was also residing to recuperate from illness. Chekhov substituted once again in the Zvenigorod hospital for a few days and was summoned by authorities to perform a forensic autopsy. Not well himself, he was extremely busy and returned periodically to Moscow on business. Most reviews of *Motley Tales* were positive, but in the thick journal *Northern Herald* (*Severnyi vestnik*) an anonymous piece (by A. M. Skabichevsky, though Chekhov thought its author was the weightier N. K. Mikhailovsky) placed Chekhov in 'the guild of newspaper clowns' and called his book the 'sad and tragic spectacle of the suicide of a young talent'. This was the article Chekhov would long remember and cite as having predicted that he would finish 'as a squeezed-out lemon, and like a squeezed lemon, he will end up dying by a wall somewhere, utterly forgotten' (*Letopis'* 1, p. 252).[25]

When the Chekhovs returned to Moscow in the autumn, it was once again to a new home. For several years they had ended their leases and avoided rental payments while summering elsewhere, which meant moving when the dacha season ended. This time Maria found a home they would keep for four years, the two-storey brick wing of a wooden house (no longer extant) of a Dr Korneev on what is now Sadovaya-Kudrinskaya Boulevard. This is the site of today's Moscow Chekhov House-Museum.

After this move Chekhov forewent hanging the doctor's sign on his door, as he would for the rest of his life. Still, he kept busy with medicine as well as literature. In inviting a provincial literary figure to visit, he wrote, 'as a doctor I receive every day from 12 to 3; for writers my door is open day and night' (*Letopis'* 1, p. 333). Among those he treated was his brother Nikolai, whom he brought home seriously ill and spitting up blood, a portent of worse to come. He also initiated a pattern of philanthropic efforts in the educational sphere in paying the St Petersburg printer Roman Golike to produce one hundred gradebooks for Ivan's school (*P* 1, p. 258; *Letopis'* 1, p. 263).

Although Chekhov never left medicine altogether, something had changed. Brother Mikhail attributed Chekhov's shift away from medicine to a traumatizing therapeutic failure. At the end of 1885, Chekhov attended the mother and three sisters of the artist Alexander Yanov, an art school friend of Nikolai. The women had been stricken by typhoid. The mother and one sister died – the latter while gripping Chekhov's hand – and according to Mikhail, 'Her cold handshake instilled such feelings of helplessness and guilt in Anton that he contemplated abandoning medicine altogether. And indeed, after this case he gradually switched the focus of his energies to literature and only treated the occasional patient.'[26] But Mikhail overstates the tailing off of Chekhov's medical career, and certainly factors other than the Yanov family catastrophe were in play. True, Chekhov professed an 'as though mystical' fear of the typhus epidemic in Moscow, which in short order killed six doctors from Chekhov's graduating class: 'I'm afraid! I'm afraid of nothing, but I'm afraid of this typhus...' (*Letopis'* I, p. 234; letter to Bilibin, 11 March 1886). But he continued to go when summoned to treat those suffering from it.

The surviving Yanov girls became frequent visitors to the Chekhovs and guests at their table. At the beginning of the new year, Maria Yanova gave Chekhov a small hand-sewn album for photographs, inscribed 'in memory of her deliverance from typhoid' (*Letopis'* I, p. 216); it is still held by the museum at the Yalta Chekhov home. Within the year, the Yanov episode had itself found its way into Chekhov's fiction, transformed into the superficially comic 'Work of Art' ('Proizvedenie iskusstva'; December 1886), a story where celebration of a doctor's therapeutic triumph is undermined by uncanny anxieties of loss and failure.[27]

Around this time Chekhov also abandoned his second project for a PhD dissertation in medicine, ceasing his two-year practice of collecting materials towards a 'History of Doctoring in Russia'. We cannot know just what Chekhov's scholarly intentions had been, as no discussion of the project was found in his extant correspondence; Chekhov's notes were found only long after his death, and memoirists do not speak of it. Still, the 79 pages of the Academy edition devoted to those notes show noteworthy breadth in defining his subject. They derive from reading published primary and secondary works dating back to medieval times, as well as significant bibliographic work to determine just what sources he should be looking at. Those range from medieval chronicles, the *Domostroi* (a sixteenth-century rulebook for household organization, in line with Church, autocracy and the patriarchal order), collections of folklore and other nineteenth-century ethnographic studies, travel accounts of foreigners in Russia, and histories like that of Nikolai Karamzin.[28] Although he dropped this project, the ambition to pursue medical research never left Chekhov, as his 1890 Sakhalin expedition and the book he wrote about it testify. For the moment, however, literary ambitions were displacing medical ones. Many of the short tales from this period, including some first published under pseudonyms, are frequently anthologized together with his finest mature work. The period 1886–7 was a watershed.

In a quite different but rather obscure arena of life, Chekhov came close to marrying at this time, going so far as to propose to his sister's friend Dunya Efros on his name day (17 January) in 1886. There is very little solid documentary evidence about his engagement, which was apparently kept secret from his family; after Chekhov's death, his surprised sister withheld what she had discovered from the public eye. Relations between the pair were stormy, and Efros was Jewish and unwilling to convert to Russian Orthodoxy. Six weeks later, Chekhov wrote to his friend Bilibin that the two had split definitively. He joked, 'But I have not yet bought a revolver and am not writing a diary' (*Letopis'* I, p. 231). In the 1890s Chekhov, Efros and the man she eventually married, the Jewish lawyer Efim Konovitser, re-established very friendly relations,[29] but at the moment he was upset.

Indeed, Chekhov's letter about the break-up contains antisemitic language that does not match common images of Chekhov's ethics and open-mindedness. His native city Taganrog was a very cosmopolitan town with a large Jewish population, and Chekhov had close Jewish friends from the earliest days. His insistence that Efros convert may have been entirely practical, as lawful marriage was otherwise impossible, but Chekhov showed no particular concern about religious propriety when his older brothers were involved with Jewish women; indeed, he urged his brother Alexander to ignore their father's harangues, as this was his personal business. He himself had a two-year affair with the Jewish woman Natalya Golden, who years later became Alexander's second wife. Later in life Chekhov would side with Émile Zola in the Dreyfus affair, but already as a gymnasium student in Taganrog he had organized a successful protest against the expulsion of a Jewish student who had slapped the face of a boy who had called him a 'yid' (*Letopis'* I, p. 51). And yet Chekhov was capable of using that derogatory term himself (albeit in a time and place where it was less hostile than today); he insisted that his fiancée convert to Orthodoxy; and around the time of his affair with Efros he published the clearly Judaeophobic 'Mire', while subsequent treatments of the Jewish theme, if not antisemitic, betrayed no little ambivalence.[30]

The story appeared in *New Times* at the end of October 1886. It opens with a young officer on leave arriving at a vodka distillery to collect, on behalf of his cousin, a debt owed for oats purchased by the late father of the distillery's current owner, Susanna. Ushered into what turns out to be the woman's bedroom, the lieutenant finds a strange, Oriental, jasmine-scented space, and the woman in an expensive Chinese robe and with her head wrapped such that he can see only her long (Jewish) nose and one (Cyclops) eye. He explains that the debts he collects for his cousin will fund a 5,000-ruble security deposit required by the army for him to marry (as an officer under 28). Susanna agrees to pay off the debt only after considerable ranting against both women and Jews – that is, herself – but when she gets the chance, she snatches the I.O.U. from the lieutenant. The wrestling that follows leads to sex and the lieutenant's return to his cousin's estate with neither funds nor document. His outraged cousin sets out to settle matters and only returns the next day, having been likewise seduced. After a week, when the lieutenant asks for a horse to go back to the woman for a visit, his cousin gives him a wad of rubles and urges him to return by post horse to his unit, which he agrees to do. Another week passes. Dull family life becomes too much for the cousin and he slips out to visit the distillery, where he finds the lieutenant (among other male captives) held like Odysseus' crew on the island of the Sirens, AWOL from the army and with marriage plans shattered.

This story came out in Suvorin's antisemitic newspaper at a time when the Jewish question was front and centre in a highly polarized public and governmental debate. Chekhov's portrayal of a Jewish woman who ruins Russian men appeared, in such a context, to lend his voice to the reactionary and antisemitic parties resisting the granting of civil rights to Jews;[31] worse, the most directly antisemitic remarks in the narrative, like the anti-feminist ones, are put into the mouth of Susanna herself.

Chekhov resisted calls for political correctness and refused to distance himself from Suvorin, whom he excused as having largely abdicated control of his paper's message to his son and the editorial staff. He was still inclined to talk about his work in correspondence in these years – that would change in the next decade – and so defended himself against the many critiques, by friends and literary critics, of both the story's politics and its sexual content. To Maria Kiseleva he wrote a lengthy defence that likened the writer to a reporter who

must do battle with his squeamishness and sully his imagination
with the grime of life [...] To a chemist there is nothing impure
on earth. The writer should be just as objective as the chemist;
he should liberate himself from everyday subjectivity and
acknowledge that manure piles play a highly respectable role
in the landscape and that evil passions are every bit as much
a part of life as good ones. (14 January 1887; *Letters*, p. 62)

Chekhov claims a professional, detached gaze on all matters, regardless of how low or immoral, an objectivity foundational, too, to his
professional identity as a physician.

Interestingly enough, the undoing of distancing, objectivity and professional identities is central to 'Mire'. Male identities collapse precisely
through contact with the wily Jewess. The fiancé's impending marriage dis-
solves, and as a military man he is defeated in hand-to-hand combat with
a Jewish woman who, moreover, at first appears ill and debilitated. His
cousin, too, is undermined as a husband and a businessman-landowner.
The lieutenant's first apprehension of Susanna involves a medicalizing
perspective proper to Dr Chekhov: she must be 'some kind of psycho-
path', he thinks; her pallor and pale gums suggest 'anemic weakness'
(*S* v, pp. 355, 366). But an access of desire weakens him and collapses
that analytical distance. Meanwhile, Susanna, in one of her antisemitic
and self-masculinizing rants, claims to be 'more like a hussar than a
Shmuel [i.e. Jew]' (*S* v, p. 367).

Chekhov's defence of his stance as a professional writer in the letter
to Kiseleva actually replicates what happens in his story:

> If I had known my criticism would go on for so long, I wouldn't
> have started in the first place.... Please forgive me!
>   We are coming. We wanted to leave on the fifth, but...
> we were held up by a medical congress. Then came St Tatyana's
> Day, and on the seventeenth we're having a party: it's 'his' name
> day!! It will be a dazzling ball with all sorts of Jewesses, roast
> turkeys and Yashenkas. (14 January 1887; *Letters*, p. 63)

The high-minded rhetoric with which Chekhov had defended himself
fizzles out in connection with Chekhov's upcoming name-day party,
with its anticipated drinking, dancing and concourse with Jewish women
(chief among them, presumably, Efros). The Yashenkas he refers to are the

two surviving sisters of Nikolai's art institute colleague Alexander Yanov, whom he had boasted about saving in the letter to Bilibin referring to his engagement with Efros. Now family friends, they also made the rounds of the Chekhov brothers: Chekhov refers to them elsewhere as 'whorelets'.[32] Thus, in this letter to the prim matron of the Kiselev family, from whom the Chekhovs rented their summer dacha at Babkino, Chekhov ends his discussion of 'Mire' by alluding to his own susceptibility to the mire of erotic adventure.

For Chekhov in this period the topic is repeatedly tied to a Jewish theme, perhaps reflecting his travails with Efros. His second *New Times* story, 'The Witch' ('Ved'ma'; 1886), was without Jewish characters; but the postal courier whom the story's namesake entices carries a sword 'similar in fashion to those depicted on *lubok* [popular woodblock] prints of Judith in Holofernes's lodging' (*S* IV, p. 380), a biblical allusion linking the story's 'witch' with a Jewish femme fatale.

As Chekhov ascended, his two elder brothers sank. Nikolai vanished for a time in summer 1885, and Chekhov resorted to leaving notes for him in editorial offices where he might stop by for commissions. Over the next year Nikolai came and went from the Chekhov family residence, disappearing to flophouses and abandoning work as a magazine illustrator and painter of theatrical sets that hopeful friends had lined up for him. Both Alexander and Nikolai would go on binges and run up debts that Chekhov had to cover (he was even summoned to court because of them in 1886; *Letopis'* I, p. 233). Alexander, who went blind for a while from drinking bad liquor, always clawed his way back; he had a family and work: after an abortive career in the civil service as a customs official he settled into the role of a journalist at *New Times*. Nikolai, though, was utterly unable to take care of himself. In March 1886 Chekhov sent him a letter urging him to change his ways, to take responsibility for his life and respect the talent 'that places you above millions of people'. Chekhov laid out the behavioural code of a decent young *intelligent*, acknowledging that their background made following it a struggle: 'It's the bourgeois side of you coming out, the side raised on birch thrashings beside the wine cellar and handouts, and it's hard to overcome, terribly hard.' This letter provides a great deal of insight into what Chekhov himself felt he had to overcome; the rules of conduct are his own:

To my mind, well-bred people ought to satisfy the following conditions:

1 They respect the individual and are therefore always indulgent, gentle, polite and compliant. [...]
2 Their compassion extends beyond beggars and cats. [...]
3 They respect the property of others and therefore pay their debts.
4 They are candid and fear lies like the plague. They do not lie even about the most trivial matters. [...]
5 They do not belittle themselves merely to arouse sympathy. [...]
6 They are not preoccupied with vain things. They are not taken in by such false jewels as friendships with celebrities [...]
7 If they have talent, they respect it. They sacrifice comfort, women, wine and vanity to it. [...]
8 They cultivate their aesthetic sensibilities. They cannot stand to fall asleep fully dressed, see a slit in the wall teeming with bedbugs, breathe rotten air, walk on a spittle-laden floor or eat off a kerosene stove. They try their best to tame and ennoble their sexual instinct...

This letter is as much about Chekhov as it is about his brother. 'If I were to abandon the family to the whims of fate,' he wrote, 'I would try to find myself an excuse in Mother's character or my blood spitting or the like.' He ended by urging Nikolai to 'come home. Smash your vodka bottle, lie down on the couch and pick up a book' (March 1886; *Letters*, pp. 50–51, 49).

Chekhov wrote similar instructions to Alexander and repeatedly urged him to take his writing seriously. A May letter, written after another emboldening trip to St Petersburg, offers an often-cited lesson in poetics. Alexander should avoid ready-made patterns and clichés, strive for objectivity, and avoid long-windedness and 'politico-socio-economic' verbiage. The inner worlds of characters should 'be understandable from the actions of the heroes', and an effect-for-the-cause, metonymic principle makes for potent, concise nature descriptions: 'For example, you'll get a moonlit night if you write that on the mill dam a piece of glass from a broken bottle glittered like a bright little star and the black shadow of a dog or wolf took off rolling like a ball, etc.' (10 May 1886). That image came straight from his own story 'Rabies (A True Story)' ('Vodoboiazn'

(Byl´)᾽, 1886),[33] and such remarks to Alexander and other mentees over the years provide valuable windows into Chekhov's own writing practices.

The year ended auspiciously. That autumn, Fyodor Korsh gave Chekhov a season's pass to his private theatre and repeatedly asked him for a comedy, which would materialize in a year with *Ivanov*. According to Alexander, Chekhov's Christmas story for *New Times*, 'On the Road' ('Na puti'), created a furore in Petersburg;[34] Suvorin and Alexander tried to persuade Chekhov to move to St Petersburg, where, Alexander reported, 'they're expecting big things from you' (*Letopis´* I, pp. 281, 289). Meanwhile Chekhov became an export commodity: 'A First-class Passenger' ('Passazhir 1-ogo klassa', 1886), previously published in *New Times*, appeared in a Czech newspaper.

At the beginning of 1887 Chekhov attended the Second Congress of the Pirogov Society of Russian Doctors in Moscow. In the coming summer he would again substitute for a short stint in Zvenigorod and treat peasants and others while on holiday at Babkino. Later that year he boasted in a letter to Alexander that he was now doctoring in aristocratic homes – he had been summoned a couple of times to treat their servants (29 October 1887). Also to Alexander, in a postscript to a letter written on his name-day, he deployed a metaphor for his dual career that would reappear in correspondence and conversations: after signing 'Anthony and Medicine Chekhov', he appended, 'Besides a wife – medicine – I also have literature, a lover.' He continued, mimicking their father in a dig at the cohabiting Alexander, 'I won't mention her [the lover], for those living outside the law also perish outside the law' (17 January 1887). In March Alexander summoned an apprehensive Chekhov to Petersburg, where a raging typhoid epidemic had hit his family; they recovered well, though, and a long visit with Suvorin resulted in a plan for a volume of his *New Times* stories and the promise of a 300-ruble advance. He also visited Grigorovich, who was suffering from angina.

As spring approached, Chekhov began planning a trip south to recuperate from overwork and poor health and seek new material for his writing. In early April he departed for his birthplace of Taganrog and other locales of childhood memories; lengthy letters back to his family would serve as travel notes after his return. The climate at first struck him as delightful and wholesome. He loved the natural surroundings, the sea and the steppe, with its Scythian burial mounds and familiar birdlife. The family of his uncle Mitrofan, Pavel's kind brother, was warm and very proud of his success. Their diet did not agree with him, however, and he quickly fell ill when the weather turned cold; soon he was suffering from haemorrhoids, diarrhoea and the painful inflammation of a vein in his leg. The old family home, which he refers to as Selivanov's, was 'empty and abandoned. Just looking at it is boring, and I would not agree to own it for any amount of money. I'm amazed: how could we have lived in it?' (*Letopis'* I, p. 304).

Contradictory letters show Chekhov reconnecting with his past while also seeking separation. To Leikin he wrote, 'Such Asia all around that I simply can't believe my eyes. 60,000 inhabitants have the sole occupation of eating, drinking, being fruitful and multiplying, and no other interests' (7 April 1887). He criticized the local consumption of the Santorini wine that he himself quite enjoyed and would stock in his own homes. As a child, churchgoing had been enforced by his father and he had felt 'like a convict' singing in the choir, but now he attended Mass willingly and delighted in the Easter service. His gut resumed orderly function once he got away from Taganrog, heading east through Novocherkassk for a visit to the Cossack farm of the family of his former pupil Petya Kravtsov. Chekhov rather grandiosely called the area 'at the center of the Donetsk escarpment' the 'Don Switzerland'; 'hills, gullies, woods, streams and steppe, steppe, steppe...' (to Leikin, 5 May 1887). He enjoyed a thorough sense of well-being there and sang its praises, in spite of the crudeness of life. (Kravtsov's father was a retired cornet, and there were vicious dogs and constant gunfire as fowl was shot from inside the house; Chekhov's former pupil would himself die as a Cossack major-general at the Battle of Tsaritsyn during the Russian Civil War.[35]) From the farm Chekhov went back to Novocherkassk for the wedding of a doctor colleague's sister, returned to the Kravtsovs for another ten days, and then pushed on to Slaviansk (today's Sloviansk, in the northern part of Donetsk Oblast of Ukraine). There Chekhov had a chance encounter with the lively Alexandra (Sasha) Selivanova, whose uncle had taken their house; she too had boarded with the Chekhovs for a while to study in Taganrog.

From Slaviansk he proceeded to the high point of his trip, the ancient monastery at Sviatye Gory by the city of Sviatogorsk, on the chalky hills overlooking the Seversky Donets River (not far northeast of Slaviansk). Some 15,000 pilgrims came to pray on St Nicholas Day, and Chekhov stood through the long church service and participated in a holy procession that took place in boats on the water. He loved visiting monasteries (and graveyards) and especially enjoyed the Easter liturgy, with the bells and singing, and he always spent Moscow Easter eves wandering from church to church. A year earlier, Chekhov had set the poetic and symbolic *New Times* story 'Easter Night' ('Sviatoiu noch'iu') in a monastery; now one of his finest stories from this period derived from Sviatye Gory: 'Tumbleweed' ('Perekati-pole (Putevoi nabrosok)'), in which a converted Jew tells his story, was inspired by a police spy who had roomed with Chekhov at the monastery (*Letopis'* I, pp. 310–11). Like 'On the Road' of the previous winter, this story features a wanderer; but whereas the earlier story's central character had been presented as quintessentially Russian, rootlessness has a quite different valence in this story.

What stands out in 'Tumbleweed', indeed, is not the monastic setting, river rites or general chaos, but the personality and story of the 22-year-old stranger with whom the unnamed narrator shares his room. The narrator finds something familiar but unfathomable about this character, whom he cannot identify as any 'type'. Why? It emerges that his identity has been dislocated by conversion to Russian Orthodoxy. Isaak, now Alexander, explains, 'I'm a Jew, a convert' (*S* VI, p. 257), a formulation suggesting that, baptism notwithstanding, he remains a Jew. And in fact, he cannot seem to find a place for himself. His parents refused him any education beyond the Talmud; interest in the greater world, including the Russian language, was cause for beating: 'Of course, you can't do without fanaticism, because every people instinctively preserves its national identity' (*S* VI, p. 258). This wandering Jew, in the monastery for two weeks now, hopes to become a schoolteacher now that his religious status is sorted out. But behind him already lies an impressive series of provisional professions: he has trained to be an engineer, a veterinarian or physician, and a mine director. Judaism is finished, he says, and any thinking person with a religious sensibility must be a Christian; but he sounds unconvinced, and in making such remarks seems to seek the narrator's affirmation. Cut off from his family since leaving home, he especially misses his sister, who, he repeats, must be married by now. Rather than changing identities, he has lost his altogether.

Something about this odd character strikes the narrator as uncannily familiar, which suggests that, in spite of the overwhelming otherness of the wanderer, there is the possibility of an overlap or identity between the two of them. In play here is a psychological dynamic recalling Freud's understanding of the uncanny and déjà vu, feelings that arise from encountering a staging of something repressed within oneself. And even though this pertains most directly to the frame narrator, who is unnamed and cannot be identified directly with the person of Anton Chekhov on any textual basis, this christened Jew does echo his author in certain ways. Chekhov has abandoned his family to take the trip south. The convert introduces himself as someone knowledgeable about art, death and physiology: his first words to the narrator are 'There are no bones like that', as he points out the anatomical incorrectness of the representation of a skeleton in a painting, *Reflections on Death*, that the narrator is contemplating. For this man has, like Dr Chekhov, 'seen bones' – he has visited the anatomical theatre in Kharkov, as well as the morgue. This man has also been diagnosed with tuberculosis, and in telling it says what Chekhov knows about himself but will keep unspoken for another decade. He has lived and worked in the underworld of mines that captures Chekhov's imagination and which will help draw him to Sakhalin and guide his depiction of it; and he has already experienced his own death, so to speak, having fallen to the bottom of a mine shaft in a bucket whose chain was severed. That is to say, this expert on death knows at first hand, not from a distance, the meaning of the breaking string that haunts Chekhov's last major play, *Cherry Orchard*.

In 'Mire', sexual attraction had trumped financial self-interest and identity differences. In this story, where money and sex are not in play, some undercurrent of identification with the other undermines manifest differences. On the surface, though, Chekhov represents the converted Jew as a lost soul, the walking dead. A dismally failed conversion figures centrally in the major play Chekhov would soon write, *Ivanov*. Lost souls are everywhere in Chekhov, however, and not unique to the Jewish theme in his work, which by 1886–7 was free of constraints imposed by earlier publishing venues and acquiring ever more seriousness and profundity.

Chekhov returned to Moscow in mid-May and then joined his family in Babkino for the summer. The next year of writing further exploited the impressions and childhood memories aroused by the journey. Among works infused with imagery and themes from the trip were 'Happiness' ('Schast′e', 1887), evoking steppe life and lore in plotless, poetic prose much praised by critics; the longish 'Lights' ('Ogni', 1888), which involved the theme of 'going home again'; and the ambitious 'Steppe' ('Step″, 1888), which marked an important turning point in his career. That summer, while back in Moscow for a bit, Chekhov met Alexei Pleshcheyev, another elder statesman of Russian literary life, now an editor of the Petersburg *Northern Herald*, who was passing through Moscow. Like Grigorovich, Pleshcheyev had a Dostoevsky connection: almost forty years earlier he too had been arrested, convicted, sentenced to death (commuted at the last moment) and then exiled in the Petrashevsky affair. Chekhov promised to write for the *Northern Herald*; in the coming months he was urged to place material in this prestigious, liberal 'thick journal' also by its leading critic, N. K. Mikhailovsky.

At the very end of his stay at Babkino, Chekhov read the proofs of Dr Arkhangelsky's forthcoming book on psychiatric institutions. He remarked that a similar book on prisons might be useful as well – a thought that would grow into his Sakhalin project.

By autumn, when Chekhov returned to the family's Moscow lodgings, his new volume of *New Times* stories, *In the Twilight* (*V sumerkakh*), was drawing high praise, and his Petersburg patrons were scheming to enter it for the prestigious Pushkin Prize. Meanwhile, for a quick 150 rubles Chekhov agreed to let *Cricket* (*Sverchok*) issue a volume of his comic tri-fles, *Harmless Utterances* (*Nevinnye rechi*), though he asked his brother to keep *New Times* from announcing the book's publication. A less embar-rassing opportunity to increase earnings and raise his profile arose when, again buttonholed by Korsh for a play, Chekhov sat down and within two weeks had drafted *Ivanov*.

In this period the leading prose author Vladimir Korolenko visited to echo Pleshcheyev's invitation to write something long for *Northern Herald*. Chekhov reflected on the lightheartedness and mercenary moti-vations with which he had embarked on his publishing career. Korolenko recalled, 'He looked at his desk, grabbed the first thing that came to his sight – it turned out to be an ashtray – put it in front of me and said, "If you want, tomorrow there will be a story... Its title: *The Ashtray*"' (*Letopis'* 1, p. 332). *Ivanov* was written with proportionate quickness, but Chekhov's attitude was far from dismissive. When it was finished, authorial pride and commercial instincts both spoke. Chekhov arranged an announcement regarding the play in the theatrical chronicle of *New Times*. Everyone he had shown the play to had liked it, he told Alexander.

> The plot is well shaped and not dumb. I end each act like my stories: I bring all the action along peacefully and quietly, and in the end give it the audience on the mug [...] I've created a type that has literary significance; I have given a role [...] in which an actor can develop and demonstrate his talent. (*Letopis'* 1, p. 339)

The play's premiere on 19 November created a sensation,[36] with the author being summoned to the stage multiple times. But the acting was poor, he complained to Alexander: 'Only Davydov and Glama knew their parts; the rest of them relied on the prompter and inner conviction' (20 November 1887; *Letters*, p. 72). By the second performance, though, the actors had found the groove. A euphoric Chekhov calmed himself down and got back to a story-writing routine. Days later, after 'the dust has finally settled', he signed a letter to Alexander, 'Your Schiller Shakespearovich Goethe' (24 November 1887; *Letters*, p. 73). Amusingly, the established playwright and critic Viktor Krylov had the gall to visit Chekhov and propose that he help rewrite the play in exchange for co-author status and half the royalties; Chekhov declined (*Letopis'* 1, p. 351). *Ivanov* did need reworking, however: after a few more performances in Moscow, Korsh pulled it from the theatre, though it was published (in lithograph) and continued to make Chekhov money in the provinces. A year later, Chekhov would revise the play before its 1889 staging at the Alexandrinsky Theatre in St Petersburg and journal republication. This version, subtitled a 'drama', is the one generally available in English translation and discussed here.

In many ways the most conventional of Chekhov's major plays and very neatly plotted, *Ivanov* is also one of the most personal. Once a progressive young landowner, and married to a converted Jewish woman suffering from consumption, Ivanov has broken under the weight of challenges assumed. Now he is pursued by Sasha, the daughter of a neighbouring landowner, who tells him, 'You need someone close to you to love you and understand you. Only love can reinvigorate you.'[37] The play tests this prescription, which fails: Ivanov was finished before the action began.

Guilt towards his wife (formerly Sara; now Anna Petrovna) becomes the heaviest of Ivanov's burdens. She has lost her religious identity and been cut off by her parents and relatives, and her dire medical prognosis, withheld from her, weighs on Ivanov. The others gossip relentlessly and assign him the basest motivations: in their view, his pursuits first of Sara and now Sasha have been about money. Anna Petrovna's young doctor, Lvov, proves the most self-righteous and moralizing among them, and the most central to the plot. At the end of Act Two, Sasha declares herself to Ivanov, and to his horror his wife witnesses the ensuing embrace. Act Three is composed of Ivanov's attempts to reassure her and suppress his attraction to Sasha, but towards its end Sasha comes to see Ivanov, and once again their meeting is discovered by his wife. Her rebukes provoke a violent reaction at the play's turning point. 'Sara, shut up, get out, or else I'll say something I'll regret! It's all I can do to keep from calling you something horrible, humiliating... (*Shouts.*) Shut up, yid!'[38] The act ends with Ivanov, further inflamed, telling her that the doctor says she will die soon, which then happens between acts.

At the start of Act Four, nearly a year after the crisis of Act Three, Ivanov is about to marry Sasha. Lvov is determined to prevent this, perhaps through recourse to a duel. In the end, though, Ivanov dies onstage without Lvov's intervention: in the original version, he merely lies down and expires (his heart having given out, presumably); in the 1889 revision he shoots himself.

Chekhov told Alexander that he 'did not portray a single villain or angel (though I could not refrain when it came to buffoons), did not indict or acquit anyone' (24 October 1887).[39] Nevertheless, critical reactions invariably vilified either Ivanov or Lvov, missing the extent to which these two characters are alike; for that matter, Sasha's infatuation with Ivanov, which involves the fantasy of resurrecting his progressive heroism, in some ways replicates Sara's. But whereas Sara and Sasha never confront one another, Ivanov and Lvov, the tapped-out *intelligent* and the young energetic physician, are doubles. Dr Lvov's criticism of Ivanov offers nothing more penetrating than his target's self-reproaches, and it is Ivanov's own inwardly directed analytical gaze that eventually proves fatal. Meanwhile, Lvov is blind to his own emotional investment in a situation that he claims to be addressing with an objective medical eye. (Ivanov's uncle, Shabelsky, suspects him of an erotic interest in his patient.) 'No, Doctor,' Ivanov declares, 'each of us has far more cogs, screws, and valves in him than to enable us to judge one another on first impressions or a few outward signs. I don't understand you, you don't understand me, we don't understand one another. You may be an excellent general practitioner – and still have no understanding of people. Don't be so smug and look at it my way.'[40]

When staging this play in London and New York in the 1960s, John Gielgud wrote, 'One feels that Chekhov must have seen something of himself both in the character of Ivanov and that of Doctor Lvov, the two most intelligent men in the play, whose attempts to understand each other and win each other's confidence result in such violent mutual destruction.'[41] There is something to that, especially if one thinks of Dr Chekhov still struggling to get a grip on his feelings regarding Efros, which also may account for the play's antisemitic language. In speaking to Lvov, Ivanov blames his decline on his marriage: 'Dear friend, you got your degree only last year, you're still young and vigorous, but I'm thirty-five.

I have the right to give you advice. Don't marry Jewish girls or neurotics or intellectuals, but pick out something ordinary, drab, without flashy colors or extraneous sounds.'[42] Sara was just such a triple threat, but she is also a victim and tragic figure: she will die young, mistakenly certain that her husband has betrayed her, and unreconciled with her parents. In another twist, most of the play's many antisemitic remarks are directed towards Sara by Shabelsky, who clearly loves her and is the kindest to her. Why are such utterances cruel invective from others and enjoyable banter from Shabelsky? Perhaps Sara recognizes that his malicious tongue teases all and sundry, and so his remarks to her provoke laughter rather than offense; perhaps she sees him as parodying the antisemites all around for her enjoyment. Another possibility: in sharing Jewish jokes the two foreground an identity that her conversion and marriage were supposed to have erased, but which does remain part of her self.

All of these questions resonate most deeply in the context of the play's likely biographical significance. Whereas Chekhov was infused with anger at Efros when he wrote 'Mire', it has been argued, *Ivanov* was conciliatory. In fact, Efros, by then married, attended the play's premiere, and Chekhov autographed her programme: 'To Evdokia Isaakovna Konovitser (Efros); the (whistling) spectator, from the author. 17 January 1888.' Elena Tolstaia calls it 'a parting gift to Efros, as though Chekhov was proving to her: don't regret, it wouldn't have worked out with us anyhow'.[43]

Chekhov would have resisted any interpretation broaching his personal life. In later years he was notoriously reluctant to explain himself beyond what was already offered in the text itself – his remarks would be cryptic and provocative rather than explanatory. In the case of *Ivanov*, however, he wrote letter after letter about the play, especially to Alexander and Suvorin, who was on site and standing in for the author as the play was revised and prepared for staging at the Alexandrinsky Theatre. In particular, Chekhov contested reflexive interpretations of Ivanov as a reiteration of the superfluous man character, a Russian literary cliché over half a century old. He did not address the play's Jewish theme.[44]

By the end of November, Chekhov had left the furore in Moscow for St Petersburg, where he stayed in Alexander's appallingly disordered apartment while hobnobbing with Russia's literary elite, including Suvorin, the poet Yakov Polonsky, such leading (and social-minded) authors and critics as Korolenko, Gleb Uspensky, Kazimir Barantsevich, Mikhailovsky, the painter Ilya Repin and, perhaps most significantly at this juncture, Pleshcheyev. Networking with fury, Chekhov faced an ever-expanding horizon and was again encouraged to write something big for *Northern Herald*. Leikin invited him for a meal and Chekhov stayed over, a 'respite from the filth' at Alexander's, as he wrote to his family (3 December 1887). But Leikin was losing Chekhov: with 'The Lion and the Sun' ('Lev i solntse'), a comic fable about a medal-craving provincial town head that appeared in *Fragments* while he was visiting, Chekhov would end regular publication there, though he did return occasionally over the years.

Petersburg agreed with Chekhov in this phase of his career. In the letter to his family he declared himself in 'seventh heaven' and lamented that he could not live there, an idea that he entertained for a few years. In Petersburg, Suvorin told him, his *Ivanov* would be understood; the city's intellectual and literary milieu was of an entirely different calibre than Moscow's. While there, Chekhov managed to finish one of his best short stories of the period, 'The Kiss' ('Potselui'). The story put to good use observations of garrison life among the artillery officers he met in the Babkino and Zvenigorod summers near Voskresensk, while broaching themes of existential loneliness and the fluid boundaries between fantasy and reality that far outstrip the military context. After Chekhov returned to Moscow, another masterpiece, 'Kashtanka', came out in *New Times* before the end of 1887. Because the story's central character is a dog who gets lost from its original owner and ends up being trained for a circus act along with other tame beasts, it has always been catalogued as a children's tale. This led to profitable reprinting over the years, as well as gifting by Chekhov to a number of children of his friends. But Chekhov averred that he did not write children's literature as such: 'I don't like what is known as children's literature; I don't recognize its validity. Children should be given only what is suitable for adults as well' (21 January 1900; *Letters*, p. 372). 'Kashtanka' involves a profound meditation on time, memory and – in the version revised in 1891 for subsequent republication – death. The story's original title, 'In Learned Society', hints at a larger meaning for the trained menagerie, where the dog is well cared for and among friends. In the story's denouement, instinct and the tug of the past trump all that this educated dog has learned, and she rejoins her previous master, even though he had treated her poorly.[45]

Although Chekhov had turned down Krylov's cheeky offer to rewrite *Ivanov*, the next few years saw him repeatedly propose dramaturgic collaborations with writer-friends and others. Playwriting was by its nature a social activity, and as Chekhov's involvement in the theatrical world grew, he increasingly made commitments to specific impresarios and actors, for whom he often conceived the roles he was creating. Staging his plays also involved much give and take with directors and actors, some of which has become legendary. And though Chekhov's major plays were not in any sense co-authored, Chekhov repeatedly proposed collaborating on dramatic projects with friends. As *Ivanov* was being readied for the stage, A. S. Lazarev (Gruzinsky) had a vaudeville in mind for the Korsh theatre, to be titled *Hamlet, the Danish Prince*; he and Chekhov exchanged ideas about it for a time before Chekhov cooled on Korsh and the project was dropped (*Letopis'* 1, pp. 249, 353). At one time, Pyotr Tchaikovsky proposed that they collaborate on an opera adaptation of Mikhail Lermontov's 'Bela', with Chekhov writing the libretto.[46] *The Wood Demon* (*Leshii*, 1890) was first conceived as a collaboration with Suvorin, and the one-act *Tatyana Repina* (1889) was a kind of parodic epilogue to Suvorin's full-length play of the same name, inspired by the story of an actress who, spurned by her upper-class lover, took poison and died on the Kharkov stage. Chekhov sent the play to Suvorin as a gift, never meaning for it to be published or staged.

As with Chekhov's prose practice, long and ambitious works were balanced against brief, usually light ones. At the beginning of 1887 he published a one-act monologue, *Kalkhas*, which refashioned an 1886 short story by that title. With slight revisions it then appeared in lithograph as *Swan Song* (*Lebedinaia pes'nia*, 1888), and the following year in the journal *Artist* (*Artist*). He had published another one-act monologue, *On the Danger of Tobacco* (*O vrede tabaka*), in the *Petersburg Gazette* in February 1886, and now he was embarking on a whole series of such efforts. Early in 1888, 'having nothing to do', as he put it to Polonsky (22 February 1888), he dashed off *The Bear* (*Medved'*), which would be published in the summer in *New Times*. Over the next few years there would be others – *The Proposal* (*Predlozhenie*, 1888) and *The Wedding* (*Svad'ba*, written 1889) – some of which were adaptations of earlier short stories. Written quickly, these one-act plays generated outsized royalties due to frequent staging, and *The Bear*, *The Proposal* and *The Wedding* are still in the theatrical repertoire.

The more seriously Chekhov was taken, the more he seemed to need to joke around as well; while he sweated over longer works, he still felt the urge to pen what he would call a trifle, a duality that remains visible at the very end of his career in the unique tension between the farcical and the tragic in *Cherry Orchard*. This practice also meant wasting as little as possible: working both ends of the creative spectrum enhanced Chekhov's productivity by making useable otherwise ephemeral ideas for a story or play. Although we only have notebooks from Chekhov's later years, during this period he showed his friend Lazarev (Gruzinsky) one that he always kept at hand for jotting down story ideas, and he advised him to do the same (*Letopis'* 1, p. 364).

In fact, the period of 'nothing to do', when Chekhov wrote *The Bear*, saw intensive work on the long, poetic narrative that would mark Chekhov's entry to literature's top ranks. 'Steppe' was Chekhov's answer to those who had been urging him to write a long, serious piece for *Northern Herald*. 'The thought that I'm writing for a thick journal and that they'll look at my trifle more seriously than they should prods my elbows like the devil does a monk,' he wrote (to Leontyev (Shcheglov), 1 January 1888). Pleshcheyev offered an advance from *Northern Herald* if that would save Chekhov from writing small stories, but such diversions were necessary also to Chekhov's creative economy. Chekhov had just spent half a day knocking out the troubling 'Sleepy' ('Spat' khochetsia') for the *Petersburg Gazette*. Far from a comic trifle, however, the frequently anthologized little story complemented 'Steppe' and other undertakings of the period in its focus on child psychology and the phenomenology of dreams and hallucinations. Its theme of psychological trauma and child abuse remains sadly gripping.

'Steppe' was the most important of the works inspired by Chekhov's trip south. The story lyrically evokes the beauty of the steppe through the fresh vision of a child; it is also a profound meditation on a child's first experiences of nascent sexuality and loss, including intimations of the reality of death. Among several studies in child psychology, including the remarkable short stories 'Sleepy' and 'Vanka' ('Van'ka'), 'Steppe' was Chekhov's most sustained effort. Appropriately ambitious for a debut in a 'thick journal' that featured prominent Russian writers, no major narrative work by Chekhov operates on so many levels. He had explained to Korolenko, 'On your friendly advice I have begun a short novelette for the *Northern Herald*. For a start I have undertaken to describe the steppe, the people of the steppe and the things I experienced in the steppe' (9 January 1888; *Letters*, p. 89). Beyond returning Russian readers to the distinctively Russian topography indicated by its title, however, the steppe becomes endowed with rich symbolic meaning in this work of poetic prose. Crossing it is an existential life journey;

apprehending it builds a child's mind; reading it means traversing a kind of literary space in what is also a very self-reflexive narrative.

The plot involves a nine-year-old boy's journey by buggy and haycart from home and his widowed mother to a big city (identified by scholars as Rostov), where he will lodge with a childhood friend of his mother's and be schooled. Yegorushka travels for three days, at first with his uncle (Kuzmichev) and a kindly old priest (Father Christopher), both of whom have business dealings along the way, and then with carters transporting their wool to be sold. He becomes overwhelmed by impressions of the steppe and its people; these impressions link up in associative fashion to create semantic and psychological tensions that intensify and sicken him in the story's climax. Here Chekhov likely follows Herbert Spencer's associationist theory of mental development and education, as laid out in *Education: Intellectual, Moral, and Physical* (1861), which Chekhov had praised half a decade earlier when conceiving his dissertation proposal on gender disparity in human evolution. The journey metaphor for mind-building appears in Spencer, and his metaphoric association of intellectual assimilation with eating and digestion is picked up in 'Steppe', beginning when Father Christopher calls learning 'spiritual food' (*Novels*, p. 13); carefully developed in the course of the story, it culminates when, overstuffed with impressions, Yegorushka becomes ill in the story's climax and vomits. As a study in psychology, the story also presents a kind of initiation rite, with the steppe a liminal space crossed by a child who has been wrenched from his mother and placed in the world of adults. There he assimilates as best he can new knowledge of death, loss, Eros and aggression; consciousness expands, but not without errors and pain.[47]

A landscape painting of stunning poetic texture, the story systematically repeats imagery and words or parts of words and boasts a deliberately constricted vocabulary that tests the narratological limits of sameness while conveying the boredom and sameness of the steppe landscape. Translators who correct Chekhov's style by introducing more variation in the story's lexicon undermine the story's poetic dimension, draining its undercurrents of symbolic associations. One striking example of this involves Chekhov's use of words involving circular motion, as in the verb *kruzhit'sia*. If that is translated sometimes as 'knocking about', as Ronald Hingley does in a passage regarding the wealthy and important steppe character Varlamov, then the linkage between his movements and others involving the 'circle' lexeme is lost.[48]

The story is also a profound intervention in the cultural mythology of Russian space, the social and psychological significance of Russia's massive landmass. Shortly after sending in the story, Chekhov responded to Grigorovich's urging that Chekhov take up the theme of youth suicide. In discussing the causes of this phenomenon, a result of the 'terrible struggle' between man and nature 'possible only in Russia', Chekhov wrote:

> On the one hand, physical weakness, nervousness, early sexual
> maturity, passionate thirst for life and truth, dreams of action
> as broad as the steppe, anxious analysis, a poverty of knowledge
> combined with a sweeping flights of thought; on the other,
> a boundless plain, a severe climate, a grey, stern people with
> its painful, cold history, the Tatar yoke, officialdom, poverty,
> ignorance, the dampness of the capitals, Slavic apathy, etc...
> Russian life hits a Russian man such that not even a damp
> spot remains, like a thousand-pood stone. In W[estern] Europe
> people perish because it's too crowded and suffocating to live;
> but with us it's because there is too much space... So much space
> that the little man lacks the strength to orient himself... That's
> what I think of Russian suicides. (5 February 1888)

Yegorushka confronts this excess of space in slowly crossing the steppe.[49]

'Steppe' is also a deliberate experiment in the handling of narrative point of view and voice.[50] The story's focalization alternates between the approximately nine-year-old main character, Yegorushka, and an older and wiser, reminiscing narrator whom some interpret as a hardened and reflective adult Yegorushka. Chekhov himself associated Yegorushka's journey across the steppe with those he had made as a child;[51] according to his brother Mikhail, the Jewish inn episode was based on the Jewish hostel where Chekhov had been cared for when he fell ill with peritonitis while visiting the steppe farm of the renter Selivanov's brother.[52]

Finally, among the metaphoric aspects of the steppe (and by no means exhausting the possible list) is its representation of textual space, which makes crossing it a metaliterary journey. The story begins with a transparent allusion to the literary 'tsar of the steppe' (as Chekhov put it), Nikolai Gogol; as readers have long noticed, the story's opening echoes the description of the carriage with which Gogol began *Dead Souls*. 'I know that Gogol will get angry with me in the other world,' Chekhov wrote to Grigorovich; 'I snuck into his property with good intentions, but committed all sorts of nonsense' (5 February 1888). 'Steppe' proceeds to reflect on its own narrative devices. As in the just-cited letter, space in the story represents (also) literary space, and the journey across the steppe was no less a rite of initiation for Chekhov, as an author aspiring to greater things, than it is for Yegorushka.[53]

Although Chekhov's literary ambition was well and truly lit by now, he had few illusions about the elite spheres he was entering. In a letter to Pleshcheyev he complained about the 'insider, party-minded tedium' that 'reins in all our thick journals' (23 January 1888). Chekhov's unwillingness to adhere to any party line would have killed his career had his talents not been so outstanding. The next decade would see him more and more oriented towards *Northern Herald* and other 'thick journals'. 'Sleepy', which he published as A. Chekhonte, would be the last work Chekhov placed in *Petersburg Gazette*. Meanwhile, he wrote to Lazarev (Gruzinsky) that 'Steppe' would earn him 1,000 rubles, quite a taking for one month's writing, which had been difficult: 'I don't know whether it was successful or not, but in any case, it's my masterpiece, I'm not able to do better' (4 February 1888).

The period 1888–9 proved another watershed for Chekhov, though the next long story he wrote, also connected with the trip south, flopped. 'Lights' presented an argument against philosophical nihilism and a lesson in ethics through the confession of a seducer. It received poor reviews, and Chekhov later omitted it from the first complete collection of his works, a dishonour generally reserved only for his early writings. And yet it is a very interesting and revealing story, one important to Chekhov at the time he wrote it. In narrative manner it recalls the frame tale 'Tumbleweed': an unnamed narrator, in this case a doctor, unexpectedly spends the night with an engineer and his assistant at their railway building site in the middle of the steppe. The empty, vast space surrounding them on a dark night; the anxieties of their watchdog, who barks at ghosts; the knowledge that whole civilizations have arisen, vanished and lie buried under this land; and the utter uselessness of their own efforts viewed against a millennial time horizon – all this and a few cynical remarks by the young assistant lead the engineer to tell a story about his callous seduction and abandonment of a childhood friend when visiting his hometown, and the resulting moral turn.[54] The story's sole female character appears in the embedded tale. Bright, soulful, and proud of the town's boys who have gone on to do something in their lives, Kisochka is trapped by gender in a loveless, abusive marriage and deadening provincial town. To keep herself intellectually alive she studies mathematics on her own. Her former schoolmate seduces her with the fraudulent promise that he will take her away from this place; racked by guilt afterwards, he rejects his prior cynicism.

Although Chekhov criticized the story's 'philosophizing', he defended himself vigorously when taken to task for its last line, 'You can't figure anything out in this world.' Answering rebukes that 'it is certainly the writer's job to figure out what goes on in the heart of his hero', and that 'neither the conversation about pessimism nor Kisochka's story help to solve the problem of pessimism', Chekhov argued in a letter to Suvorin:

> In my opinion it is not the writer's job to solve such problems
> as God, pessimism, etc.; his job is merely to record who, under
> what conditions, said or thought what about God or pessimism.
> The artist is not meant to be a judge of his characters and what
> they say; his only job is to be an impartial witness. I heard
> two Russians in a muddled conversation about pessimism,
> a conversation that solved nothing; all I am bound to do
> is reproduce that conversation exactly as I heard it.
> (30 May 1888; *Letters*, pp. 106, 104)

Though claiming to have overheard what in fact came from his own imagination, Chekhov here reiterates previously avowed principles: the author's task is to pose the problem, not solve it; and the cooler his stance towards his material, the greater the emotional response elicited from the reader. As he put it in a letter that year to Suvorin, 'You are right to demand that an author take conscious stock of what he is doing, but you are confusing two concepts: *answering the questions and formulating them correctly*. Only the latter is required of an author.' He was fond of a legal analogy: 'It is the duty of the court to formulate the questions correctly, but it is up to each member of the jury to answer them according to his own preference' (27 October 1888; *Letters*, p. 117).

During the summer of 1888 Chekhov holidayed with his family at a new preferred site in eastern Ukraine, near Sumy. The Chekhovs rented a dacha from the fascinating and admirable Lintvarev family, which included two young women physicians. From there Chekhov set out on his own for travels through Ukraine, after which he visited the Crimea and Suvorin's dacha at Feodosia, and then took a trip through the Caucasus with Suvorin's son Alexei.

In October 1888 Chekhov learned that his volume *In the Twilight* had won him the prestigious Pushkin Prize, awarded by the Division of Russian Language and Letters of the Imperial Academy of Sciences. The news came from Grigorovich, proud 'discoverer' of Chekhov and member of the award committee. Grigorovich again rebuked Chekhov for not appreciating his own talent and stooping to lowbrow publishing venues. But Chekhov always felt that one of his major accomplishments was having blazed a trail for others from the 'small press' to the most serious heights of Russian literature. He knew that without the inside help of Suvorin and Grigorovich he would not have received the award – as it was, he split the 1,000-ruble prize with joint winner Korolenko, whom he himself viewed as more deserving – and he did not think his writings would be remembered for more than a decade or so.

Was this false modesty? After all, Chekhov was feeling his oats and growing increasingly assertive with editors and in censorship matters. Only on condition that neither censors nor editors 'cross out *a single word*' would he offer his story 'Breakdown' (or 'Attack of Nerves'; 'Pripadok') for a volume memorializing Vsevolod Garshin, perhaps the leading young prose writer of the 1880s, who had thrown himself down a stairwell in March, shortly after Chekhov had attempted to meet him in St Petersburg. The story featured a trio of university friends – budding professionals in art, law and medicine – visiting the Moscow brothel district. The experience leads to mental collapse in the law student, who possesses Garshin's capacity for feeling the sufferings of others. The volume's editor, Pleshcheyev, admired the story, but he did worry about the censorship (*S* VII, pp. 660–61).

Chekhov made similar demands with his story 'The Name-day Party', also sent to *Northern Herald*. In addition to governmental censors, Chekhov was bothered by the fashionable political correctness of the intelligentsia, which the liberal editorial board of the *Northern Herald* was inclined to enforce. His back was up from personal attacks for his continued association with Suvorin and his reactionary and unscrupulous *New Times*. Now that Chekhov had the best thick journals at his disposal, why did he continue to publish with such venues? Chekhov's October 1888 letter to Pleshcheyev contains his most famous statement about the relationship between politics and literature:

The people I am afraid of are the ones who look for tendentiousness between the lines and are determined to see me as either liberal or conservative. I am neither liberal, nor conservative, nor gradualist, nor monk, nor indifferentist. I would like to be a free artist and nothing else, and I regret God has not given me the strength to be one. I hate lies and violence in all of their forms [...] Pharisaism, dullwittedness and tyranny reign not only in merchants' homes and police stations. I see them in science, in literature, among the younger generation... [...] I look upon tags and labels as prejudices. My holy of holies is the human body, health, intelligence, talent, inspiration, love and the most absolute freedom imaginable, freedom from violence and lies, no matter what form the latter two take. Such is the program I would adhere to if I were a major artist. (4 October 1888; *Letters*, p. 109)

Chekhov was never a 'free artist and nothing else': a physician to the end of his days, he did think about treatment as well as diagnosis. Further, 'absolute freedom' will always be a fantasy, though that fantasy might deeply impact one's life and view of the world. But resistance to 'tags and labels', to reflexive, readymade understandings of all sorts, was a constant target of Chekhov's art and thought. At the same time, he was socially active from his earliest mature years, doing good works when and as his financial resources and remarkable skill set allowed. A decade later he would write to his physician colleague Ivan Orlov, 'I have faith in individuals, I see salvation in individuals scattered here and there, all over Russia, be they intellectuals or peasants [...] They do not dominate, yet their work is visible (22 February 1899; *Letters*, p. 341). Chekhov was such an individual.

Above all, Chekhov was now his own man, and this was reflected in the tone of his letters. Gone was the polite submissiveness with which he had addressed Russian literary giants when they first started paying attention to him. No matter the grief from liberals, he would maintain his connection with Suvorin and *New Times*: he was genuinely attached to the old man and found him intellectually stimulating. For his part, Suvorin appears to have loved Chekhov like a son, if not more than his own sons. He offered jobs and other assistance to every one of Chekhov's siblings at one time or another, and Alexander and Mikhail would both work for him. He even proposed, perhaps not entirely in jest, that Chekhov marry his minor-aged daughter. Politics did eventually divide the two, but not for another decade, and never with finality.

In January 1889 the revised *Ivanov* was successfully staged in St Petersburg. Chekhov had been heavily involved in preparing the play for production, largely through his proxy Suvorin. His letters expressed preferences regarding the assignment of roles, interpreted the play for members of the cast, provided lengthy explanations of his intention, and he even offered to give a talk before the Russian Literary and Theatrical Society of St Petersburg. With success and visibility came new professional associations and duties, as well as greater ambition. Chekhov began refereeing and editing the fiction that other writers submitted to *New Times*, an activity that widened to other venues and consumed more time in years to come. In late February he was proposed as a full member of the Society of Lovers of Russian Literature, and in March he was elected a member of a committee of the Society of Russian Playwrights and Opera Composers.

While also conceiving a new venture for the stage, Chekhov now began working on a novel. Literary history tells us that Chekhov was operating in a period when the short form was dominant, but this was not clear at the time, and Chekhov had internalized urgings that he produce the novel required for entry to the literary pantheon. We know very little about this project, provisionally titled 'Stories from the Lives of My Friends'; it never came to fruition and his letters offer no details. Now and then Chekhov claimed to be making good progress, but he generally destroyed drafts, and none remain from the project (though some of his late stories may derive from it).[55]

This was when Chekhov wrote the revealing letter to Suvorin, cited earlier, in which he averred that he was glad he had not tried to write a novel until mature, when he felt the necessary 'personal freedom'. Speaking obliquely of himself, he suggested Suvorin write the story of a young man who with great difficulty had 'squeezed the blood of a slave' from his veins. That image tells us much about the hard-won dignity and self-assurance that distinguished Chekhov from his immensely talented older brothers. It would be a mistake, however, to view the transformation described in that letter to Suvorin as complete by the beginning of 1889: the struggle and self-disciplining it involved were lifelong.

The family member least capable of that struggle was Nikolai. By the spring of 1889 his disordered life was waning: he was suffering from typhoid fever, tuberculosis and the ravages of alcoholism. Chekhov took him to the family's current summer retreat at the Lintvarev estate, where he also worked on his next major play, *The Wood Demon* (1889). He had rescued Nikolai more than once, finding him commissions, fending off creditors, dealing with his military draft-dodging, bringing him home deathly ill from a flophouse. Nikolai's health had been so precarious for so long that this outcome was inevitable. Already in 1883 Chekhov had announced to Alexander that 'a fine, powerful Russian talent is perishing, perishing for nothing... A year or two more, and the song of our artist will have been sung' (20 February 1883). By spring 1889 Nikolai's demise was certain. Although Chekhov misled the patient into believing that he would recover from the typhoid also afflicting him – it was common medical practice to withhold dire information from patients themselves – his correspondence shows that he had given up hope; in question only was how long the tubercular infection would take to wreak full havoc.[56] Letters also show him more irritated by than sorry for his dying brother: he repeatedly complains of the noisy coughing and the demands of caring for him. In mid-June, misjudging the time remaining, he took advantage of his brother Alexander's visit and departed for a respite at the estate of friends in Poltava province. The day after he left, Nikolai died. Had Chekhov wished, at some level, to be away for the event? Alexander claims that the whole family discounted Nikolai's sufferings and did not see the end coming; he got no help in caring for the brother who died in his arms. There is something of a pattern here. Chekhov wrote to Pleshcheyev, 'Our family had not yet known death, and had to see a coffin at our place for the first time' (26 June 1889), apparently repressing the 1871 loss of his beloved toddler sister. At Nikolai's funeral Chekhov demonstrably tamped down emotion. In a letter written after the funeral in Sumy to their father, who was still working in Moscow, Alexander reported that among the family only Anton had not cried, 'and that is awful'.[57] Both Chekhov's mother and his sister later alleged that Chekhov never cried in his life. And Chekhov would essentially go away for the end of his own life as well, avoiding familial emoting.

After the burial, Chekhov spent a month in the Crimea. In the wake of Nikolai's death he wrote the long, bleak 'A Boring Story' ('Skuchnaia istoriia', 1889), in which the first-person narrator is a very accomplished professor of medicine suffering from a fatal illness still undisclosed to others. He is painfully alienated from his family and tortured by consciousness of his declining competence at work.

'Boring Story' could not be more different from 'Steppe', and yet Chekhov's two most ambitious narratives to date make a complementary pair, the first being a study of a critical phase of expanding consciousness in childhood, and the second, of an aged but brilliant and critical mind very cognizant of its own decline. 'Steppe' ends with the words, 'What sort of life would it be?' (*Novels*, p. 113); 'Boring Story' with a farewell to life, as the narrator parts with his former ward Katya, the person closest to him (*Stories*, p. 107). Indeed, this scene's placement at the end of a narrative structured by fatal illness makes her leave-taking a substitute for death itself, with the 'treasure' to whom the professor bids farewell a kind of double for his own life. The poetic 'Steppe' experiments with a variety of voices and points of view, whereas 'Boring Story' confines us with the voice and dismally critical perspective of the dying professor of medicine, Nikolai Stepanych. If boredom is a central motif of 'Steppe', which tempted the reader to become as bored as Yegorushka and the carters during a journey in stifling heat that flirts with motionlessness, in the very title of 'Boring Story' Chekhov recasts and reissues the challenge. How bold of Chekhov to invite the critical response that, yes indeed, it is a 'boring story'! In fact, Chekhov was warned by Pleshcheyev, who read the manuscript, that 'to the majority the tale will doubtless seem boring' because of its lack of conventional plot and excess of argumentation (*S* VII, p. 673).

Just what is the valence of the Russian *skuchnaia* (boring) in this story? Like 'Steppe', the narrative experiments with plotlessness. Illness functions as a kind of natural plot, but the denouement of that line of action remains out of sight: instead of progressing or leading to death, it underlies an existential situation explored by the narrator. The story's several potential subplots, such as the romance and engagement of the narrator's daughter with a reprehensible young man and the depressed and lost state of his former ward Katya, also come to naught: exploiting their dramatic potential would require the narrator to intervene in some way, and that is beyond him.

Instead, 'Boring Story' depicts a downward trajectory of increasing isolation and alienation from family and friends, juxtaposed with recollection of the appealing routines, now spoiled, of prior everyday life. During Chapter Four, the habitual and repetitive (but *not* boring) gives way to narration of progressive action, linear time; we now have real movement towards an ending, though without the attending plot tension or payoff, by comparison, of Tolstoy's 'The Death of Ivan Ilyich', published only a few years previously. This shift from gratifying daily cycle to discrete events in irrevocably advancing time involves interesting shifts in verbal tense (and, in the Russian original, verbal aspect), which structure the narrative's temporality. Along the way, the narrator's relentlessly analytical perspective on his own life and those of his family and close associates also results in a cascade of quotable aphorisms, such as: 'If no progress is to be seen in small things, it would be futile to start looking for it in major things' (*Stories*, p. 71); 'If a young scholar or writer begins his activity by complaining bitterly about scholars or writers, it means he's already worn out and not fit for work' (*Stories*, p. 73); 'purity and virtue scarcely differ from vice, if they're not free of malice' (*Stories*, p. 76); 'You can be a gentleman and a privy councillor a hundred times over, but if you have a daughter, nothing can protect you from the bourgeois vulgarity that is often introduced into your house and into your state of mind by courtships, proposals, and weddings' (*Stories*, p. 77).

'Boring' encompasses the anxiety and insomnia that the professor calls 'the main and fundamental feature of [his] existence', now defined by decline and mortality (*Stories*, pp. 56–7). 'Boredom' thus indicates not the absence of events but the anxiety of anticipating a feared event. Death comes to all, of course, so in that sense 'boring' also refers to the *commonness* of this story: even if Nikolai Stepanych is exceptional, his has become the *same old story*, the usual tale.

Another line of interpretation is suggested by Chekhov's working title for the story, 'My Name and I', which highlights the professor's feeling of disjunction between his famous name and reputation, on the one hand, and on the other the interiority of a man whose work life, family and very self are falling apart. The theme is sounded in the story's opening: 'As my name is brilliant and beautiful, so I myself am dull and ugly' (*Stories*, p. 56). Towards the end, alone in Kharkov on an abortive mission to investigate his daughter's fiancé, whom he rightly suspected a fake, the narrator finds his arrival in the city spotlighted in the local newspaper and reflects, 'Evidently, great names are created so as to live by themselves, apart from their bearers. Now my name is peacefully going about Kharkov; in some three months, inscribed in gold letters on a tombstone, it will shine like the sun itself – while I'm already covered with moss...' (*Stories*, p. 105).

The philosopher and literary critic Lev Shestov viewed the depressing story as evidence of a radical change in the mentality of its author between when he wrote 'Steppe' and the writing of *Ivanov* and 'Boring Story'. Certainly, it had been a time of trials and anxiety. The TB that had killed Nikolai was attacking Chekhov as well, and for the past year or so his relationship to the real fame coming his way had been difficult. Just how he handled his own name as an author comprised a veritable 'name drama', as one penetrating scholar puts it.[58] And Chekhov had been criticized for the lack of a guiding idea with which the professor indicts himself and his generation. All this, together with the first-person narration of the story, facilitated application of the narrator's self-analysis to Chekhov himself.[59] Chekhov objected. 'If someone serves you coffee,' he wrote to Suvorin, 'don't try to look for beer in it. If I present you with the professor's ideas, have confidence in me and don't look for Chekhovian ideas in them' (17 October 1889; *Letters*, p. 149). In other words, the 'I' that is speaking in this story is not Chekhov but the fictional professor.[60]

A larger point in the letter countering biographical interpretations offers a key to understanding just how, as an author, Chekhov handles ideas. 'The substance of all these opinions is of no value to me as an author. Their substance is not the point; it is variable and lacks novelty. The crux of the matter lies in the nature of the opinions, in their dependence on external influences, and so on. They must be examined like objects, like symptoms, with perfect objectivity and without any attempt to agree with them or call them in question' (17 October 1889; *Letters*, pp. 149–50). Although Chekhov has stories that are structured around ideological arguments, we are on the wrong interpretive path if we try to identify which side the author is on, picking a winner. Rather, Chekhov presents ideas and arguments as symptoms of the character expressing them. Psychology most often appears to be the ground floor in Chekhov: words and the ideas they express are best viewed as issuing from the situational and psychological context. This is a fundamental principle in Chekhov's construction of character and character interaction.

That autumn, Chekhov suffered a setback with *Wood Demon*. He had offered the play for a benefit performance at the Alexandrinsky Theatre in St Petersburg, but an evaluating committee, which included Chekhov's patron Grigorovich, deemed it unfit for the stage: it was odd and drawn out, lacking action, and committee members were likely offended by its portrayal of a professor of literature. Friends lectured Chekhov on theatrical conventions, telling him that such material was better suited for a novel and even suggesting he eschew writing for the stage. Chekhov swore, as he would many times, never again to write a full-length play. Nevertheless, he allowed a revised version of *Wood Demon* to be staged at the Abramova Theatre in Moscow at the end of December. While the play subsequently did well in provincial theatres, reviews of its Moscow run were poor. Chekhov returned to the play – scholars debate exactly when – and a decade later a radically trimmed, reconceived and even less dramatic version of *Wood Demon* would become the very successful *Uncle Vanya* (*Diadia Vania*).

Chekhov family, 1890, prior to Chekhov's departure for Sakhalin.
From left to right, top: A. I. Ivanenko, I. P. Chekhov, P. E. Chekhov;
middle: Masha Korneeva, Lika Mizinova, Maria Chekhova, Evgenia Ia.
Chekhova, A. Korneev; bottom: Mikhail Chekhov, Anton Chekhov.

3

Explorer and Homebody: Sakhalin Island to Melikhovo

Sometime towards the end of 1889, perhaps stimulated by his youngest brother Mikhail's studies of the penal system at university,[1] Chekhov decided to undertake a journey to study the prison colony on Sakhalin island. Exactly why remains opaque – not for lack of likely motivations, but for the multiplicity and complexity of them. For Chekhov, Sakhalin promised to solve a number of problems in one stroke. Letters to close friends and family had been expressing a need to get away and start over, to give life and work a more serious direction. Fame and the furore that came with major theatrical ventures unsettled him, and travelling to the empire's far eastern reaches meant turning his back on all that. Lika (Lidiya) Mizinova, a friend of Chekhov's sister whom he had met in 1889, and with whom he had become romantically entangled, was reproaching him for his lack of commitment, and he probably wished to escape her as well. Nikolai's death had driven home his own dire prognosis; not only would this trip mean making the most of a life likely to be shortened, but travel and change of climate was a cure some physicians prescribed for TB (in the United States, patients were sent on wagon-train journeys to the west).

The voyage also answered deep, long-standing aspirations. When marooned in Taganrog years before, Chekhov had been particularly drawn to narratives of travel and exploration. In October 1888 he wrote an obituary, published anonymously in *New Times*, for the great explorer of Central Asia Nikolai Przhevalsky, whom he lauded as an inspiration and example. Such personalities were

> living documents, demonstrating to society that in addition to people who argue about optimism and pessimism, and from

boredom write insignificant tales, useless plans, and cheap dissertations, who live in debauchery in the name of negating life and lie for a piece of bread; that in addition to sceptics, mystics, psychopaths, Jesuits, philosophers, liberals and conservatives, there are still people of another order, people of great feats of sacrifice, belief, and a clearly acknowledged goal. (*S* xvi, p. 237)

A letter to Suvorin speaks of Sakhalin as a site of 'unbearable suffering', with 'problems involving frightening responsibility'; if he were sentimental he would 'say that we ought to make pilgrimages to places like Sakhalin the way the Turks go to Mecca' (9 March 1890; *Letters*, p. 159). Chekhov's voyage to Sakhalin was just such a *podvig*, or feat of self-sacrifice.

In seeking adventure and a trial and fleeing the depression caused by Nikolai's death, Chekhov undertook a katabatic journey to the island of the damned, so as to return renewed and on terms with the death that awaited him as surely as it had taken Nikolai. Chekhov travelled to the eastern edge of the continent overland, when a less taxing and less dangerous trip by sea was possible: the hard journey, forcibly undertaken by convicts sent to Sakhalin, was itself an important aspect of the venture. Among the remarkable features of his writings about the voyage and survey is that Chekhov made himself, for the first and only time outside his letters, the hero of his own narratives.

Chekhov asserted that he was not travelling for literary purposes, but as a physician: 'I am going there absolutely secure in the thought that my journey will not make any valuable contributions to literature or science [...] I want to write at least one or two hundred pages to pay off some of my debt to medicine, toward which, as you know, I've behaved like a pig' (to Suvorin, 9 March 1890; *Letters*, pp. 158–9). Years later there were unsuccessful back-channel efforts to submit the resulting book as a dissertation at the Faculty of Medicine at Moscow University, which would have qualified Chekhov to teach. Still, no other project came close in investment to *Sakahlin Island*, by far the longest work Chekhov ever wrote. It had significant impact, provoking follow-up journalistic investigations by Vlas Doroshevich and others, government attention, and reforms.

Chekhov's disavowal notwithstanding, impressions from the trip also inspired or enriched subsequent works of fiction, such as 'Gusev' (1890), 'Peasant Women' ('Baby', 1891), 'In Exile' ('V ssylke', 1892), 'Ward No. 6' ('Palata No. 6', 1892) and 'Murder' ('Ubiistvo', 1895). Chekhov also arranged to send back travel sketches during the voyage east for imme-diate publication in *New Times*; six were written on the way, and three after he had arrived on the island.

Early in 1890 Chekhov travelled to St Petersburg to obtain permis-sions for his survey. Although he did receive a letter from the prison directorate authorizing all assistance necessary for accomplishment of his scientific and literary goals, a secret order prohibiting contact between Chekhov and certain political exiles and convicts was also sent to the administrator of Sakhalin. Preparing systematically, Chekhov composed a bibliography of 65 titles to read before his departure, and he studied topics ranging from the criminal justice system to the history of the exploration of the Russian Far East and its geology, ethnography and meteorology. Family and friends were enlisted to make notes from library books.

In the spring of 1890, before his departure, another collection of Chekhov's stories was published by Suvorin. Its title, *Gloomy People* (*Khmurye liudi*), lent itself to a depressive typecasting of Chekhov's work that persists to this day. Chekhov dedicated the volume to the composer Tchaikovsky, whom he had met just a year and a half earlier. The two maintained warm and mutually admiring relations until Tchaikovsky's death in 1893.

Less than two weeks before setting out for Sakhalin, Chekhov sent an uncharacteristically angry and unrestrained letter to the editor and publisher of the Moscow journal *Russian Thought*, where a review had labelled Chekhov as one of the 'priests of unprincipled writing'. Rather than criticism, Chekhov declares, this is 'libel, plain and simple. I might have let even libel to go by, except that in a few days I will be leaving Russia for an extended period, perhaps never to return, and I lack the strength to refrain from responding.' Chekhov attaches no great value to most of what he has published, he writes, but he refuses to be ashamed of his work. 'I never show my face in editorial offices without an invita-tion, I've always tried to have my friends think of me more as a doctor than a writer – in short, I was a modest writer, and the letter I am writing you now is my first immodest act in the ten years of my career as a writer' (10 April 1890; *Letters*, pp. 165–6). The offensive words had appeared precisely when Chekhov's careers as writer and doctor were to merge on a truly difficult and ambitious journey reflecting serious social commit-ment. A few years later the publisher, Vukol Lavrov, made amends and the two became close, and Chekhov placed fine, important works in *Russian Thought*.

Chekhov departed Moscow on 21 April 1890. Friends and family accompanied him during the first short rail stage to Yaroslavl. From there he travelled by river steamer to Perm, by rail to Ekaterinburg and Tiumen, and then by light, horse-drawn carriages through Omsk, Tomsk, Karsnoyarsk and on to Irkutsk. His travel sketches and letters home describe abysmal roads, torturous cold and truly harrowing moments such as the crossing of flooded rivers and a collision with a government troika that was speeding in the opposite direction with its driver asleep. In the end he travelled by horse-drawn carriage more than 4,000 versts – 2,667 miles (4,292 km), roughly the equivalent of crossing the continental United States. His entire round-trip voyage covered 10,000 miles (16,000 km). From the trans-Baikal city of Sretensk he was able to steam the rest of the way, first along the Amur river to the eastern shore of Siberia, the port town of Nikolaevsk, and from there across the Tartar Straits to Sakhalin. When Chekhov arrived, many fires were burning in the taiga, rendering his final destination uncanny and hellish; a kind of hell was exactly how he had conceived Sakhalin in letters about the project before going there and in the travel sketches penned en route.

While in Tiumen, Chekhov sent a letter to the chairman of the Taganrog city council, informing him about books he had arranged for the city library to receive and promising more in the future. In an anonymous editorial on poverty, Chekhov had remarked that the recipients of scholarships never gave a thought to repaying this debt once they had made their way in the world. He himself behaved otherwise, and meaningfully so: the library had been his refuge during his solo years in Taganrog, and he knew what the institution could mean to young people and what it needed. Over the years he cajoled publishers into donating books, contributed valuable author-signed editions and some 2,000 volumes from his own personal collection, and even persuaded the sculptor Mark Antokolsky to create a statue of Peter the Great – founder of the city of Taganrog – for the library grounds in connection with the city's 200th anniversary. When he returned from Sakhalin he also undertook to have thousands of books shipped to the schools and library on the island. Many of these books he bought himself, while his name and personal connections obtained further support for his charitable projects from others.

Once on Sakhalin, Chekhov was taken under the wing of the Alexandrovsk settlement doctor, and he was able to meet with the top

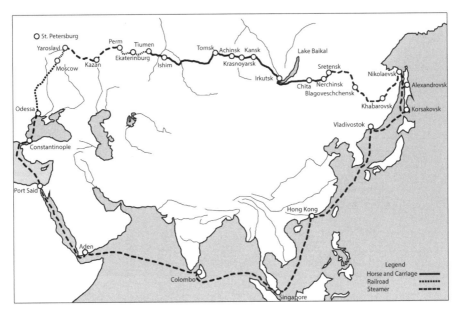

Map of Chekhov's voyage to Sakhalin.

administrators of the island as well as with Baron Korf, the governor-general of the entire Russian Far East. There were frank discussions about the penal colony and promises of cooperation and assistance; Chekhov could do virtually anything he liked other than meet with political prisoners and exiles. He soon arranged for the printing of approximately 10,000 census cards with spaces for place of settlement, address, title, name, age, religion, place of birth, year of arrival on Sakhalin, chief occupation, level of education, marital status, assistance received from authorities, and ailments. As Chekhov wrote to Suvorin while sailing from North Sakhalin, where he had spent two months, to the southern part of the island,[2] 'the conditions I worked under were as favorable as could be.' He claimed to have taken 'a census of the entire population of Sakhalin' and to 'have records of about ten thousand convicts and settlers by now. In other words, there's not a single convict or settler who hasn't talked with me' (11 September 1890; *Letters*, pp. 170–71). Chekhov exaggerated a bit: his own narrative in *Sakhalin Island* tells of settlements that he skipped, and scholars have only been able to account for approximately 7,400 completed cards. Nevertheless, his effort was stunning. He was particularly proud of the data collected on children, and in the book his sections on women and children are quite gripping and disturbing.

Census card from Sakhalin research project.

Scholars have had a hard time with *Sakhalin Island*, which strikes some as dry and unreadable, and they are generally befuddled by the book's overarching shape. Chekhov himself told Suvorin, in the letter cited above, 'I have the feeling I've seen it all, but missed the elephant,' perhaps a reflection of the irrational, ultimately ungraspable phenomenon he was studying.[3] Statistics, so fundamental to a putatively scientific approach, are poorly articulated, and it is often difficult to understand their import. Chekhov explains that his 'main aim in conducting the census was not its results but the impressions received during the making of it':[4] gathering the numbers was chiefly a pretext for talking with individuals and getting their stories.

Still, there is a definite logic to the organization of the book. The first fourteen chapters hang on the skeleton of Chekhov's own travels on the island. It begins with his arrival in Nikolaevsk, his departure point from the mainland, and follows him to and around the island, disposing of historical, geographical and meteorological overviews along the way. The following seven chapters are organized thematically and get at the institutional and social structures comprising the place. These include treatments of what remained of the indigenous population (and the horrifying atrocities committed against them by the colonizers), practices regarding escapees, and – in the highly marked position of the book's ending – illness, mortality and medical infrastructure on the island. The book's genre has long been debated, but a convincing argument places it in the nineteenth-century tradition of medical geography, a hybrid form that melds narratives of travel and exploration with medical and sociological study of the relationship between environment and human health.[5] Appropriately, Chekhov presents himself as a physician in the work, and he argues that physicians should have been consulted when settlement sites were chosen.

Damning conclusions pervade the study. Voluntary colonization on southern Sakhalin has failed – those who can, make their way to the mainland. The communal life that Dostoevsky celebrated in his memoir of life in a convict labour prison is portrayed negatively: living in cabins independently would always be better, even if the convicts had to build their own living spaces as soon as they reached the island.[6] Chekhov being Chekhov, however, understatement prevails, and the most horrifying facts appear without haranguing commentary. Thus, at the book's end, after describing the dismal health of the population, their poor treatment and the awful conditions in the prison infirmary, Chekhov relates official statistics regarding medicaments shipped to the island, dryly remarking that 'the population of Sakhalin can brag that, in 1889, they all underwent the most enormous dosing.'[7] It is left to the reader to ponder official theft and embezzlement. Likewise, in the book's final paragraph, Chekhov cites without comment two articles of law pertaining to convict health: the first states that convicts cannot be assigned labour that affects their health in a harmful manner; the second exempts pregnant and nursing women from work. The reader is trusted to contemplate the contradiction between these laws and the practices exposed in the book.

If one compares *Sakhalin Island* with Chekhov's two abandoned projects for a dissertation in medicine, the most striking distinction to be borne in mind is that, for this project, Chekhov actually went there. He invested his entire self into the project in ways utterly unprecedented in all his writings, let alone the two earlier scientific projects. The authority of Chekhov's voice in this work derives from the fact that he himself undertook the hard journey to get to Sakhalin: he suffered all manner of dangers and discomforts and exhausted himself with great physical effort to see it with his own eyes and talk to the people. He himself experienced a portion of the bodily punishment involved in being sentenced to Sakhalin: travelling there. This was not the theorizing of 'History of Sexual Dominance' or the scholarship of 'History of Doctoring in Russia'; Chekhov's bodily self was very much on the line in this project.

True, there was preliminary research with textual sources, and Chekhov had help from others in this. But both the first and the last pages of the book drive home the point that he made the hard journey himself. He traversed the terrain he describes, entered spaces of the damned and dialogued with the lowest of the low, trying to understand their lives from their points of view. The goal of entering the point of view of his subject is perhaps most evident in the central chapter where one of the convicts – an innocent man, as it emerges – tells his own tale, in his own language ('Yegor's Tale', or 'Rasskaz Egora').[8]

Chekhov's voyage to Sakhalin gave his representation of the island's inhabitants, and the system of penal servitude and colonization through exile, great authenticity. In August 1895, during his first visit with Leo Tolstoy, Chekhov felt sure enough to correct Tolstoy's handling of Katerina's sentence to penal servitude in the first draft of the novel *Resurrection* (the specific combination of term and punishment was not possible).[9] Everywhere in the book one encounters information undergirded by implicit or explicit assertions that might be formulated such: I went there, and I saw this; I met him or her, and he or she told me this.

This means that the biographical Chekhov is the hero of *Sakhalin Island*, a massively significant fact if one considers the rest of his literary production, where he strove to keep his 'I' out of his fiction and drama. This norm was quite programmatic and spelled out in letters with pithy how-to advice to other writers (such as Maxim Gorky, and especially his brother Alexander), in which keeping the author out of the picture was a central theme. As he wrote to Alexander, 'the main thing is to watch out for the personal element [...] Who's interested in knowing my life and your life, my thoughts and your thoughts? Give the people people, not yourself' (8 May 1889). Chekhov was not tempted by the genres of autobiography and memoir. In an 11 October 1899 letter to Dr Grigory Rossolimo, who had asked for an autobiographical sketch to accompany a photograph for an album commemorating the 25th anniversary of their medical faculty class's graduation, he famously diagnosed himself as suffering from 'autobiographophobia'. Even when he wrote opinion pieces (in Russian, *publitsistika*), which expressed personal views on matters of public concern, Chekhov generally signed with pseudonyms.

Sakhalin Island, and the travel sketches Chekhov wrote about getting there, stand out as looming exceptions to this picture. There Chekhov's person is everywhere central; only in his letters and in photographs is his 'I' more visible. This is an extraordinarily suggestive aspect of the book and the larger project behind it. It is also consistent with what Chekhov had told Bilibin many years earlier about saving his proper name for publication of medical research.

To be sure, the journey to Sakhalin had an element of hiding to it: it was conceived at least in part as an escape from his growing fame. Not long after his return he bought an estate south of Moscow that further restricted his visibility to the public. Nevertheless, in the *medical* study that he published as a result, and there only, Chekhov presented himself as the hero of his own narrative. For anyone with an interest in Chekhov's creative biography, that is a remarkable fact. It suggests that the particular self that is presented in *Sakhalin Island* most closely approximated the way he wished to be seen by his public.

On 13 October 1890, Chekhov boarded the steamer *Petersburg* at Korsakovsk for his voyage home via Vladivostok, Singapore, Colombo, Hong Kong, the Suez Canal, Constantinople and Odessa; a cholera epidemic kept him from visiting Japan. A letter to Suvorin thrills at having been to 'hell itself' and then, on Ceylon (Sri Lanka), a heaven that included erotic adventure:

> Here in paradise I traveled more than a hundred versts by train
> and had my fill of palm groves and bronze women. When I have
> children, I'll say to them, not without pride: 'Why, you sons of
> bitches, I've had relations in my day with a black-eyed Hindu
> girl, and guess where? In a coconut grove, on a moonlit night!'
> (9 December 1890; *Letters*, p. 173)

Chekhov returning from Sakhalin with mongoose, accompanied by
midshipman G. N. Glinka, whom Chekhov met on the voyage home.

The mythopoetic motif of the hero's descent to the underworld, which
runs through much of Chekhov's art and life, requires the trial of a detour
through hell for the ascent to heaven.[10]

On the way to Singapore, Chekhov witnessed two burials at sea,
reporting to Suvorin that the sight makes 'you grow frightened and somehow start thinking that you are going to die too and that you too will be
thrown into the sea' (9 December 1890; *Letters*, p. 174). During a typhoon

the ship's captain recommended that Chekhov keep his revolver handy, so as to guarantee himself a quick death if they went down. But in the Indian Ocean Chekhov devised a bold entertainment that challenged the very notion of death at sea: a line was draped from the stern of the steamer, and Chekhov would dive into the water from the prow and catch the line as the ship passed by. Once he was approached by a shark, which together with the burial at sea featured in the first story he published after Sakhalin, 'Gusev'. That story, conceived on Ceylon, is narrated from the point of view of a dying peasant soldier being shipped back from the Far East. His superstitious, ignorant and fatalistic world view is contrasted with that of another mortally ill returnee, an *intelligent* critical of the social and political order that has put them where they are. Interpretations of the work tend to view Chekhov as preferring one or the other position, but the story's contrapuntal presentation of two world views may be more to the point. One remarkable feature of this story is its adherence to the peasant character's point of view beyond death, but in such a way that rules out any notion of an afterlife. The ending feels poignant and uncanny; its final images, paradoxically, represent a highly personified nature freed of any human consciousness apprehending it. The ending both demands interpretation and mocks the human propensity for reading the world as a forest of symbols at one and the same time.

When Chekhov arrived in Odessa on 1 December, he had been gone for longer than seven months, with more than three of them spent on Sakhalin. His mother and brother Mikhail met him at the train station in Tula on 7 December, and the following day he was installed in the Moscow apartment to which his family had moved in his absence. He claimed to have been healthy all during his time on Sakhalin, where his routine had been to rise at five in the morning and retire late after a frenetic day's work, but now he was suffering from the strenuous voyage's after-effects. In letters to Suvorin and Leikin he complained of a cold, painful haemorrhoids and general exhaustion. What really worried him, though, was his heart: 'Every minute my heart stops for a few seconds' (to Suvorin, 24 December 1890); 'it feels like there's a rubber ball present in my chest' (to Leikin, 27 December 1890). He had long complained of haemorrhoids, headaches and flashing in his eyes, and he suffered terrible breathlessness towards the end of his life, but it would be heart failure that actually killed Chekhov.

At the end of January 1891, Chekhov had his first epistolary contact with Ivan Bunin, whom many consider to be Chekhov's successor; they would not meet for almost five years, after which they became close friends. It began with Chekhov responding favourably to Bunin's request that he read and comment on some stories, though Bunin never sent them (*P* IV, pp. 445–6; *Letopis'*, p. 401).

In March Chekhov arranged for some 2,200 books to be sent to the Sakhalin library and left for St Petersburg, where he admired the Italian star Eleonora Duse in Shakespeare's *Antony and Cleopatra*. From there he departed for his first tour of western Europe, with Suvorin and his son. He saw Vienna, Venice, Bologna, Florence, Rome, Naples and Paris. He gambled (and lost) in the casino at Monte Carlo, but he proved immune to the addiction that had tormented Pushkin, Dostoevsky and the young Tolstoy.

After returning to Moscow at the beginning of May, Chekhov and his family left for a new summer dacha south of Moscow on the Oka river. They had chosen poorly: the place was cramped and without such amenities as an indoor toilet. Soon they moved to Bogimovo, the run-down but charming and expansive estate of Evgeny Bylim-Kolosovsky, whom Levitan and Mizinova had met on their way to visit the Chekhovs. There Chekhov had grand working space and engaging neighbours, including the eminent zoologist Vladimir Vagner. Chekhov set up a rigorous writing schedule: he would rise early, at 4 a.m., and work through the morning; in the middle of the day he would join the leisure activities of the others and rest; then, beginning in the late afternoon, he would sit to his work until a late supper and the night's entertainments. Three days a week were dedicated to *Sakhalin Island*, three days to the long story under way, 'The Duel' ('Duel''), and one day for short fiction. That productive summer turned the Sakhalin voyage to considerable literary profit.

'The Duel' also benefited from Chekhov's proximity to Vagner. The two carried on extensive discussions of the theories of evolution and degeneration, which had long been of central intellectual and personal interest to Chekhov. According to his brother Mikhail, Chekhov argued that the taints of inheritance could be overcome by individual effort, 'that no matter how irreversible degeneration may seem to be, it could always be overcome through personal will and education'; this was a position of deep personal significance for a man who was suffering from and had lost family members to TB, a disease that, in spite of the discovery of the bacillus causing it by Robert Koch in 1882, was still understood as having a weighty hereditary component. Vagner, by contrast, 'asserted that nature did not joke around – once there were signs of degeneration, that was it, there was no return'.[11] The sociobiological perspective proper to theories of evolution and degeneration applies throughout *Sakhalin Island* and is central to 'Duel'.

'The Duel' is Chekhov's longest work of fiction (excepting the early serialized potboiler *The Shooting Party*) – so long that Chekhov's literary colleagues grew irritated at his monopolization of the space for fiction over the eleven instalments of *New Times*. The story is more compositionally complex and novelistic than 'Steppe' or 'A Boring Story', each of which focuses on one character. 'Duel' comprises a number of intersecting storylines, and a narrator who moves systematically among the internal perspectives of various characters. On the way to the tense culmination promised by the title, Chekhov treats tried and true themes of the nineteenth-century Russian literary tradition: duelling and the ideological debate, fundamental to the masterpieces of Dostoevsky and Turgenev, between the materialist world view and philosophical idealism. This debate has been updated, however, so as to reflect the impact of late nineteenth-century theories of biological and cultural degeneration.[12] Urgently personal for Chekhov, the topic also reverberated on a larger social and political scale: thus, in his book on Sakhalin, the colonial project represented by the island appears as a grand exercise in bio-social devolution.

From the time of his first dissertation proposal, Chekhov had been deeply invested in evolutionary theory. After his journey to Sakhalin he maintained his optimism about the human potential to master, in an ethically positive way, the workings of biological inheritance and the evolution of our species, as well as the development of individuals. A case study of failure, the Sakhalin book nevertheless asserts that results could be different with a rational, scientific approach. It is no surprise, then, that most scholarly treatments of Chekhov's attitude towards degeneration read 'The Duel' as a continuation of Chekhov's debate with Vagner. But it does not follow that certain characters and the ideas they hold reflect Chekhov's own position, or that the shooting duel with which the story culminates resolves the duel of ideas, leaving the reader to declare a victor. Instead, opposing world views are balanced against one another, and each is undermined through correlation with psychological weaknesses of its holder. The positive characters in this story are those whose views of and responses to others are unideological, unprofessional and humane.

The chief characters are Ivan Layevsky, a lapsed student of philology who has taken a civil service job in the finance ministry in the seaside Caucasus town; Nadezhda Fyodorovna, who left her husband to live with Layevsky; Alexander Samoilenko, an army doctor who is friend to all and at whose home some of the characters take meals; and Nikolai von Koren, a zoologist who visits the seaside town annually to study the embryology of jellyfish, and who is planning an exploratory voyage to the far northeastern, Arctic areas of the empire. After two years of cohabitation, Layevsky has tired of his mistress and is wracked by guilt, while she has become entangled in a sordid affair with a police captain and a rather exploitative flirtation with the son of a merchant to whom she is in debt. Neither Layevsky nor Nadezhda Fyodorovna has a clue as to the other's emotional state, but their situation is reaching a crisis: Nadezhda Fyodorovna's husband is now dead, which puts marriage on the table and makes Layevsky all the more desperate to escape; and Nadezhda Fyodorovna's lover refuses to end the affair, while the young victim of her flirtation grows jealous and in the story's turning point will lead Layevsky to the room where his partner and the police captain are in bed together.

The metaphoric and literal duels of Layevsky and von Koren activate a grand theme of Russian literature, where duelling was a defining episode for the Romantic hero and a frequent occurrence in Russian actuality as well, with Pushkin and Lermontov perishing in duels. It continued to appear in later periods, though most often as an anachronism and with irony (for example in Turgenev's *Fathers and Sons*).[13] At the time of Chekhov's story, however, the practice of duelling was making a European comeback. In Russia in 1894, duels among military officers were declared not to be crimes but affairs to be taken up by committees of honour and even encouraged, as happens in Alexander Kuprin's *The Duel* (*Poedinok*, 1905). The characters in Chekhov's tale are not military officers, however, and their duel is no affair of honour. Both Layevsky and von Koren are highly conscious of literary precedents for their duel – they refer to duels in Lermontov and Turgenev – and like every other duel in the grand Russian literary tradition, theirs is highly irregular, an aberration from start to finish.

The same may be said of the ideological duel playing out between the two characters, the relation between the arts and the sciences, between 'the humane sciences' and the 'exact sciences' in von Koren's formulation (*Novels*, p. 206). This replays the conflict between the mindsets of the generations of the 1840s and the 1860s, as portrayed in Turgenev's

Fathers and Sons, but with a *fin de siècle* twist that updates the theory of evolution (fundamental to the materialist position) with social Darwinisim and the theory of degeneration. Chekhov's own position was extremely nuanced. He was critical of the theory of degeneration but clearly influenced by it all the same, and he was a qualified defender of science and materialism. Thus, in a letter to Suvorin, Chekhov faults the 'pretentious crusade against materialist doctrine' in Paul Bourget's novel *Le Disciple* (1889):

> Everything that lives on earth is necessarily materialistic. In animals, in savages and in Moscow merchants everything that is elevated and non-animal is conditioned by unconscious instinct; everything else in them is materialistic – and not by their own choosing, certainly. Creatures of a higher order, thinking humans, are also necessarily materialists. They search for truth in matter because there is nowhere else for them to search: all they can see, hear and feel is matter. They can necessarily seek out truth only where their microscopes, probes and knives are effective. Prohibiting materialist doctrine is tantamount to preventing man from seeking out the truth. Outside of matter there is no experience or knowledge, and consequently no truth. [...] [P]sychic phenomena are so strikingly similar to physical ones that it is almost impossible to figure out where the former start and the latter end. It seems to me that, when a corpse is being dissected, even the most inveterate spiritualist must *necessarily* come up against the question of where the soul is. And if you know how great the similarity is between mental and physical illnesses and when you know that both one and the other are treated with the very same remedies, you can't help but refuse to separate soul from body. (7 May 1889; *Letters*, pp. 143–4)

Making the case to Suvorin was one thing, however, and representing characters who argue it in his fiction quite another. 'Duel' offers striking cautions and complications.

Thus Chekhov's irony is appreciable when von Koren overreachingly refers to himself as a 'zoologist, or a sociologist, which is the same thing' (*Novels*, p. 163). The young deacon Pobedov, who like von Koren takes his meals at Samoilenko's table, furthers this association when, observing the duel, he is reminded of von Koren's remarks about territorial moles fighting underground. But for the man of the cloth, humans behaving like animals is a degradation of their humanity, rather than scientific evidence of a fundamental sameness. He is particularly appalled by von Koren's argument that, having diminished the struggle for existence and natural selection, 'we ourselves must take care of destroying the feeble and unfit, or else, as the Layevskys multiply, civilization will perish and mankind will become totally degenerate' (*Novels*, p. 142; see also pp. 206–10). Chekhov's handling of Layevsky is similarly ironic. The philologist calls himself a 'superfluous man' and a 'Hamlet' and persistently refers to literary models, including Anna Karenina, by way of self-explanation (*Novels*, pp. 119, 131, 127). Above all, however, he seeks alibis and so willingly resorts to those offered by a scientific perspective. He calls himself 'a pathetic neurasthenic, an idler...', and he adopts central precepts of degeneration theory in blaming 'the degree to which we're crippled by civilization!' (*Novels*, p. 120).

As is his wont, Chekhov complicates the thought of both characters by exploring their psychological foundations. While a perceptive (if unkind) appraiser of the other, each is blind to his own self's investment in just how the other is viewed, and neither quite understands the human potential for change, which turns out to be the story's astonishingly positive moral. In a revealing passage, the arrogant, narcissistic von Koren poses with a pistol from Samoilenko's shelf and gazes at himself in the mirror: 'He was very pleased with his face, and his handsomely trimmed little beard, and his broad shoulders, which served as obvious proof of his good health and sturdy build' (*Novels*, p. 132). But he is utterly incapable of empathetic understanding of others, even those whom he likes: he proposes that the deacon have his new young wife tonsured as a nun so he might join von Koren's scientific expedition to the far northeast as a hieromonk, and he cannot comprehend the deacon's demurral. In the duel, when he is told of the shock Layevsky just suffered – the night before, he had found Nadezhda Fyodorovna with the police captain – rather than accepting the notion that this combat might not make sense under the circumstances, disgust takes such hold of him that he aims to kill Layevsky, who has already shot into the air. He had told Samoilenko that nothing would come of the duel, but now acts in the grip of unconscious impulses, 'and for the first time that morning looked at Laevsky with hatred' (*Novels*, pp. 152, 225).

Meanwhile, in the characters of the ignorant but good-natured Dr Samoilenko and the prone-to-laughter deacon, the story celebrates, in a minor key, the Rabelaisian enjoyments of meals, drinking, storytelling and laughter. The deacon plays a pivotal role in the story's culminating moment: he cannot resist the sin of observing (in secret) the duel, and then distracts von Koren at the moment of his shot, likely saving him from committing a murder.

With more than a century's backward perspective, it proves easy to see the connection between the pseudoscientific truths of social Darwinism and the theory of degeneration and social and political injustices of the time. In 'Duel', Chekhov already makes this visible by correlating von Koren's scientific sureness regarding the inferiority and racial hygienic danger of Layevsky with the scientist's megalomaniacal tendencies.

The ending of this story, which involves a reconciliation between von Koren and Layevsky some time later, after Layevsky has buckled down to work and normalized relations with Nadezhda Fyodorovna, strikes many readers as artificial and unpersuasive. Yet it is utterly consistent with the characters Chekhov has constructed, the theme of the duel, and Chekhov's own poetics. Layevsky's rehabilitation has started even before the duel. When he sees Nadezhda Fyodorovna in bed with the police captain, rather than anger or jealousy he is confronted with his own guilt and shame. What he saw when he looked through that doorway was a staging of his own guilt: 'He clearly recalled what he had seen that evening in Miuridov's house, and it gave him an unbearably creepy feeling of loathing and anguish. Kirilin [the police captain] and Atchmianov [the merchant's son] were disgusting, but they were merely continuing what he had begun; they were his accomplices and disciples' (*Novels*, p. 215). This scene – a Freudian primal scene – has functioned rather like Hamlet's mousetrap, or like the bedroom scene witnessed by father and son sailors in Chekhov's very Hamletian 'At Sea (A Sailor's Tale)'. Rather than buttressing a self with sureness in his radical difference from the others he is observing, Layevsky sees himself, and his own failings, in these others. That is what begins his rehabilitation. For him the duel ultimately works precisely as a duel is supposed to: one restores one's honour or dignity not by killing one's opponent, but by standing manfully under that opponent's fire.[14]

Von Koren too now sees anew. At the end of the story, he passes by Layevsky's window on his way to the steamer that will take him away. He is astonished by the sight of Layevsky hard at work at his desk. 'His marriage, this all-day work for a crust of bread, some new expression in his face, and even his gait – it's all so extraordinary to such a degree that I don't even know what to call it.' This stunning admission of epistemological humility from von Koren is further emphasized by Layevsky's last thoughts, 'No one knows the real truth,' a repeated motif in the story's final pages (*Novels*, pp. 233, 236–7).

In mid-June, Chekhov sent *New Times* his story 'Peasant Women' ('Baby'), a bleak tale of adultery, murder and betrayal inspired by the Sakhalin experience. As in the book on Sakhalin, gender inequality and the abysmal treatment of children are underlined, and the smug story-teller, Matvei Savvich, who is the tale's villain, deploys a self-serving religious rhetoric reminiscent of Alexander Ostrovsky's merchant *samodur* characters: petty, ignorant, high-handed tyrants.

In September of this same year Chekhov was back at work on another long project, which became 'Story of an Unknown Man' ('Rasskaz neizvestnogo cheloveka'); because it touched on the underground revolutionary movement and treated the possible assassination of a high government official, he worried that it might be blocked by the censors. Chekhov also published an anonymous denunciation of the scientific pretentions of the inhumanely managed research station at the Moscow Zoo, 'Tricksters'('Fokusniki').

In October, Chekhov's kind, beloved aunt Fedosya Dolzhenko died of the family disease, TB. 'Of course,' Chekhov wrote Natalya Lintvareva, 'we'll all die, but it's sad nonetheless' (25 October 1891). Chekhov was sleeping poorly and read *War and Peace* at night. Its central theme of death caught his attention; he wondered at Prince Andrei's long suffering from a fatal wound that he himself could have treated successfully: 'Tolstoy, while he was writing his thick novel, must have been saturated by an unwitting hatred of medicine,' he told Suvorin, while also tempering his overarching admiration with a critique of Tolstoy's tendentious, inauthentic representation of Napoleon's mind (25 October 1891).

By the end of 1891 Chekhov's attention had turned to the countryside. He was helping to raise funds for peasant victims of famine in the Nizhegorod and Voronezh provinces. A January trip to the area to see for himself and organize efforts left him ill with what he called a cold, though the pains in his upper chest suggest progress in his lung disease; he went back there with Suvorin in February. For a benefit volume he donated a chapter on runaways and vagrants from the Sakhalin book he was writing.

Meanwhile, Chekhov had begun looking for a small estate to purchase. He hoped to escape the expense of living in Moscow and renting summer dachas, and he thought that residing in the country might improve his declining health.[15] Ever increasing demands were being made on his time by visitors, who might be kept distant if he relocated, and a new environment could also advance his writing. Something had to change, as he complained to Suvorin: 'If I'm a doctor, I need patients and a hospital; if I'm a littérateur, I need to live among the folk, and not on Malaya Dmitrovka [a street in Moscow] with a mongoose. [...] This life between four walls, without nature, without people, without a homeland, without health and an appetite – this isn't life' (20 October 1891). (Chekhov had picked up what he thought was a pair of mongooses in India on his voyage home from Sakhalin. However, one of the pair turned out to be an unsociable palm civet that was killed when it bit painters; the rascally mongoose was eventually donated to the Moscow zoo.) At the end of autumn he suffered a month-long bout of the flu, and he wrote and published a lengthy pseudonymous feuilleton, 'In Moscow' ('V Moskve'), the satirical tone of which further separated him from the capital and its intelligentsia as he contemplated moving to the country.

At the beginning of February 1892, Chekhov signed a contract to purchase the 575-acre (230 ha) estate of Melíkhovo, located in the Serpukhov district, about 80 kilometres (50 mi.) south of Moscow. The mortgage interest would cost him half of what he paid annually in rent for an apartment in the city and a dacha in the summer, he told Alexander (*Letopis'*, p. 310). He moved there with his extended family at the beginning of March and began work on another long story in part inspired by Sakhalin, 'Ward No. 6'.

In January Chekhov had published 'The Fidget' ('Poprygun'ia'), a story about a flighty, celebrity-crazed woman who fails to respect her devoted and hardworking physician spouse and humiliates him with an open affair with a painter. Only after her husband contracts diphtheria from sucking membranes from a sick child's throat with a tube and himself dies does she understand that he was in fact an enormously talented researcher for whom his colleagues expected a brilliant future. Readers in the know quickly identified the adulterous pair of the story as caricatures of Chekhov's friend the artist Levitan, and the wife of another friend and medical colleague, Dmitry Kuvshinnikov. The trio had been among those seeing Chekhov off on his trip to Sakhalin two years earlier, when Dr Kuvshinnikov had presented Chekhov with a flask of cognac to drink when he reached the Pacific Ocean. This was not the first time Chekhov had made literary use of the lives of his friends, and it would not be the last, but it was the most explosive: Levitan considered challenging him to a duel, and their relations were severed for several years, as was Chekhov's friendship with an actor who found himself represented unflatteringly in a member of the fidget's circle. As always, Chekhov denied his guilt, perhaps protesting too much. In a letter to the writer Lidiya Avilova he complained, 'Can you imagine, one of my acquaintances, a 42-year-old lady, has recognized herself in the twenty-year-old heroine of my "Fidget" [...] and all of Moscow is accusing me of a pasquinade' (29 April 1892). In an amusing irony, a few years later Chekhov would overtly parody Avilova in *Seagull*, and long after Chekhov's death (1940) Avilova would publish a little book spinning her relationship with Chekhov into a major, but impossible, romance.

In May, another fine short story emerged from Chekhov's Sakhalin trip, 'In Exile' ('V ssylke'), in which two opposing stances towards the existential pain of Siberian exile are contrasted: a deliberately acquired callousness, immune to loss and void of desires for self or others; and the painful, hopeless struggle to remain a feeling human being and to love. Chekhov also sent an odd, parabolic animal tale to his dismissed venue *Fragments*. As in old times, 'Fishy Love' ('Ryb'ia liubov'') was signed with the pseudonym 'Man without a Spleen'. The piece, in which an old carp falls in love with a young woman, gets himself hooked but then tears free, losing some of his lip, ran into difficulty with the censors.

In the summer of 1892, Chekhov signed on as an unpaid *zemstvo* doctor in Serpukhov and dedicated himself to battling the cholera epidemic threatening the area. In addition to the medical station he opened at Melikhovo (which received supplies from the *zemstvo*), he had charge of 25 other villages, four factories and one monastery (*Letopis'*, p. 324). He travelled jolting roads to educate locals about the disease and its transmission and to supervise preventive and preparatory measures, such as stocking supplies and organizing space for the care of those who would be stricken; money to fund all this was cajoled from factory owners and landholders. In the mornings Chekhov received local peasants who needed doctoring.

Apparently, the Sakhalin venture alone had not been enough to repay his debt to medicine: Chekhov was working full-time as a physician when traditionally he would be holidaying with his family and focused on his writing. Progress on the Sakhalin book and other projects was delayed until mid-October, when the cholera danger abated and the official infirmary at Melikhovo was closed after serving at least a thousand people. The summer's meagre literary achievements notwithstanding, Chekhov felt that he 'had spent no other summer as well as this one' (*Letopis'*, pp. 327, 324–25), and he did the same next summer. The intensive involvement in public health and larger social problems animating the Sakhalin voyage thus continued over the following years. If Chekhov's earlier medical activities were largely split between theorizing (his unrealized dissertation projects) and the clinical treatment of ill individuals, now he was acting as a public health physician. Most biographers see the post-Sakhalin Chekhov as more socially and politically engaged, and much of that engagement is refracted through medicine.

In January 1893 Chekhov was visited by Tolstoy's son Lev; the two talked about travelling to the World's Fair in Chicago together, a trip Chekhov would renounce for lack of funds but assign to a character in the long story 'Three Years' ('Tri goda'), for which he was making notes. Chekhov managed to publish two lengthy works of fiction during the winter of 1892–3, both in the leftist *Russian Thought*: the extraordinarily powerful 'Ward No. 6', perhaps Chekhov's most anthologized long story; and 'The Story of an Unknown Man' (1893), a politically daring work that, over the years, has been inadequately appreciated by readers.

'Ward No. 6' was something of a sensation. The tale of a physician and hospital chief, Dr Ragin, who acquiesces to corruption among his medical staff and foul conditions in his hospital, and in the end is himself committed to the psychiatric ward and beaten to death by a caretaker, reportedly caused impressionable female readers to faint and deeply disturbed no less a figure than Vladimir Lenin.[16] Chekhov's tricky narration facilitates strong reaction: he begins the story with a chatty narrator but imperceptibly slots the reader into Ragin's perspective through a gradual shift to free indirect discourse. When Ragin's beating and death are depicted from within, the shock is all the greater. Instead of attending to what the story's form might tell them, however, readers generally focus on the central philosophical debate between Ragin and Ivan Gromov, an inmate of the hospital's psychiatric wing. As with 'Duel', the story's ending is typically interpreted as Chekhov's resolution of their argument: the passive Ragin ends up committed as a patient in his own institution, which refutes Tolstoy's doctrine of non-resistance to evil while validating Gromov's stance of active protest. It matters, though, that the philosophizing happens in a madhouse: ideas are not the bottom line here. Opposing positions create a kind of intensifying contrapuntal rhythm, around which other motifs in the story cluster in thematic harmony, but the ideas themselves are neither validated nor rejected as such; instead, they are undermined from the start by their flawed articulators. Before the story's action is under way the reader knows full well the awfulness of the institution that Ragin, a physician who never wished to become one and avoids clinical practice, is supposed to be supervising; Gromov's paranoiac madness is also a given. Most interesting are the connections Chekhov establishes between personal history and personality and these characters' ideas.

With individual psychology the ground floor here rather than philosophy, utterances by characters become symptomatic behaviour, signifiers on the plane of personality. This is not to say that the ideas do not matter: the stoic philosophy of Marcus Aurelius, whom Chekhov read in this period, is cited in Ragin's arguments with Gromov and in the narrator's aphoristic remarks in free indirect discourse tied to the point of view of Ragin. Scholars have also found echoes of Schopenhauer and Tolstoy. But rather than operating as disembodied logics with a disputable relation to some truth, ideas serve the inner needs of those who express them. This is connected with the story's lengthy biographical digressions on the two chief characters. In each case, the personal history of the individual speaks to who he is and what he is arguing now.

Ragin had been compelled by his physician father to study medicine; his real calling was theology and philosophy. He was never beaten as a child, and Gromov attributes his quietism to this fact: 'You're totally unacquainted with reality, and you've never suffered [...] while I have suffered constantly from the day of my birth to this very day. Therefore I tell you frankly that I consider myself superior to you and more competent in all respects' (*Stories*, pp. 199, 201). But Ragin's loss of avocation was indeed a traumatic blow to which he is arguably still responding. His distaste for and withdrawal from his position as physician and administrator – malpractice, really – belatedly resist his forced career. His father insisted he become a doctor; well then, he would be a very bad one, in spite of natural gifts and empathic disposition. In the story's supreme irony, Ragin is actually doing his job, and doing it well, precisely when his junior colleagues come to the self-interested conclusion that he has 'gone completely loony'. It is because he sits on the bed of a psychiatric patient and addresses him as an intelligent, thinking human being that the others conclude he is himself mad; whereas his conversation actually provides a kind of therapy and even succeeds in talking Gromov out of paranoiac delusions (*Stories*, pp. 202, 196).

Gromov, the narrator states authoritatively, 'suffers from persecution mania'; but he is also 'polite, obliging, and of extraordinary delicacy in dealing with everyone except Nikita [the brutal ward caretaker]' (*Stories*, p. 173). His illness was preceded by one severe emotional blow after another: while studying in St Petersburg, his brother died of consumption; his father, who had been supporting his studies very generously, was arrested for forgery and embezzlement; and Gromov, suddenly poor, had to quit the university and seek work (as a court bailiff) to support himself and his mother (*Stories*, p. 174). He had always been sickly, and his illness may have been caused by inherited syphilis: when he breaks down he is first put into a ward for venereal diseases (*Stories*, p. 178). Nevertheless, Chekhov provides details that suggest a connection between his personal history and the particular form his mental illness takes. On encountering two prisoners being escorted by soldiers, 'For some reason it suddenly seemed to him that he, too, could be put into chains and led in the same way through the mud to prison'; in the spring, when the corpses of a violently murdered old woman and boy are discovered, he becomes possessed by the delusion that he is suspected of having committed the crime and is being sought by the authorities (*Stories*, pp. 176, 178). That 'for some reason' is a riddle towards whose solution the text offers hints. The delusion that others will consider him guilty indicates that, at some level, Gromov must indeed be suffering from feelings of guilt. Based on what is actually there in the story, we might infer, by way of sources for such feelings, that Gromov either identifies with his criminal father or feels himself responsible for the family's catastrophe, or both. After all, he was well supported in St Petersburg by his father's ill-gotten funds.

Thus the psychopathology of both characters is given roots in family history and, in particular, their relations with their fathers. Ragin refuses to become his father – he does not invest himself in the professional identity which was his father's and for which his father insisted he train. The Christ-like Gromov is the son who suffers for the sins of the father. There is indeed something evangelical about him in the narrator's description:

> When he speaks, you recognize both the madman and the
> human being in him. It is hard to convey his insane speech
> on paper. He speaks of human meanness, of the violence that
> tramples on truth, of the beautiful life there will be on earth
> in time, of the grilles on the windows, which remind him

every moment of the obtuseness and cruelty of the oppressors. The result is a disorderly, incoherent potpourri of old but still unfinished songs. (*Stories*, p. 174)

'Ward No. 6' reflects a serious interest in psychiatry on Chekhov's part. He had read galley proofs of his colleague Dr Arkhangelsky's study of Russian psychiatric institutions; he urged young author-protégés to study psychiatric literature; and had his own literary career not diverted him from medicine, he said that he would likely have specialized in psychiatry. As the narrator tells us, the abysmal institution and patterns of (mis)treatment represented in the story were anachronistic aberrations even in Russia of the 1880s, and it is easy for today's reader to view them as utterly impossible in developed nations today. Nevertheless, the story remains utterly compelling. Its themes especially engage readers with an interest in medicine, and the work is a staple of medical humanities courses in the United States.

'The Story of an Unknown Man', Chekhov's only major work set in St Petersburg, depicts an aristocratic milieu quite alien to Chekhov. Its first-person narrator is an ex-naval officer turned revolutionary who is posing as a wealthy Petersburg aristocrat's butler so as to gain information about his employer's father, a top government minister. There had been publicity about former revolutionaries in this era of political stagnation, and Chekhov had met a former naval officer and revolutionary who had since converted while he was on Sakhalin. But the topic was quite unusual for Chekhov, and he was rightfully anxious about censorship. That his character eventually abandons the cause gave reason for him to also fear the wrath of liberal critics.

Chekhov's undercover operative suffers from consumption (like Chekhov), and for reasons he does not quite fathom, his determination to complete his mission begins to fail. With life ebbing, he has become something of a dreamer who craves personal happiness: travel, new sights, romance. At the story's climax he quits his mission and offers to whisk abroad the deceived and pregnant mistress of his employer, Orlov. She fastens to him quickly, attracted by his adventurous revolutionary past and infatuated with the idea of becoming involved in the movement herself; but in fleeing with her he has left this all behind, and their relations sour. She poisons herself on having delivered the baby of her former lover, and the story ends with his return to Petersburg with her baby, whose future he attempts to settle with Orlov.

Critics have emphasized the story's association with Turgenev, and in particular the novel *On the Eve* (*Nakanune*, 1860), in which the hero's revolutionary fervour fades as he sickens from TB and dies in Italy. They often find Chekhov's story derivative and unsatisfying, itself infected by Chekhov's tuberculosis, 'a strange, febrile work that reads as if it had been written nonstop in the heightened state of consciousness that tuberculosis has been said to induce in artists'.[17] Beyond the TB theme, however, what connects the story with Chekhov's person is the overarching theme of spying. Chekhov was famed for his powers of observation, and the motif of the gaze and situations of peeping are everywhere in his works; this is especially true in the early pseudonymous humorous stories. Chekhov had vowed to his brother Alexander to write 'from a crack in the wall', that is, as a voyeur or observer who keeps himself out of the action (13 May 1883).

For the revolutionary, peeping is an aggressive activity intended to result, through the detour of feigned servility, in mastering the situation he observes – perhaps through murder. But assuming that servile position, even in role-playing, proves dangerous: he loses his edge and abdicates when he has the chance to kill his target. Here we might do well to recall again Chekhov's famous letter to Suvorin about a young man's process of 'squeezing the blood of the slave' out of his veins. The unknown man's letter to Orlov blames his decline on biological degeneration, nervous exhaustion or neurasthenia, fashionable medical concepts with which TB was connected in both the popular and medical imagination (in spite of recent scientific discoveries regarding its infectious origins).[18] The unknown man's weakness and dreaming, which he does not understand, evokes this entire complex of biological and psychological regression. TB may be its cause, but it is just as easily understood as one more symptom. Playing the role of the slave turns out to have been dangerous for the unknown man not because of the risk of discovery, but because it involved susceptibility to a process exactly opposite to that of 'squeezing the blood of the slave' out of one's veins: becoming infected with slavishness.

The anonymous narrator and fictional author of the story is quite a writer, as we see also in the denunciatory letter he leaves for Orlov; Orlov in turn is presented as a detached and ironic reader. The narrator's letter pairs them as literary doubles: 'You and I have both fallen, and neither of us will ever get up, and my letter, even if it were eloquent, strong, and fearsome, would still be like knocking on a coffin lid...';

'Why are we worn out? Why do we, who start out so passionate, brave, noble, believing, become totally bankrupt by the age of thirty or thirty-five?' (*Novels*, pp. 298, 300). If there are features of the unknown man suggestive of Chekhov, then this is true, too, in regard to Orlov. His ironic detachment, his womanizing, his defendedness – all these echo reproaches that women (especially Mizinova) launched at Chekhov.

Politics entangled Chekhov's personal life that March, when he broke off relations with Suvorin for a time. Suvorin's son Alexei (often referred to as the *dauphin* in Chekhov's letters) had walked into the office of *Russian Thought* and slapped Lavrov in response to criticism in the liberal journal, now becoming Chekhov's most important venue. Chekhov and the elder Suvorin were reconciled by the end of April – being able to blame the son for the sins of the father's publishing empire helped – but their ideological differences and the utterly unprincipled conduct of Suvorin's newspaper weighed on their friendship and would eventually sink it. Although he continued to do business with Suvorin's press (always with accounting problems), Chekhov's connection to his newspaper *New Times* was coming to an end.

In June Melikhovo again became the site of a temporary medical station for the battle against cholera, which Chekhov was helping 'catch by the tail', as he wrote (*Letopis'*, p. 394). Autumn saw him return to literary activity, including a three-week Moscow whirlwind of banquets and new acquaintances (including Tatyana Shchepkina-Kupernik), as well as further progress on *Sakhalin Island*, some of which was coming out in *Russian Thought*. The fine story 'A Woman's Kingdom' ('Bab'e tsarstvo') would also appear in that same journal in January. This Christmas tale explores the inner world of a 25-year-old factory heiress who lacks the will to take charge of her enterprise and her own life. She can neither address the oppressive injustices she sees in the kingdom she commands, nor pursue her ordinary longings for personal happiness. As an exploration of a young woman's desires it recalls Chekhov's very brief 1892 story 'After the Theatre' ('Posle teatra', originally 'Happiness', or 'Radost''), in which a girl comes home from a performance of *Eugene Onegin* and, inspired by Pushkin's Tatyana, sits down to write a love letter. As a story tackling the social and economic problems caused by rapid industrialization and the migration of peasants from land to factory, the focus of 'Woman's Kingdom' was quite unorthodox, addressing the unhappy inner life of the privileged rather than proletarian sufferings. Chekhov would do something quite similar in his later short masterpiece 'A Medical Case' ('Sluchai iz praktiki', 1898).

At the end of the year, the story 'Big Volodya and Little Volodya' ('Volodia bol'shoi i Volodia malen'kii') came out, but only after severe editing of its overt sexual content; when Chekhov's French translator took up the story, Chekhov urged him to wait until he could send him an uncensored variant (*Letopis'*, p. 361). In it a sensitive young woman who has married a wealthy older man is seduced by an old friend of both only a few months after the wedding. In December, Chekhov also completed 'The Black Monk' ('Chernyi monakh'), which in a letter to the critic M. O. Menshikov he called an '*historia morbi*' and 'study of megalomania' (15 January 1894). Chekhov had been pursuing his long-standing interest in psychiatry with intensive reading in the new field. There had not been a department of psychiatry at Moscow University when Chekhov studied, and S. S. Korsakov's pathbreaking *Course of Psychiatry* was published only this year. Chekhov told Yasinsky that he would probably have become a psychiatrist if literature had not diverted him;[19] Shchepkina-Kupernik reported Chekhov as telling her that if she wanted to become a 'real writer', she should 'study psychiatry – it's essential' (*Letopis'*, pp. 352, 353). In 'Black Monk', which came out in *The Artist* in January 1894, the hallucinated monk signals a break with reality in the main character, a university scholar in philosophy; the monk derived from a disturbing dream the author reported to his brother Mikhail.[20] Motifs of incest contribute a Gothic stratum to the story, while its setting in an anti-Edenic, hellish garden elicits symbolic patterns that run through the whole of Chekhov's writings. In coordinating the story's psychological theme with trendy theoretical debates regarding biological and cultural degeneration, Chekhov returns again to that theme, accentuating in this instance the connection between genius and madness elaborated by Cesare Lombroso and Max Nordau. No mere case study, this rich, poetic story was disliked by the editor of *The Artist*, but he could not pass up an opportunity to publish Chekhov, 'a big name' (*Letopis'*, p. 353). Among close friends, 'Black Monk' aroused worries about Chekhov's own mental health. To Suvorin he declared himself 'psychologically fit': 'Every time an author depicts a mental patient, it does not mean that he himself is ill.' He called the story a coldly conceived depiction of megalomania (25 January 1894).

In mid-January, Chekhov wrote to Menshikov that he now 'has the right' to set medicine aside and focus on accumulated story ideas (*Letopis'*, p. 355). These few years of intensive medical activity validated Chekhov's witticism on the benefits of maintaining both wife and mistress: while working tirelessly as a physician and researcher, and therefore writing little, he jotted notes that would fuel his last decade of literary activity. Meanwhile, February saw the publication of another short masterpiece, 'Rothschild's Fiddle' ('Skripka Rotshil'da'). A return to the Jewish theme, it has not a hint of the Judaeophobic or ambivalent tone of his earlier 'Mire' and *Ivanov*. Instead, Jewishness becomes associated with the emotive potential of music, which transcends ethnic differences. The story's central character, a coffin-maker whose overriding concern is money not made, and therefore lost, connects with the two terms of the story's title, Jewishness and music, and this creates a pathway to the restoration of his memory and a selfhood that was long distorted by trauma. Key is the story's pivotal allusion to the 137th Psalm, concerning the Jewish people's traumatic loss, 'By the rivers of Babylon'.[21]

By now Chekhov's cough had become troubling enough that he left for the Crimea towards the end of winter. Once there, heart palpitations added to his health complaints, which continued after he returned to Melikhovo; to Suvorin he reported an episode when he momentarily thought he might be dying (21 April 1894). While in Yalta he wrote an Easter piece, 'The Student' ('Student'), published first under the title 'In the Evening' ('Vecherom'), which he himself counted as one of his best. This brief masterpiece shares many features with his early comic sketches. As in 'Death of a Clerk', professional identity comprises the story's title and point of departure; naming a character in a way that implies rank or social status had been a frequent principle of narrative organization in the sketches or 'little scenes' (*stsenki*) that Chekhov cranked out as a novice in the 'small press' where he began his publishing career. The setting of 'Student' on Good Friday also recalls the seasonal pieces featuring the corresponding social rituals demanded by the 'small press'. But such allusions to the cultural code are handled differently in the mature work. Instead of evoking readymade meanings that are manipulated to comic effect, they excavate metaphysical depths. The student finds his own way to participate in the Easter holiday; this involves attaining a place in the world that is not given or preordained by Orthodox theology, or any other ideology, and conceiving a cosmos with an open horizon and the possibility of progress.

Many of Chekhov's early stories, including 'Death of a Clerk', work a theme of communication failure to comic effect. 'Student' features profoundly successful communication. A rather fallen seminarian returning home from an inappropriate hunt on Good Friday has paused to retell Peter's denial to two widows, mother and daughter. Before the encounter, as dusk approached and it became bitterly cold, he had not wanted to return to his impoverished home and peasant parents. His thoughts turned to bleak, unchanging Russian history, in which context even the cyclical repetition of the holiday on the church calendar leads to the darkest possible interpretation of the present moment. But his telling connects with the two women, who respond quite emotionally, and this causes the student's spirits to rise. His inner, euphoric ascent is spatially mirrored by a climb from the low, swampy area he had been traversing.

How Chekhov narrates 'Student', and how the student tells his story, may be key to what happens in it. The story opens and closes with passages narrated by means of free indirect discourse attached to the student's point of view, a much studied feature of Chekhov's mature stylistics.[22] This technique subtly, and at times trickily, merges the consciousness of the reader with that of the character, more so than first-person narration; it facilitates empathic identification of reader with character, rather than creating the comic, satirical distance from which we view, by contrast, Cherviakov in 'Death of a Clerk'. And the student's framed tale replicates Chekhov's storytelling manner: just as Chekhov invests us into the perspective of this meditative young man, the student himself tells the story of Peter's denial in a way that facilitates identification of his listeners with Peter: 'In the same way [as me, as us] Peter warmed himself by a fire on a cold night'; 'Peter stood by the fire with them and also warmed himself, as I'm doing now' (*Stories*, pp. 264, 265).

The student also shifts the focus of the Gospel tale from Jesus Christ to Peter, and to the sufferings of guilt and shame aroused by his denial of Christ. Peter's denial and the student's own denials of his faith and his family, which are overtly, though minimally, sketched, may further resonate with the briefly outlined situation between the two women.[23] This strategy of facilitating identifications and arousing empathy is precisely what Chekhov does *not* do in such early comic works as 'Death of a Clerk', which make fun of their characters.

Interestingly, the narrative strategy relates in a very obvious and instructive way to what Chekhov was thinking that he, with his skills as a storyteller, might be able to offer medical students as a lecturer at the medical faculty of Moscow University. Around the time of writing 'Student', his medical school colleague Dr Rossolimo, now on the faculty, investigated the possibility of accepting *Sakhalin Island* as a dissertation in medicine and assigning Chekhov a position in internal medicine. Chekhov proposed, as Rossolimo later put it, 'to read lectures in medicine as though sitting in the skin of the patient under analysis [...] to render a subjective coloration to the medical question being illuminated before the audience' (*Letopis'*, p. 587). Thus, in contemplating lecturing on medicine, Chekhov envisioned bringing techniques he had developed as an author of fiction to the medical faculty of Moscow University.

During this period, in a letter to Suvorin, Chekhov made an often-cited statement about Tolstoy's influence:

> Tolstoy's moral philosophy has ceased to move me [...] I have peasant blood flowing in my veins, and I'm not the one to be impressed with peasant virtues. I acquired my belief in progress when still a child [...] because the difference between the period when they flogged me and the period when they stopped flogging me was enormous. [...] But Tolstoy's philosophy moved me deeply and possessed me for six or seven years. It was not so much his basic postulates that had an effect on me [...] it was his way of expressing himself, his common sense, and probably a sort of hypnotism as well. But now something in me protests. Prudence and justice tell me there is more love for mankind in electricity and steam than in chastity and abstention from meat. War is an evil and the court system is an evil, but it doesn't follow that I should wear bast shoes and sleep on a stove alongside the hired hand and his wife [...] (27 March 1894; *Letters*, pp. 261–2)

Chekhov's reference to a period of Tolstoyan influence has been overblown. To be sure, he read Tolstoy and admired him even when rankled by his tendentiousness, and he alluded to Tolstoy (among others) in his writings. In Chekhov's last years, he would also have considerable personal contact with Tolstoy. Above all, however, what Chekhov learned from Tolstoy had to do with prose stylistics; as he says here, it was the manner of expression that chiefly attracted him. Chekhov was never an orthodox follower of any programme.

In spite of Chekhov's stated intention to abandon medicine, in May he attended a congress of Moscow district *zemstvo* physicians, and in June was voted in as a member for a term of three years. That spring Chekhov had a small outbuilding erected where he could have a place to write away from the hubbub in the cramped main house, and where some of the many guests visiting Melikhovo might sleep. The tiny 'wing' (*fligel'*) was outfitted with a flag that indicated when Chekhov was available to treat local peasants in need of medical assistance. But as daily life at Melikhovo became organized, the desire to again get away only grew. He wrote to Suvorin about wanting 'to live', that 'some power, like a premonition, is hurrying, wanting him to speed up. Or maybe it's not a premonition, but just sorrow that life is flowing so uniformly and listlessly' (11 July 1894). While chapters of *Sakhalin Island* were coming out in issues of *Russian Thought*, Chekhov worked on the complete book version.

In September, after asking Suvorin to intervene with Odessa author-ities, who were blocking his international passport, Chekhov left for a month-long trip to western Europe, beginning in Vienna, from where he proceeded to Abbazia (today Opatija, Croatia), Trieste and Venice, and crossing Italy to Milan, Genoa and Nice before proceeding to Paris. In Venice Chekhov was impressed by an Italian stage adaptation of *Crime and Punishment* (*Letopis'* III, p. 546). In Paris he failed to visit Mizinova, blaming missed letters, not knowing her exact location, and that he was travelling with Suvorin. Lika had reached the crisis point in an affair with Chekhov's friend, the prolific writer Ignaty Potapenko, who had left her pregnant to return to his family; he also holidayed with Chekhov in Moscow and along the Volga to Nizhny Novgorod and then Sumy in late July and August. Her letters imploring Chekhov to come refer

Anton and Mikhail Chekhov on the steps of the Melikhovo 'wing', 1895.

obliquely to her situation and urge him not to discuss it with others; she wants to see only him, because he is not judgemental. Chekhov had lamented losing her in a letter from Vienna – 'Obviously, I've dropped the ball with my health, just as I did with you' (18 September 1894) – a flattering way of saying that their time has passed. Chekhov's correspondence with Mizinova at times makes painful reading for Chekhov idolaters: he was capable of emotional cruelty, and any notes of affection are invariably accompanied by mockery. Mizinova was fully capable of repaying him in kind, but more often her rather manipulative and guilt-tripping attempts at provoking some sort of declaration express pain and confusion. Just what was going on is of course impossible for us to know, but it was no straightforward matter of fending off a woman for whom one does not have feelings, or of a celebrity protecting himself from an admirer: for a while Chekhov keeps Mizinova on call, as it were, and there are times when he desires her company and asks his sister to bring her to Melikhovo, as another item on a Moscow shopping list that might include Santorini wine, plantings for the garden, and fishing paraphernalia.

When Mizinova gave birth to a girl in November, Potapenko snuck away to visit her in Paris, writing to Chekhov to ask for at least 200 rubles, explaining only, 'otherwise I'll be thinking about suicide' (*Letopis'* III, p. 565). Estranged from his legal spouse and living with yet another woman who fought to hold on to him, Potapenko was still making promises to Mizinova. She neither believed him nor blamed him, it seems, and she implored Maria Chekhova not to speak ill of him. Chekhov and Potapenko remained very close. Mizinova's little girl, left in the care of a great aunt in Tver province, died at two.

Something of the affair between Mizinova and Potapenko would be incorporated into *Seagull*, already gestating in Chekhov, but without causing the hard feelings provoked by 'Fidget'. Those became ancient history when, on the spur of the moment, Shchepkina-Kupernik persuaded Levitan to join her in visiting Melikhovo at the very beginning of 1895, and Chekhov and Levitan resumed their prior friendship 'as if nothing had happened'.[24]

Chekhov spent a good part of that winter in Moscow and Petersburg. It was during a Petersburg visit in February that, in Avilova's telling, Chekhov's unhappy passion for her reached its peak. After he returned to Moscow, Avilova had a book-shaped pendant made and engraved with a bibliographic reference (volume, page, lines) that encoded the message: 'If you ever need my life, then come and take it' (*Letopis'* IV.I, p. 69); a few years later Chekhov would parody both gesture and message in *Seagull*, where they lead to an offstage affair. There does seem to have been some interest in Avilova (beyond as a writer with important connections) on Chekhov's part, even if her self-depiction as the love of his life rings false. In this period Chekhov disclosed that, nowadays, he had amorous relations 'almost exclusively with married, that is to say proper, women', presumably to avoid serious entanglements.[25] In March, Leikin recorded in his diary that Avilova was 'in despair': she had written to Chekhov, asking him to come to see her in Moscow, and he did not respond (*Letopis'* IV, p. 86). Among memoirists and biographers, only Bunin accepts Avilova's portrayal of Chekhov's deep attachment to her. But Chekhov certainly enjoyed the company of beautiful and refined women, a category into which Avilova fit very well. So did the actress Lidiya Yavorskaya, with whom Chekhov had a lengthy affair. It is likely there was also intimacy with Tatyana Shchepkina-Kupernik, another female writer seeking patronage from Chekhov, who was herself also involved with Yavorskaya.[26]

However, Chekhov was very discreet; so much so that for almost a century after his death, his dominant image was quite ascetic. When glasnost and the fall of the Soviet Union opened archives in the late 1980s and 1990s and Russian scholars were freed of worry about censorship, his image took a Don Juanish pendulum swing.[27] But by the mid-1890s Chekhov was clearly ill, with coughing that never abated, and he was anything but oversexed (though that was one of the stereotypical symptoms of tuberculosis in popular and literary consciousness). After a visit to Levitan's studio with his sister, Chekhov wrote to Suvorin, who was urging him to marry, 'I think that women have worn him out. Those nice creatures give love, and just take a little from a man: just his youth. [...] If I were a landscape artist, I'd lead a nearly ascetic life: I'd have a woman once a year and eat once a day' (19 January 1895). His next extant letter to Suvorin picks up the theme: 'Phew! Women rob men of their youth, but not me. [...] I've had few affairs; I'm about as much like Catherine the Great as a hazelnut is like a battleship. And the only excuse I can see for silk underwear is that it's softer to the touch and therefore more comfortable. I have a penchant for comfort, but debauchery doesn't tempt me [...]' (21 January 1895; *Letters*, pp. 265–6). A few months later:

Very well, then, I shall marry if you so desire. But under the
following conditions: everything must continue as it was
before, in other words, she must live in Moscow and I in the
country, and I'll go visit her. I will never be able to stand the
sort of happiness that lasts from one day to the next, from one
morning to the next [...] I promise to be a splendid husband,
but give me a wife who, like the moon, does not appear in
my sky every day. I won't write any better for having gotten
married. (23 March 1895; *Letters*, pp. 272–3)

Meanwhile, the wife of a depressed Suvorin wrote to Chekhov, asking
him to 'tempt' Suvorin to visit him in Moscow, since 'apart from you,
he loves and values no one' (*Letopis'* IV.1, p. 20). Chekhov followed up,
promising to make the rounds of cemeteries with Suvorin and go to the
circus. When abroad, too, the two of them would visit cemeteries, a
favourite activity for Chekhov. The relationship with Suvorin remained
Chekhov's most important for now.

At the beginning of 1895, Chekhov's 'Three Years' came out, a long
story that was serialized in *Russian Thought*. Once again Chekhov found
himself fending off *roman à clef* interpretations. The depressing story was
set in the Moscow merchant milieu where Chekhov's father had worked
until a few years earlier, and it gave a bleak picture of marriage and family
life. The story did not do well with critics and remains underappreci-
ated to this day. In time span, array of characters and coordinated plot
lines, 'Three Years' is perhaps the most novelistic of Chekhov's mature
works. It also explores notions of inheritance and familial bondage in
ways that evoke Chekhov's biography. Chekhov unconvincingly denied
any association between the merchant patriarch of that story and his own
father, whom he called 'a man of middling calibre and limited range', or
between the bluestocking music teacher Rassudina and his friend and
sometimes mistress Olga Kundasova (to Suvorin, 21 January 1895). But
years later he wrote to Bunin, apropos of his own frail health towards the
end of his life, that peasants and the merchant class degenerate terribly
fast, directing, 'Read my "Three Years".'[28]

The story's wealthy Laptev family patriarch recalls the playwright
Alexander Ostrovsky's *samodur* merchant characters as well as Chekhov's
father; like Chekhov's, the family descends from serfs. The central character, Alexei Laptev, cites this heritage to explain why he and his brother
Fyodor, in spite of their fine education, wealth and freedom, appear

weak and lacking self-assurance. They have been shaped by the brutal patriarchal order of both family and business, endless browbeating and frequent physical violence, as well as ritualized patterns of servility. He tells his bride, after introducing her to his father:

> You're surprised that a big, broad-shouldered father has such undersized, weak-chested children as me and Fyodor. [...] Father married my mother when he was forty-five and she was only seventeen. She went pale and trembled in his presence. [...] Fyodor and I were conceived and born when mother was already exhausted by perpetual fear. I remember my father began teaching me, or to put it simply, beating me, when I was not yet five years old [...] and every morning when I woke up, my first thought was: 'will I be whipped today?' (*Novels*, pp. 369–70)

When his brother, already suffering from mental illness and struggling to intellectualize a measure of dignity for himself, refers to their 'respectable merchant family', Laptev explodes:

> Distinguished family! Landowners thrashed our grandfather, and every last little official hit him in the mug. Grandfather thrashed our father, father thrashed you and me. What has this distinguished family given us? What nerves and blood have we inherited? [...] I'm afraid at every step, as if I'm going to be whipped. [...] I'm afraid of everybody, [...] because I was born of a cowed mother, I've been beaten down and frightened since childhood!... You and I would do well not to have children. (*Novels*, pp. 418–19)

No matter that the two have become wealthy and independent, and their father decrepit and benign.

The central theme of degeneration recurs in peripheral episodes and characters. The lawyer Kostya, who was raised by the Laptev siblings when his alcoholic father died and orphaned him, subjects himself to a rigorous regime of weight training and takes unspecified medications with a worried look. He is disciplining his body in the hope of evading his biological inheritance and defeating the workings of degeneration. The chemist and philologist (a telling combination) Yartsev, Laptev's closest friend, is writing a historical play set in old Muscovy. He experiences the hallucinatory vision of an attack on Russians by the Polovtsy, during which a Russian maiden is tied across the back of a horse and abducted. It is a flashback returning him to events that preceded his birth by centuries, but which nevertheless inhere in the historian's phylogenetic make-up. 'Moscow is a city that has much suffering ahead of her,' he says, as if degeneration can also occur as a historical phenomenon to a traumatized social entity (*Novels*, pp. 407–8).

In spite of calling degeneration theory nonsense and denouncing its most famous popularizer, Max Nordau, as a charlatan,[29] Chekhov persistently employed the theory's concepts and rhetoric in comments about himself and, in *Sakhalin Island*, both individuals and social entities. Degeneration theory pervades 'Three Years', but this does not render the story its affirmation. It was everywhere in the milieu Chekhov represents in that story, too, and what Chekhov is showing us is how his characters make use of the theory to understand themselves and the world around them.

Indeed, by the end of the story Laptev has broken through the pessimistic view of himself entailed in that theory and manned up, stepping into his father's shoes. The overarching plot of the story brings him to an unwilling command of the firm after his father goes blind and his brother descends into fatal illness and insanity. It is not a happy ending. Laptev dreams of simply walking away from it all, but in the end, and at the insistence of his wife, he puts himself in harness and assumes the boss's role. Contrary to what Kostya and he himself had said earlier, he proves fit for struggle.

Aligned with this plot line is the austere and ironic romance between Laptev and Yulia, the daughter of the doctor treating his cancer-afflicted sister, who does not share his feelings but agrees to be his wife. After a few difficult years, which include the loss of a child and Yulia's short-lived retreat to her father's provincial home, she comes to love her husband very much; but by then he has grown detached. At the end of the story, Laptev is observing his good friend Yartsev's obvious infatuation with his wife as they lunch on the terrace of the dacha where she is spending the summer, and he thinks that 'maybe he was to live another thirteen or thirty years... And what were they to live through in that time? What does the future hold for us? [...] Time will tell' (*Novels*, p. 432). Poignant and sad, this open-ended conclusion is nevertheless a relatively happy one for a Chekhov story. Laptev's sister has died of cancer; some neurological disorder is killing his brother; the father is blind and infirm;

and Laptev has lost his former passion for Yulia. But these characters are kind and respectful to one another, and this closing reference to the life yet to be lived together holds at least as much hope as it does anticipation of ill fate.

Chekhov's involvement with the local *zemstvo*'s public health initiatives continued. He participated in meetings and, when at Melikhovo, provided medical services to area peasants, who were always grateful; in contrast, a government official presented with a nasty cut and, after the wound was cleaned, stitched and bandaged, instead of thanking Chekhov departed with a haughty 'Good-bye' (*Letopis'* IV.I, p. 146). There were other good works, too. In early March Chekhov shipped some 160 volumes from his private library – many of them autographed gifts to Chekhov from their authors – to the Taganrog public library, which established a special collection. This led to a brief, revealing flap when the local Taganrog newspaper published an article that cited some of the inscriptions; an infuriated Chekhov viewed it as equivalent to making his private mail public, though – as the article's author pointed out – Chekhov had himself put these inscribed books into a public library (*Letopis'* IV.I, pp. 373–4, 378, 379). The incident speaks to a central contradiction of Chekhov's life: achieving spectacular, hard-won success in a field that defined success by breadth of circulation and self-exposure, he was the most private of public figures. His patronage continued nonetheless. He sent many more books, and he encouraged other prominent former Taganrog natives, like the journalist and former revolutionary Ivan Pavlovsky (living in Paris), to send books and memorabilia of interest.

Chekhov's philanthropy largely focused on health and education. He was a generous trustee of the *zemstvo*'s nearby Talezh school, for which by the end of September he had bought new student desks, contributed more than 100 rubles towards other needs, and planned a new building at considerable personal expense. He supplied local schoolteachers with books, journals and newspapers, and he allowed them to borrow from his personal library. That autumn he also sought funding for the medical journal *Surgical Chronicle* (*Khirurgicheskaia letopis'*), arguing in a letter to Suvorin that the survival of a good surgical journal would be more valuable than performing 20,000 successful operations (21 October 1895).

It was a difficult summer for Chekhov. A visit to Tolstoy at Yasnaya Polyana, where Tolstoy immediately invited his guests to bathe, left him with a debilitating migraine and, to top it off, a toothache that did not abate until a dentist in Serpukhov pulled out the offender. He sent 'Ariadne' and 'Murder' ('Ubiistvo') to Lavrov's *Russian Thought*; 'Ariadne' was to have been published by *The Artist*, and Chekhov had taken an advance, but when *The Artist* collapsed its assets were acquired by *Russian Thought*. As the title suggests, this is one of many Chekhov works invoking the mythological framework of the hero's descent to the underworld, though in a highly ironic, inverted way: the male hero who travels to lower (southern) lands to rescue his beloved knowingly becomes her captive, desperate to be released at the story's end. This frame tale, which culminates with the embedded narrator's rant advocating women's education, may parody Chekhov's student project for a medical dissertation, 'A History of Sexual Dominance'. It is no stretch to see in it, too, Chekhov imagining what might have been had he actually tried to rescue Mizinova.[30] 'Murder' is very different: a bleak tale fusing rote religiosity, venality and violence, it ends with the guilty parties on Sakhalin and is tightly connected with Chekhov's observations there.

In May Chekhov offered to write a play for a new theatre in Petersburg sponsored by Suvorin: the Literary-Artistic Circle (Literaturno-artisticheskii kruzhok). He wanted to observe the troupe in rehearsal and then write 'something strange' (5 May 1895). *The Seagull* was beginning to take shape in his mind, and by autumn he would be working on it intensively; but it would not be staged by Suvorin's theatre.

In June *Sakhalin Island* came out as a book, but to little acclaim. Chekhov generously distributed autographed copies to friends, family, both literary and medical colleagues, and even his attendant in the Grand Moscow hotel, where he often stayed (*Letopis'* IV.1, p. 235). Later that month he was summoned as both physician and close friend to the Turchaninov estate in Tver province to care for Levitan, who had tried to shoot himself. Chekhov had cared for Levitan during a suicidal crisis a decade earlier as well.[31] Now the artist, a kept man with a house to himself in the woods by a lake, had managed to become entangled not only with his patroness but with one of her daughters, and it was all too much. The situation and the setting both fed into the play Chekhov was writing.

In mid-November Chekhov finished a draft of *Seagull* and had two copies of it typed out. He wrote to Suvorin, as though to forestall criticism, 'I began it *forte* and finished it *pianissimo* – against every rule of dramatic art. It's turned out more like a novella. I am more dissatisfied than satisfied, and reading through my newly born play convinces me more than ever that I am not a playwright' (21 November 1895).[32] In mid-December he read the play to a sceptical audience in the large living room of the Moscow hotel room of Yavorskaya. The theatre owner Korsh told Chekhov that 'it's just not theatrical: you have a man shoot himself offstage and don't even let him say a few words before his death!' (*Letopis'* IV.I, pp. 273–4). A very nervous Chekhov visited Nemirovich-Danchenko to hear what he had to say about the typewritten copy he had given him. To Suvorin he wrote that his play 'had failed without being staged', particularly upset that Suvorin and others had seen a portrayal of the Potapenko and Mizinova affair in it (17 December 1895). Nevertheless, in March 1896 he sent two copies of the reworked play to St Petersburg, for consideration by the official committee that sanctioned performances in imperial theatres. The approval process would drag on for an abnormally long time: it was suspended during the new tsar's coronation ceremonies in Moscow, and the censors were troubled by the character Treplev's knowledge and acceptance of his mother's affair (*Letopis'* IV.I, pp. 478–9).

It had been a hard winter, with poor health and much financial stress, some of it caused by the miserable bookkeeping of Suvorin's publishing and bookselling enterprises. With the advent of spring, Chekhov's lungs loosened up and he suffered a bout of blood spitting. Whether grounded in physiology or metaphoric thinking, Chekhov came to associate the spring thaw with death: as the ice melted and rivers began flowing freely, the blood flowed from his lungs. Letters often complained about his health, even if he tended to belittle the significance of coughing up blood, presenting it as an ongoing, chronic condition to which he had become accustomed rather than symptomatic of a worsening mortal illness. Friends who knew him well were growing increasingly concerned, however. For instance, the architect Franz Shekhtel responded to this spring's reports by questioning why Chekhov did not take therapeutic measures: if he himself had such obvious symptoms, he wrote to Chekhov, he would head for sunshine and healing. Can Chekhov really be so imprudent as to remain in the cold, damp north? (*Letopis'* IV.I, p. 391).

In mid-April 1896 *Russian Thought* published the story 'House with a Mezzanine' ('Dom s mezoninom'), initially conceived for a volume benefiting impoverished artists and their families. Chekhov's early remarks about the story are intriguing and, in their autobiographical import, quite unique; they are also something of a red herring. He wrote to Yelena Shavrova, an attractive young author whom Chekhov had met in Yalta in 1889, when she was still an adolescent, and who had become one of his literary protégés: 'I'm writing a little story: "My Fiancée". At one time I had a fiancée... My fiancée was called "Missius". I loved her very much. This is what I'm writing about' (26 November 1895). The story's narrator is an artist who becomes bitterly opposed to the socially active daughter of a landowner near his summer dacha, Lida, who questions the value of his artistic activity; the character 'Missius' is Lida's wispy, innocent young sister, whom Lida sends away at the story's end in order to protect her from the narrator's advances. For all the echoes of real people and places in the story that critics have proposed – Levitan is often adduced as the artist's prototype – none of these associations prove helpful in explaining a story that is one of Chekhov's most poetic and allegorical. It is a story of failed communication, where the erotic spark that characterizes the narrator's first encounter with Lida takes a perverse turn: the artist ends up deploying extreme arguments in which he himself has no confidence, while Lida moves to diametrically opposing positions. As is often the case when Chekhov's characters mix it up in the realm of ideas, readers tend to reduce interpretation to siding with either or the other. Instead, something far more complex and ambiguous is happening in 'House with a Mezzanine': it opens with a fascinating motif of déjà vu and closes with an access of nostalgic longing, and its poetic repetitions (including character doubling) bear more structural weight than the argument opposing the arts and a life of the spirit to nose-to-the-grindstone social activism ('small deeds', as Chekhov himself put it elsewhere). Readers wondering why Chekhov does not present more positively the story's doer of good deeds miss what the story is really doing.

For Chekhov himself, this was a period of continued good deeds, both small and large. As a school trustee he attended student exams and kept at least one from failing, thus sparing also the teacher grief, by intervening when the inspector posed unfair questions (*Letopis'* IV.I, p. 420). As with medicine, his interest in education took a sociological turn: he conceived and gathered materials towards a survey (unrealized) of the day-to-day operations of all sixty *zemstvo* schools in his district (*Letters*, p. 288). He also erected a bell tower for the church, whose bells had been perched on poles, and he organized the building of a new school in the village of Talezh, working on the design, gaining necessary approvals, managing the building project and paying roughly 1,000 rubles (half the total cost). The local peasants were not always appreciative, and some were caught having stolen building materials, but when the new school was consecrated on 4 August, a touched Chekhov was presented with four loaves of bread and a silver salt-shaker (the traditional bread and salt), as well as a holy icon. He soon began working on a school for the village of Novoselki, which was consecrated in July 1897. (A sympathetic *zemstvo* official sent him a limerick about Chekhov building a school where, by order of the Holy Synod, none of his own writings were approved for reading therein; *Letopis'* IV.2, pp. 267–8.)

The tribulations and gratifying completion of the Talezh venture were reflected in the long story 'My Life' ('Moia zhizn''), but Chekhov asked friends who knew what he was doing to tell no one: he did not want to read about himself in *News of the Day* (*Letopis'* IV.1, p. 462). Likewise, Chekhov repeatedly tried to keep secret his philanthropic efforts on the Taganrog library's behalf. In June he sent books for a Russian student reading room in Heidelberg, and he hatched plans to send one hundred schoolchildren and their teachers to Nizhny Novgorod for a national exposition of industry and arts. He also took active part in getting the miserable road from Lopasnia (Melikhovo's closest train access) paved to a point nearby, which meant covering the portion of expenses pledged by local peasants as well as his own (*Letopis'* IV.1, pp. 619, 428, 441, 490).

At the start of September, Chekhov was officially appointed a 'counter' in a section of the Serpukhov district for the first complete census of the Russian Empire. The torturous job would involve more than three weeks of intense effort in January and February 1897 and, in addition to making the rounds himself in miserable cold, overseeing and provisioning fifteen other census workers. Chekhov would receive a medal for these efforts; his real reward, though, was furthering his public health and educational missions, for both of which meaningful statistics were key. Nationwide, some 150,000 counters participated in the massive undertaking (*Letopis'* IV.1, pp. 19, 23, 43–4, 52, 55, 188).

On 17 October *The Seagull* had its premiere. Chekhov's stature and impact on Russian and world drama and theatre are tightly connected with the story of that play's legendary failure at the Alexandrinsky Theatre and, two years later, its spectacular success in the hands of the new Moscow Art Theatre (MAT). The image of a gull would become MAT's official emblem.

The play's early history was painful. By the time the Alexandrinsky in Petersburg had permission to stage the play and a script to work with, only nine days remained for preparation. This was not unusual for the theatre, which typically managed only seven rehearsals before rolling out a new performance, but this time even fewer took place – only a couple.[33] Chekhov anticipated the worst and tried to dissuade his sister and Mizinova from travelling to Petersburg for the premiere; indeed, the actors did not know their lines and performed poorly. Even worse, that evening's audience was packed with fans of an ageing comedic actress who was starring in a three-act comedy that followed Chekhov's play, and for whom this was a benefit performance. Stars typically received the larger part of their earnings from benefits, and on those days the audience came to see *them*. The rowdy crowd hooted, laughed and whistled through *Seagull*, unsettling both actors and author. Even Vera Komissarzhevskaya, who played Nina Zarechnaya and whose rehearsals Chekhov had praised highly in letters, was flustered and flat.[34] After the third act, Chekhov reportedly told the play's director, E. P. Karpov, 'The author has failed' (*S* XII, p. 370). Chekhov returned late to Suvorin's mansion, where he was staying, and left the next day for Melikhovo. Both Chekhov's sister Maria and his brother Mikhail blamed this traumatic humiliation for the collapse of Chekhov's health the following March.[35]

In some respects, Chekhov had invited bewilderment from his audience. Like the aspiring young playwright depicted in *Seagull*, he was doing something new and provocative, and he had boasted about transgressing theatrical conventions. This flaunting of expectations takes place in a work whose overarching themes include success and failure in the literary and theatrical worlds. The play, rife with allusions to the Western literary tradition – in particular to *Oedipus Rex* and *Hamlet*, and to contemporaries Maupassant and Ibsen – takes as central themes the vulnerabilities involved in writing for the stage and the hazards of pushing boundaries. In this regard, it arguably predicted its own initially negative reception. Chekhov's artistic anxieties and ambitions, most intense in connection with the theatre, find their way into the play – often ironically.

So too, in spite of Chekhov's disingenuous claims to the contrary, do the lives in art and love of several of his friends, as mentioned above, appear in the work.[36] The most salient case, already noted, involves Mizinova and Potapenko, and especially Mizinova's failed singing career and trials and tribulations in Paris. By the time Chekhov wrote *Seagull*, Mizinova may have given up on him, but Potapenko was not the only friend of Chekhov with whom she would have a liaison, perhaps wishing to get a rise out of Chekhov. In any case, Mizinova saw herself in the play and was moved; far from being offended, she seems to have been flattered to make it into Chekhov's art. Potapenko, then living in Petersburg, had

Vera Komissarzhevskaya
as Nina in *The Seagull*,
1896.

been entrusted by Chekhov with the task of seeing the play through censorship and so must have been undisturbed by any echoes of his life in it. He was not at the play's premiere, however, perhaps to avoid encountering Mizinova, who did attend; the fact that he did not witness the play's failure meant that Chekhov was comfortable seeing him the following day, and it was Potapenko who saw Chekhov off at the train station when he fled the city.

As broached earlier, the medallion scene in *Seagull* incorporates an episode from Chekhov's relations with a female admirer, Lidiya Avilova. In Act Three, before Arkadina and Trigorin leave the estate, Zarechnaya presents Trigorin with a medallion 'to remember me by', which has Trigorin's initials on one side and, on the other, the title of a Trigorin story and indication of a specific page (121) and lines (eleven and twelve). When Trigorin looks up the reference, he finds the enticing line, 'If ever you should need my life, come and take it' (*Plays*, pp. 32, 37). For the premiere of *Seagull*, Chekhov provided a prop: the inscribed medallion that Avilova had given to him, which made the same encoded proposal. Several weeks before Avilova's come-on was staged in his play's premiere,

Chekhov had promised her a response when he encountered her at a masquerade party. After seeing *Seagull*, Avilova deduced that the page and line numbers on the medallion Zarechnaya gives Trigorin referred, in addition to Trigorin's fictional volume, to a volume of her own stories that she had given Chekhov; the encrypted message to her read: 'It is improper for young girls to attend a masquerade party.'[37] This mockery was dismissed in the romantic fantasy about Chekhov's impossible love for her, a married woman with children, that Avilova detailed in the book she wrote long after his death; instead she read herself into Chekhov's unhappy love story 'About Love' ('O liubvi').[38]

There are also Levitan echoes in the play. In an 1892 letter to Suvorin, Chekhov tells of hunting woodcock during mating season with Levitan, who winged a beautiful male bird but could not bring himself to finish it off; he begged Chekhov to do the job. 'I had to obey Levitan and kill it. And while two idiots went home and sat down to dinner, there was one beautiful, enamored creature less in the world' (8 April 1892, *Letters*, p. 222). The episode likely stands behind the gull that Treplev brings down in Act Two of the play, at which time he promises, 'And soon I'll kill myself the same way' (*Plays*, p. 26). Levitan was prone to such dramatic behaviour: the house by the lake where Chekhov had been summoned to care for him after he shot himself – the tumultuous climax of his romantic involvements with both a patroness and her daughter – was very reminiscent of the setting of *Seagull*. A passionate hunter, Levitan is reported to have brought down a gull and deposited it at Anna Turchaninova's feet.[39]

But most interesting of all are the play's reflections of Chekhov's own writing practice and creative personality. The character Trigorin, roughly Chekhov's age, shares his passion for fishing, and like Chekhov he describes his writing as compulsive. His practice of maintaining notebooks echoes Chekhov's, and what we learn of his poetics comes straight from Chekhov: 'Trigorin has his devices all worked out. It's easy... He takes the neck of a broken bottle glittering on a dam, adds the shadow of a mill wheel, and before you know it – a moonlit night' (*Plays*, p. 53). Chekhov did exactly this in 'Rabies' ('Vodoboiazn' (byl')', 1886), and he explained the technique in a letter to his brother Alexander, as discussed earlier (10 May 1886).

If Trigorin reflects certain qualities of Chekhov as a mature author of prose, the vulnerable Treplev captures something of Chekhov as a playwright, especially in the early years. Treplev's authorial trajectory arcs between the two poles that staked out Chekhov's own field of creative endeavour. At the start of *Seagull* Treplev has written for the stage, and for an audience of intimates that includes authorities of the art world he wishes to enter. The actress performing his dramatic monologue is the young woman and neighbour with whom he is in love, and the setting is the lake bordering the estate of his uncle, where he lives. Treplev's self could not be more at risk in this trial performance. By Act Four, two years later, he has had some success in writing and publishing narrative prose, but this has involved adopting a highly defended position vis-à-vis his audience, sequestering himself in his uncle's home and hiding from his readers. As Trigorin puts it, 'Nobody knows your name, you publish under a pseudonym, you're as mysterious as the Man in the Iron Mask' (*Plays*, p. 50).

Chekhov consistently spoke of writing for the theatre as a risky self-exposure inviting an ugly narcissism or megalomania as well as punishing humiliation. Prose fiction was a safer enterprise: it distanced one from one's audience.[40] Thus, during the period of *Ivanov*'s production, Chekhov wrote to Suvorin that 'the stage is a scaffold upon which dramatists are executed', and he called theatre 'a form of sport. Where you have success and failure, you have sport and gambling.'[41] Chekhov often spoke of 'a particular authorial psychosis that afflicts a person putting on a play', which he suffered during the production of *Ivanov*: 'A person loses himself, ceases to be himself, and his psychological health depends on trifles of a sort that he wouldn't even notice at other times: the facial expression of the director's assistant, the way an actor exiting the stage walks.'[42] Hence his words of advice to I. L. Leontyev (Shcheglov), reported by Potapenko: 'Give up the theatre and its wings. In essence it's an infirmary of vanities. With the exception, perhaps, of a dozen real talents, they're all suffering from *mania grandiosa*.'[43]

By contrast, fiction was a comfortable workspace. 'I was not fated to be a playwright,' he wrote to Suvorin, 'I have no luck. But I don't lose heart, for I don't stop writing stories – and in that domain I feel at home, whereas when I'm writing a play I feel troubled, as though someone were poking me in the neck' (13 December 1895). Writing prose was to occupy the safe position of a peeper, an observer who is not himself seen; recall his letter to his brother Alexander: 'If I'm going to write, then it has to be from afar, from a crack in the wall...' (13 May 1883).

True, Chekhov continued to write for the stage, no matter how many times he swore not to. He had loved the theatre from his adolescent years, and his first ambitious early literary venture had been the lengthy play *Fatherlessness*. Involvement in the theatre world entailed a kind of broader network of social contacts and activities that Chekhov often complained about, but which also offered delights, including affairs with actresses; the famous photographs of Chekhov surrounded by theatre companies during a reading of his play script, or the 1893 photo of Chekhov together with actress Yavorskaya and writer Shchepkina-Kupernik, jokingly known as 'The Temptation of St Anthony', hint at this story. Finally, by the middle of his career, royalties from the performance of his plays – especially the one-act vaudevilles, as he called them – became fundamental to his financial health, a not insignificant incentive.

But Chekhov avoided premieres of his plays after the fiasco of *Seagull*. He remained most vulnerable to emotional upset by both failure and success precisely as a playwright. This became a central theme of *Seagull*, and in this sense Treplev reflects Chekhov no less than does the successful writer Trigorin.

Indeed, while the play is packed with love intrigues – all but one of them unhappy – the play is first and foremost about literature and theatre, about making a life in art, and how that iffy enterprise interfaces with individual personality. It opens with the aspiring author Treplev staging his play, a symbolist drama set 200,000 years in the future. In what we see of the play, the dramatic action features conflict and potential reconciliation between the 'universal soul', played by his beloved Zarechnaya, and 'Satan, the father of eternal matter'. Zarechnaya points out to Treplev that his play has 'no live people,' 'little action', and 'needs a love interest'; but while the content of his play is quite abstract and distant from his self, its staging is all about self-exposure. Premiering the work before intimates is a way of asserting his own artistic stature to his actress mother, and also competing for her affections with the established author Trigorin, her lover. Meanwhile, in casting Zarechnaya as the star of his dramatic monologue he hopes to blend his art and his love in a way that deepens and cements that amorous relationship. As the character Medvedenko puts it, 'Nina Zarechnaya in a play by Konstantin Gavrilovich. They're in love, and today their souls will merge in the desire to create a unified artistic image' (*Plays*, pp. 13, 10, 5).

It all goes terribly wrong, however, with Treplev dropping the curtain on his play midstream after one too many sarcastic remarks from the audience, especially his mother. This foreshadows his two subsequent efforts to drop the curtain on his own life.[44] In a play heavy with allusions to *Oedipus Rex* and *Hamlet*, Treplev is an Oedipal loser at least twice over: Trigorin commands all Treplev's mother's love and respect, it seems, and he also steals Zarechnaya from Treplev. Literary success, ever out of reach for Treplev, never fails to smile on Trigorin.

When the ensemble is again together after a break of two years – rather than 200,000 years – Trigorin has abandoned Zarechnaya. She has had a child by him that died and is still trying to make her way in the provincial theatre world, where Treplev had quietly pursued her.

The Temptation of St Antony: Chekhov with Tatyana Shchepkina-Kupernik (left) and Lidiya Yavorskaya (centre), 1893.

Trigorin congratulates Treplev on his success as an author, but he has not cut the pages of his copy of the journal where Treplev is published, and he remarks on Treplev's inadequacies to the others. Now Zarechnaya enters Treplev's study, unseen by the others, who are playing lotto in the next room. Somewhat demented, she recalls old times, alternately repeating lines from Treplev's play and the phrase 'I am the seagull,' which is the metaphoric role Trigorin had assigned to her in his idea for a short story, inspired by the gull shot by Treplev. She is still clearly obsessed with Trigorin. True, Treplev has succeeded in publishing his fiction; now, however, having encountered the same intimate audience by which he felt rejected as a playwright two years earlier, and suffering further personal rejection by Zarechnaya, he shoots himself offstage once she leaves.

In some respects, the play has come full circle. The confrontation between the world spirit and the devil in Treplev's play-within-the-play is echoed in Treplev's study by Nina, who still remembers the lines. Again, reconciliation is not to be. Interpreters of the play tend to celebrate the persistence of Zarechnaya, whom they see as having matured and embraced the struggle to become an artist:

> Now I know, Kostya, now I understand that what really counts in our work – acting or writing – is neither fame nor glory, the things I dreamed of; what really counts is endurance. Bearing your cross and having faith. I have faith, and I don't suffer so much anymore. And when I think of my calling, I'm not afraid of life. (*Plays*, p. 56)

But Zarechnaya appears utterly unbalanced: her speech is incoherent, and she compulsively repeats, only to contradict, the assertion that she is 'the seagull'. Neighbourhood gossip reports her as having been wandering the area on foot for the past four or five days. Given this and her lack of funds, she likely dissembles in saying that she has horses waiting for her at the gate. Where Treplev is a captive on his uncle's estate – like the Man in the Iron Mask, indeed – she lives as an exile, proscribed from her home across the lake. She is no less an Oedipal victim than Treplev, having lost her father to a stepmother and Trigorin to Treplev's mother. That she is on the road, so to speak, may be due less to grit and endurance as an artist than to the fact that, if she is a gull, she has nowhere to alight. When the play ends she is just as finished as Treplev.

Among the play's self-reflexive features is also its treatment of Symbolism, both as an emerging literary movement in 1890s Russia and as a literary technique or manner. Arkadina's remark, 'There's something decadent about this,' indicates no particular moral evaluation of her son's play, but rather the recognition that it reflects a new artistic movement, which in Russia of the mid-1890s was known as both 'Decadence' and 'Symbolism'.

Is Chekhov merely mocking the Decadents or Symbolists with Treplev's play? Chekhov's overt remarks about Russian Decadents were often negative, though he liked some of them well enough personally. There was much in the Symbolist world view antithetical to his own: the metaphysically inclined Symbolists were system builders and ideologues, and their thinking discounted the real world surrounding them and departed from abstractions. Their millennial or apocalyptic temporal horizon – Treplev's 'dreams of what will be two hundred thousand years from now' – discounted notions of material progress on a human time scale that might make sense to a physician with commitment to public health, a planter of trees, and a traveller to Sakhalin and social critic of what he found there.

And yet there are also deep affinities. Andrei Bely, who was the greatest Symbolist novelist and one of the movement's leading poets, critics and theorists, saw Chekhov as a proto-Symbolist. There are pervasive patterns of symbolism in Chekhov's works, like the archetypal motif of the hero's descent to hell. Thus the red eyes of the Devil that attract the audience's ridicule in *Seagull* appear again as the culminating and penetrating vision of a physician in the medical tale 'A Medical Case' (1898). Chekhov's last known idea for a play involved a character on an expedition to the North Pole who, in the final act, icebound on a huge ship, sees the spectre of his beloved glide across the snow. If the accounts of Chekhov's wife, Olga Knipper, and Konstantin Stanislavsky are to be trusted, then the play that would have followed *Cherry Orchard* looked in many respects more like a play by Treplev than one by Chekhov.

It is also worth considering the way characters in Chekhov's play as a whole produce symbolic – in the broadest sense – utterances and acts. How does the seagull, to focus on the most obvious vehicle, come to mean something other than itself for several key characters? That bird acquires different symbolic meanings for different characters at different moments in the play. These meanings accrue or in some instances are forgotten, which suggests an approach to the symbolic quite unlike that of the Symbolists. Meanings are not elusive because they are transcendental and ineffable, but because they are so tied to an individual's life story, so grounded in contingencies and susceptible to forgetting. Such symbols comprise as much a locus of collapse and scatter of meaning as one of coherence. What the seagull means for Zarechnaya when Treplev throws it to her feet is different from what it means when Trigorin muses on it as the organizing device for a possible short story; and both differ from what it stands for, on the one hand, as a stuffed memento presented to Trigorin by Shamraev, and on the other, in Zarechnaya's repeated references to herself at the end of the play as a seagull, or as *not* a seagull.

This makes of the seagull above all an incitement to recollection, both among characters in the play and for its audience. Trigorin doesn't remember what the seagull was or why Shamraev is presenting it to him; his forgetfulness reflects an immunity to the workings of conscience for the pain he has caused others. It is unclear whether Treplev remembers killing the gull and throwing it at Zarechnaya's feet when he remarks on her references to the gull in the play's last act, but Zarechnaya definitely remembers all too well. For the play's reader or viewer, too, registering this involves remembering past occurrences of gull imagery, be they verbal or visual. This fact of reception dynamics has a way of integrating the play's imagery and action into the experiential memory of the audience, not as a message, not as meaning, but in the same way the call of a certain bird might be recognized. The seagull's function in the play may be less to *mean* than to be *remembered*.

This is a device Chekhov uses also at the level of characterization. Verbal and behavioural tics and petty obsessions often define his characters; we come to know them not because we delve into their psyches but because these repetitions anchor them in our memories. To the extent that such behaviours do reveal undercurrents in characters – or, perhaps more accurately, provoke us to infer or construct psychic peculiarities lurking behind them – then they do so symptomatically or synecdochically, as effect for cause or part for whole.[45]

One thing is certain: *Seagull* treats the struggling young Symbolist author Treplev with a great deal of sympathy. For all the similarities between the character Trigorin and the author Chekhov, one cannot imagine Chekhov offending a young author's self-esteem so carelessly as does Trigorin, who presents Treplev with a copy of a journal containing both their latest works, having cut the pages only of his own. The patron and critic of an ever-increasing number of aspiring young authors, Chekhov remarked that it would be shameful not to read their works carefully and respond as best he could. In the end, Treplev's problem is less his writing than his vulnerable personality, his inability to modulate his sense of self in the face of a severe or indifferent public, and the conflation of familial relationships with those between author and public.

The St Petersburg audience did not grasp *Seagull*. Its director, E. P. Karpov, laid blame at Chekhov's feet: had he arrived in Petersburg before the script's first reading, he might have imparted much guidance to the actors (*Letopis'* VI.I, p. 509). Contrary to what is often written about Chekhov's handling of the play's failure, he did not flee the theatre before the play had ended: he watched the last act from backstage, and when it was over he shook Karpov's hand and only then left (*Letopis'* IV.I, p. 531). After a solitary restaurant supper he wandered the streets, returning to his room at the Suvorin house at two in the morning to tell his host, 'If I live another 700 years, then even then I won't give any theatre a single play. That's it. In this arena there's no success for me' (*Letopis'* IV.I, p. 534). The following afternoon he departed for Melikhovo, seeing nobody other than Potapenko, who accompanied him to the train station.

Chekhov was shaken enough to forget some of his belongings on the train when he exited at Lopasnia, but letters show him regaining balance quickly. He remained doubtful, however, when word started flowing in of truly successful subsequent performances of the play in Petersburg, and then in Kiev and elsewhere (including Taganrog). As the journalist and critic A. V. Amfiteatrov put it, although *Seagull*'s initial failure was painful, Chekhov was hardly buoyed by successes, either, accepting them 'somehow sadly, sceptically. Not without sad secret laughter at himself' (*Letopis'* IV.I, p. 555). Success was almost as unsettling to Chekhov as failure.

The scandalous failure and the press brouhaha that followed actually helped at the Alexandrinsky box office for a while, but the play was pulled from the theatre's repertoire after its fifth performance. Adding insult to injury, the theatre's contract with Chekhov conveyed royalties of less than the going rate, and the theatre delayed paying Chekhov for many months (*Letopis'* IV.2, pp. 74, 90, 99). Chekhov kept the play at a distance: he asked Yelena Shavrova, who was involved with an amateur theatrical group, to renounce a plan to perform the play in Serpukhov, as that was too close to home for Chekhov (*Letopis'* IV.I, p. 589). It took a great deal of persuading before *Russian Thought* gained Chekhov's permission to publish the play, though bootleg copies were already circulating and performances being staged in provincial theatres – including in Taganrog – without the playwright's permission. When the play did come out in

Cover of *Fragments* after the *Seagull* fiasco, 1896.

print, it was without the dedication that Chekhov had promised to Suvorin's wife; as the play was 'connected with one of my most unpleasant recollections [...] its dedication would make no sense' (to Suvorin, 4 January 1897).

If nothing else, the controversy that erupted in print and in literary circles over *Seagull* made clear just who Chekhov's friends were. For years now he had been taken aback by the jealous hostility of many literary friends and colleagues, including some whom he had helped find work as his own profile rose. As he wrote to Suvorin, 'it justified Leikin's writing me a letter of condolence for having so few friends, and enabled *The Week* [*Nedelia*] to query, "What did Chekhov ever do to them?" and *The Theatergoer* [*Teatral*] to print a whole article [...] claiming that my fellow writers had staged a demonstration against me at the theater' (14 December 1896; *Letters*, p. 287). The cover illustration of Leikin's *Fragments* depicted Chekhov flying astride a large seagull, being shot at by all and sundry with guns, bows and arrows, and cannon (no. 43, 26 October 1896; *Letopis'* IV.1, p. 565). As he prepared to publish *Uncle Vanya*, a demoralized Chekhov lamented to Suvorin about having wasted his material on another play; he should have used it for long tales (7 December 1896).

Fame and a reputation for good works brought Chekhov further irritations. Impostors borrowed funds in his name in far-flung corners of the empire, and their creditors pursued him in Melikhovo for repayment (*Letopis'* IV.2, p. 33); strangers as well as local peasants wrote to ask Chekhov for money, and poor students needed support; relatives of unfortunates in penal servitude on Sakhalin sought information and connections; and literary associates requested that Chekhov use his influence with Suvorin to get them jobs. When responding to aspiring young authors who sent manuscripts for his judgement, Chekhov typically began with some positive remark and then turned to criticism, generally making concrete suggestions for revision, at which correspondents sometimes bristled. Chekhov also continued to take a very active part in the civic life of his region, focusing particularly on matters of education and public health; in addition to his school-building, he was heavily involved with the Serpukhov *zemstvo* sanitary council.

Chekhov's most important literary work from spring 1897 reflected his investment in social problems. 'Peasants' ('Muzhiki') touched sore points all around, and Chekhov rightly anticipated trouble with the censor: one page was ordered to be cut, on pain of 'arrest' of the issue of *Russian Thought* in which it was to appear (*Letopis'* IV.2, pp. 77, 124). As was often the case, the excised passages were restored very soon thereafter when Suvorin published the story on its own: censorship demands were lighter on books than on journals, because they were more costly, narrowly distributed and less accessible to the lower classes. But the truly censorious reactions came from critics with a populist orientation. Many who had found Chekhov's lack of engagement with the era's most pressing social issues – an absurdity, if one considers Chekhov's life and work as a whole – now cavilled that, when he did take on the biggest problem of the day, the peasantry, he did so in a kind of vacuum, without showing the historical, social and economic causes of their present state, and without depicting the positive attributes that both leftist and conservative ideologues had been assigning the peasants for the last half-century. Tolstoy called the story 'a sin against the peasants. He doesn't know the folk' (*Letopis'* IV.2, p. 139). Others accused Chekhov of a naturalism that focused on sordid details without making sense of them from 'a defined world view'; Mikhailovsky turned the words of Nikolai Stepanych in 'Boring Story' against Chekhov: because of the absence of 'an overriding idea or the god of a living man', his enormous talent would never develop to its full potential (*Letopis'* IV.2, pp. 175, 249).

'Peasants' begins with the return to his peasant family home of Nikolai Chikildeyev, afflicted by a degenerative neurological illness of some sort and no longer able to work as a waiter in Moscow's Slaviansky Bazaar hotel. 'It was easier to be ill at home, and it was cheaper living there; and not for nothing is it said that there is help in the walls of home.'[46] But he, his gentle, religiously inclined wife Olga, and their young daughter Sasha – all of them literate and urbanized – are appalled by the poverty, apathy and brutality of life in the village. Their relations treat them poorly: Nikolai is viewed as a malingerer and parasite. His drunken brother beats his wife, terrorizing the entire household; the contemptuous wife of a brother serving in the army dallies with workers on the estate across the river; the grandmother verbally and physically abuses the children; the family is not paying its *zemstvo* taxes and has its samovar confiscated. The story covers a year, touching on typical features of a peasant's life, largely as seen by Olga and Sasha. It moves systematically through the portions of the 24-hour day and the calendar year, which is organized by the seasons and the cycle of Church holidays. Towards winter Nikolai dies after being cupped by a local healer, and the story ends in the spring with Olga and Masha on the road as pilgrims returning by foot to Moscow. Olga has changed: 'thinner and plainer, her hair had gone a little gray, and instead of her former attractive appearance and pleasant smile, her face now had the sad, resigned expression left by the sorrows she had experienced, and there was something obtuse and wooden about her gaze, as though she were deaf'.[47] That description links her with the white cat that lost its hearing after a beating, which the Chikildeyevs encounter when first arriving at the family home.

Many details, like the fire that erupts midway through the story, derived from Melikhovo life. Indeed, Chekhov told Suvorin when he decided to sell the estate that, 'from the belle-lettristic point of view' it had been used up by 'Peasants' (26 June 1899). Still, the story's most remarkable features involve not the transcription of reality but its poetic density, Chekhov's construction of a deep symbolic structure under the literal surface. Spatial organization is key to this, with the river separating the hellish village from the heavenly *over there*, where the landowners' manor and the church sit. In the climactic fire episode, the metaphoric association of the village with hell becomes concretized through a proliferation of hellish and apocalyptic motifs.[48]

It was the sharp decline in Chekhov's health that would distance him from Melikhovo. In March 1897 he sat down to dinner with Suvorin at the Slaviansky Bazaar restaurant in Moscow, where he had stopped on his way to St Petersburg, and suffered a severe lung haemorrhage. From this time forward, Chekhov would be more patient than doctor. He spent two nights in Suvorin's room in the hotel and one in his own at the Grand Moscow, after which Dr Obolonsky, the friend and colleague who had been caring for him, took him to the university clinic of his former professor Dr Ostroumov, near the Novodevichy Monastery. Chekhov was particularly concerned that his parents not learn of his dire condition. Visitors were restricted, as Chekhov had to avoid speaking so as to not irritate his throat; even so, the blood flowed for something like ten of his fifteen days there (*Letopis'* IV.2, p. 178). He carried on his voluminous correspondence, though he had to write while lying down. Among the notes wishing him well was a postcard from Leontyev (Shcheglov), uncannily touching a sore point: his get-well ditty implored the gods to help Chekhov 'vanquish all the bacilli' and 'under the roof of a luxurious villa' – that is, somewhere in the south, where sufferers of TB went for their health – write a 'big novel', which is to say, do that which Chekhov

Chekhov recovering in his study at Melikhovo, April 1897.

had not managed to accomplish even when in his best health, and now never would (*Letopis'* IV.2, p. 133).

Among those who dropped by to see him was Lev Tolstoy, who eschewed pleasantries and discoursed on immortality. Chekhov found it fascinating, but he rejected Tolstoy's 'Kantian' understanding, as he later wrote Menshikov, according to which

> all of us (men and animals) will live on in some principle (such as reason or love), the essence of which is a mystery. But I can only imagine such a principle or force as a shapeless, gelatinous mass; my I, my individuality, my consciousness would merge with this mass – and I feel no need for this kind of immortality, I do not understand it, and Lev Nikolayevich was astonished that I don't. (16 April 1897; *Letters*, pp. 301–2)

Tolstoy stayed far longer than was permitted, and that night Chekhov paid with another haemorrhage.

Just how Chekhov could have ignored his illness for so long has been a rich field for psychobiographic speculation. Why had he refused to be examined by other physicians from after his first significant blood spitting in 1884 until this critical moment? Why did he undertake the difficult journey to Sakhalin? Why had he not organized his life with an eye towards resisting TB? When I speculated on an unconscious denial of his illness in a 2004 interview with the psychiatrist and psychoanalyst Dr Robert Coles, I was brought up short:

> Look, he was a doctor and he had an illness that is not silent and secret. I know as a physician what tuberculosis is. I treated some tuberculous patients many years ago in medical school, and you *know* when you have tuberculosis. You cough up blood. You feel chest pain. There is an illness there – we're not talking about something spreading like cancer cells for a long time that aren't even known. This is a tangible, physical, concrete, palpable phenomenon of the body that Chekhov knew; he knew it as a physician, and he also knew it because at that time tuberculosis was a major prevalent illness. Of course he knew it. He knew that he was dying. He knew he was dying as a human being knows.[49]

Downplaying his affliction prior to March 1897 had involved courage and stoicism and perhaps a bit of Russian fatalism, but not an unconscious disavowal of its reality. And at moments worries did show through in Chekhov's letters.

Thus, in February, the actress Liudmila Ozerova – with whom Chekhov may well have had an affair, though he called her 'a little queen in exile', 'uneducated and a bit vulgar' – had written to him that she 'cannot believe that some sort of bacilli have dared to take over your organism' (*Letopis'* IV.2, pp. 66, 68). Chekhov apparently told her that he was infected *before* he was publicly and irrevocably stricken, perhaps by way of extricating himself from intimacy, or perhaps to warn her of the risks it might entail. And just before departing for Moscow on 21 March, he had written to a neighbour who had sent an ill worker for him to examine that he himself was unwell and spitting blood (*Letopis'* IV.2, p. 101). Thus the attack that befell him the following day cannot have been much of a surprise, and those of us who have speculated about Chekhov's psychic blindness to his own state of health have been off the mark.

In any case, Chekhov was now in the hands of other physicians and, as he told Suvorin in a letter of 1 April, his life would have to change. He anticipated ceasing the practice of medicine and curtailing his *zemstvo* activities. He could not join the Novoselki teacher on a spring woodcock hunt: 'Everything interesting has been forbidden' (*Letopis'* IV.2, p. 121). But Chekhov did not let up on his school-building project, and in May he again helped with *zemstvo* school exams, which exhausted him. He also took an active part in designing the school and finding building materials, as well as acquiring all the necessary permits and organizing philanthropic support; 'In this district I'm now something in the nature of an architect,' he wrote to Leikin (26 May 1897). He himself paid for fuel to keep the buildings heated and clean, for bookshelves and student desks, and he arranged for all sorts of gifts for the children and their teachers and prizes for outstanding pupils (*Letopis'* IV.2, pp. 196, 197). He contributed roughly 1,500 rubles towards getting the Novoselki school up and running at a time when he was quite squeezed financially, drawing advances from his publishers, who served as a kind of local bank with a revolving line of credit.

The health of Chekhov's close friend Levitan was declining now as well. In an era without patient privacy, and when a patient was the least likely individual to be fully informed of a negative prognosis, Chekhov mentioned in a letter from his own hospital bed to the artist Braz, who was to paint his portrait for Tretyakov, that Levitan had 'a passionate thirst for life, a passionate thirst to work, but his physical condition is worse than an invalid's' (4 April 1897). The two old friends were very solicitous of one another, with Levitan urging Chekhov to move to a healthier clime. When Braz came to Melikhovo for two weeks in July, the painting did not go well: 'Why do you depict me as gloomy, sour; I'm a cheerful person. After all, I'm Chekhonte' (*Letopis'* IV.2, p. 260).

At summer's end, Chekhov began the doctor-ordered migrations that would define his remaining years. He left Melikhovo for Biarritz, where he had agreed to meet Vasily Sobolevsky, publisher of the newspaper *Russian News* (*Russkie vedemosti*). After a day in Moscow and four in Paris he arrived in the coastal resort. He had asked Sobolevsky for detailed travel instructions because he was unfamiliar with the route and linguistically challenged: 'You see, I can speak all languages other than foreign ones' (18 August 1897). He found the setting delightful, though, and while there were other Russian acquaintances on holiday there, he particularly enjoyed becoming closer to Sobolevsky. After three weeks the weather turned poor and Chekhov moved to Nice, where he stayed in the Pension Russe, to which he would return a few years later.

Chekhov with one of his dachshunds (Quinine), May 1897.

Money worries were chasing Chekhov, who thought he might have to return to Melikhovo if he did not buckle down to work. At one point he asked Suvorin for advice in obtaining some sort of governmental subsidy of 3,000 to 4,000 rubles a year (25 October 1897). Nevertheless, he bristled when friends such as Levitan undertook to arrange large 'loans' from wealthy admirers of Chekhov; Levitan, accustomed to such favours from patrons, was shocked when Chekhov returned funds that Levitan had solicited from one of them, Sergei T. Morozov.

By mid-October Chekhov was writing again: to the Nice autumn and winter belong 'In the Cart' ('Na podvode'), 'At Home' ('Doma'), 'Pecheneg' ('Pecheneg') and 'At Acquaintances' ('U znakomykh'), all set in the Russian countryside with the common theme of landowners in decline. 'In the Cart' features a provincial schoolmistress who has been trapped in a miserable, lonely and loveless existence by the collapse of her own family. She glimpses the potential of a new life when, on a provisioning trip, she encounters a bachelor landowner who is himself very much on the skids; that soap bubble bursts as soon as it takes shape in her mind, however, and notwithstanding her personal unhappiness, she remains a responsible, committed teacher. 'At Acquaintances' is told from the point of view of a Moscow lawyer who has been summoned to the estate of old friends whom he had served as a tutor in his student days. They are on the verge of bankruptcy and view him as their only remaining saviour, but he has no legal tricks up his sleeve and he is past marrying the family member with whom he had once been in love. Key motifs of this story will reappear in *Cherry Orchard*.

The French Riviera largely agreed with Chekhov. Like Dr Dorn of *Seagull*, he loved to observe street life. He looked forward to Mardi Gras and an upcoming musical competition featuring the stars Patti and Sarah Bernhardt; he told Suvorin that 'every dog here smells of civilization' and that, so long as he was living, he would regularly leave Russia once October arrived (10 November 1897). Although his letters complained of laziness and blamed the strange desk for his inability to work, he did buckle down. A new friend, the progressive sociologist and exile Maksim Kovalevsky, observed that after some days holed up to write, Chekhov always looked wan and pale when he reappeared for meals at the Pension Russe (*Letopis'* IV.2, p. 360).

Kovalevsky and Chekhov made plans to travel to Algiers after the new year, not for his health, Chekhov averred, but for the voyage; in the end, Kovalevsky wrote to Chekhov from Paris, begging off due to his own illness, which disappointed Chekhov greatly. He spoke of heading for Corsica, but that too came to naught. Chekhov may not have been in shape for such voyages. In the autumn he had a three-week bout of blood spitting, which recurred in mid-December, and with the new year suffered tooth problems that included a failed extraction and extremely painful abscess. Although he described his health reassuringly to his family, and Russian newspapers proclaimed his recovery, he moved to a lower room in the pension because of his cough and blood spitting. On his visits to Monte Carlo he tended not to gamble, because, though he liked observing the action and the people, gambling meant standing at the tables for protracted periods, which 'physically exhausted' him (*Letopis'* IV.2, p. 596). In keeping with Chekhov's legendary self-control, when he did go to the casino – usually to accompany visiting friends – he played very little. Small wins did not seduce him into larger stakes, and he was more interested in watching than playing. His friends bet enthusiastically, though: the visiting Potapenko was sure that he could come up with a winning system, but of course lost, and the actor and dramatist Alexander Sumbatov (Yuzhin), whose business plan for building a theatre involved winning a few hundred thousand francs, instead left 7,000 on the gaming table, losses that he implored Chekhov to keep secret (*Letopis'* IV.2, pp. 567, 570).

Among the old acquaintances with whom Chekhov associated in Nice was Vasily Nemirovich-Danchenko, novelist brother of the soon-to-be-cofounder of the MAT. The two discussed the painter Valery Yakobi, who was also in Nice and, like many Russians lodged elsewhere, frequented the inexpensive but tasty table at the Pension Russe, where conversation was in Russian. Chekhov told Nemirovich-Danchenko that Yakobi would die soon, and one could see the horror in his eyes. 'We're all sentenced,' he said. 'I mean myself... Sometimes it seems to me that all people are blind. They see at a distance, and to the sides, but right there beside them, elbow to elbow, is death, and, purposely, nobody notices or wants to notice' (*Letopis'* IV.2, p. 339). Chekhov griped but obeyed doctor's orders, which in particular forbade being outside at dusk and consuming alcohol. Most close family and friends warned Chekhov to stay away from the miserable Russian weather, though not all understood the stakes: his mother urged him to return to Melikhovo for a few months, and his father suggested he come for Christmas and then return to Nice (*Letopis'* IV.2, pp. 426, 457). Back home a horse died, as did the two huskies that Chekhov had recently got from Leikin, murdered in turn by neighbourhood boys who fed them needles and glass shards wrapped in bread; his

Osip Braz, *Anton Chekhov*, 1898, oil on canvas.

writer's retreat was remodelled; his brother Mikhail had his first child in Yaroslavl (and, making Chekhov her godfather, requested the godfather's traditional payment for christening expenses); his mother's dental plate broke; the cook Masha was delivered of an out-of-wedlock baby (and handed her over to a foundling home, though Chekhov emphasized that it was welcome to live at Melikhovo); the postmaster was reading Chekhov's letters and, 'very naively', reporting their contents to Masha (*Letopis'* IV.2, p. 501); and so on. Chekhov was kept informed, and every Russian acquaintance returning home was asked to carry a few gifts back – Chekhov constantly sent small gifts to his family, friends, servants and other acquaintances. All this was noted in the diary kept by Chekhov's father, who seems to have been chagrined when, on 21 November, he received 'a wallet without money' (*Letopis'* IV.2, p. 410).

The painter Braz visited Nice, funded by Tretyakov to make a second try at Chekhov's portrait. The result hangs in the gallery and is very frequently reproduced; Braz probably destroyed the earlier Melikhovo variant, which has disappeared. Once again, Chekhov was less than pleased with the results, finding the portrait 'not interesting. There's something in it that's not mine, and something not there that is mine' (to Maria Chekhova, 28 March 1898).[50]

In Nice, Chekhov still doctored ill compatriots. Thinking about his return to Melikhovo in early January, he asked his sister to see to it that a new flag was purchased for his writer's outbuilding, reminding her a few months later and asking that she move the cabinet with medications to its entrance vestibule, where he saw patients (6 January, 10 and 14 March 1898). He clearly looked forward to resuming medical treatment of the local peasants, though his doctors had advised he quit. He also answered all manner of requests for assistance from writers seeking venues for their works, translators asking permission to render his stories, and both acquaintances and strangers angling for positions or needing financial support for their education: a Taganrog cousin was on a monthly stipend from Chekhov while he studied, and so was a poor but talented young man from Serpukhov training in veterinary medicine. Chekhov worked from afar on his third school-building venture, this time at the village of Melikhovo. He was in good contact with Mayor Yordanov of Taganrog and purchased and posted over three hundred volumes of French classics to his hometown library (though he would despair of how the incompetent librarian catalogued and bound them). While still in France he also took charge of acquiring for the city a statue of Peter the Great, who had founded Taganrog, from the sculptor Mark Antokolsky, then living in Paris (*Letopis'* IV.2, pp. 663, 631, 684).

Chekhov's nostalgic attachment to the city of his birth included sober appreciation of its deficiencies. Friends and acquaintances travelling there were referred to his relatives and promised culinary delights. Chekhov would himself consider settling there, he wrote to Yordanov, if only the city had a proper water and sewerage system: 'I love the Donets steppe [...] and it's sad that there are no writers in Taganrog and that nobody seems to need this very fine, valuable material' (25 June 1898). He facilitated contact between city fathers and other Taganrog natives who had made good and lived elsewhere. Whereas his first Moscow years had been characterized by separation from and deprecation of his roots, his attitude later in life was quite different. For all Chekhov's vaunted faith in progress and orientation towards the future, the past also had its pull.

While in France, Chekhov closely followed the Dreyfus affair. Although his spoken French remained poor, he had been working on it and read newspapers voraciously. He quickly came to the conclusion that the Jewish officer was not guilty, and he wrote admiringly of Zola, whose famous open letter in defense of Dreyfus, 'J'accuse', appeared in *Aurore* in January 1898. Chekhov broadcast his views in letters back to Russia, where, for instance, his brother Mikhail found it difficult to get an objective grasp on the matter and had asked for guidance. He did not shy from polemics with Suvorin, whose reactionary newspaper had published a translation of Zola's latest novel without paying a dime to the author – there was no copyright agreement between Russia and France at the time – while vilifying Zola, Dreyfus, French Jewry and the international Jewish cabal. Suvorin's own column, 'A Little Letter' ('Malen'koe pis'mo'), left no daylight between himself and his rabid journalistic staff. Chekhov could no longer excuse his friend, and his letters became bitingly sarcastic: 'Zola is a noble soul, and I (I belong to the syndicate and have already received a hundred francs from the Jews) am delighted by his outburst' (4 January 1898; *Letters*, p. 311). A month later he continued,

> Let us assume that Dreyfus is guilty – even so Zola is right, because the writer's job is not to accuse or persecute, but to stand up even for the guilty once they have been condemned and are undergoing punishment. [...] [M]ajor writers and artists should engage in

politics only enough to protect themselves from it. There are enough accusers, prosecutors and secret police without them.

He offered a penetrating social-psychological analysis of scapegoating:

> When something is wrong within us, we seek the cause from without and before long we find it [...] Once the French began talking about the Yids and the syndicate, it meant they had begun to feel something was wrong, that a worm had begun to grow within, that they needed the phantoms to ease their stirred up consciences. (6 February 1898; *Letters*, pp. 317, 318)

To Mikhail he wrote,

> Just as a respectable woman who was one single time unfaithful to her husband will then permit herself a series of flagrant indiscretions, fall victim to insolent blackmail and finally commit suicide, all in order to hide her first misdeed, so is the French government forging blindly ahead, stumbling left and right to avoid admitting its mistake. (22 February 1898; *Letters*, p. 314)

Suvorin accepted Chekhov's arguments, but this did not alter the newspaper's approach, which Chekhov blamed on Suvorin's 'extreme lack of character' (*Letopis'* IV.2, p. 535). The Dreyfus episode is commonly understood as causing a final break in their friendship. Chekhov wrote to Alexander that he was fed up with exchanging letters about it with Suvorin; *New Times* had behaved 'villainously'; 'attacking Zola while he was on trial was unliterary'; and he and Suvorin had fallen into silence (*Letopis'* IV.2, p. 557). A decisive rupture would have pleased many of Chekhov's friends and associates. They could not understand how Chekhov could remain close to Suvorin or have his works appear in his reactionary and antisemitic newspaper, even if they acknowledged, as Korolenko asserted, that Chekhov himself adhered to the highest ethical standards and had never written a word of which he needed to be embarrassed.

Chekhov's political sentiments clearly leaned left, but they were also largely private. He addressed suffering, injustice and governmental brutishness with a clinical eye for what he might actually do to help rather than an ideological perspective that told him what he should write and say. He did his part to create change through private philanthropy and unrecompensed medical practice, but he avoided public statements, propagandistic art and membership in any party. In spite of their differences, Suvorin highly valued Chekhov's 'personal liberalism, which allows him to speak the truth as he sees and understands it, and not as doctrine teaches', as he wrote in his diary (*Letopis'* IV.1, p. 40). Distance was increasing between the two, but there was no final break: they met in Paris in the spring of 1898, when Chekhov was on his way back to Russia; they arranged a meeting in Moscow at the end of the summer, when he was en route from Melikhovo to Yalta for the next season of sanitary exile; and their correspondence continued.[51]

Chekhov had hoped to travel to Algeria in January and then return to Russia so as to be at home for Easter, a holiday whose spring setting, communal street activity and liturgical music (especially the bells) he greatly enjoyed. Family and friends urged him to wait until foul weather lifted, however, and it was the beginning of May before he travelled to Paris with Kovalevsky. After a brief stay he left for home, via Petersburg and Moscow. On the way, sweets offered by Kovalevsky activated the chronic digestive distress that would plague his final years.

In March 1898, responding to a letter from the theatre-obsessed Suvorin, Chekhov had claimed to be 'moving away' from it. He no longer liked actors, and while 'formerly there was no greater enjoyment for me' than sitting in a theatre, now it provokes the feeling that 'in the gallery they're yelling, "Fire"' (13 March 1898). Soon all that would change. While Chekhov was in Paris and about to depart for Russia, Vladimir Nemirovich-Danchenko sent him a letter describing his new '*artistic*' theatrical venture with Konstantin Stanislavsky and asking for permission to stage *Seagull*. Nemirovich-Danchenko had read the play's first draft at the end of 1895, knew it well and had persuaded Stanislavsky that it was right for the MAT. He promised to stage it 'with *fresh* talents freed from routine' and to accomplish a 'triumph of art' (*Letopis'* IV.2, p. 614; emphasis Nemirovich-Danchenko's).

Chekhov declined, but the persistent Nemirovich-Danchenko would not take no for an answer. He proceeded with his plans, promising to visit Chekhov to talk it over before rehearsals. Now back in Melikhovo, Chekhov urged him to visit, conceding, 'I so want to get together with you, you can't imagine, and for the pleasure of getting together with you I'm ready to give you all my plays' (16 May 1898).

Nemirovich-Danchenko's lobbying had succeeded, and though Chekhov continued to discuss play ideas with other theatre directors and make promises, in the end all the dramatic masterpieces by Chekhov yet to see the stage – *Uncle Vanya*, *Three Sisters* and *Cherry Orchard* – would premiere with the MAT. Chekhov would also marry the theatre's leading female actor, Olga Knipper. The last half-decade of Chekhov's life and his future renown as a dramatist were thus shaped by his involvement with the MAT.

Many features of Chekhov's mature drama suited innovations introduced by the MAT. That theatre famously eliminated the star system and developed an ensemble principle that shifted focus from central roles and leading actors to the relationships and interaction between characters. This was just right for Chekhov's later plays, which were not built around one or two chief characters and in which there might well be multiple dialogues going on at the same time. True, the title of *Uncle Vanya* suggests a singular character focus, but this proves a red herring, while the ensemble principle is arguably manifest in the titles of *Three Sisters* and *Cherry Orchard*.

The MAT rejected the practice of star actors making flamboyant, self-serving entries and exits or otherwise breaking the continuity of the performance by playing to the audience or taking bows; each individual was subordinated to the whole. Most famously, in the staging of *Seagull*, the viewers of Treplev's play-within-the-play were seated with their backs to the audience, whereas previously in the theatrical tradition a major actor always avoided turning his or her back to the audience. The entire performance was now defined by the authority, control and artistic vision of the director, who also invested much time and effort in coming to an understanding of the play prior to a long period of deliberate rehearsal.

Although it was painful for Chekhov to lose control of his plays, and he was often very unhappy with Stanislavsky's interpretations of his work, the role of the director in shaping the artistic object of the performance was rather analogous to Chekhov's own authorial role. In spite of the way his texts appear to represent the accidental and the prosaic everyday – this is Chekhov as a 'slice of life' writer – in a deeper sense he was very much in control of his material and always had the shape of the whole in mind. There is a lyrical and expressive dimension to his work, where what appears on the surface as accidental, superfluous, prosaic and therefore realistic, is often recuperated into subterranean systems of meaning.[52] The way Chekhov's creative personality stands behind, and is invested in and in control of, his work is echoed in the new position MAT principles created for a play's director.

On a smaller scale, the MAT also developed specific techniques that were just right for a Chekhov play. Chekhov spoke about a drama that would convey crisis through the everyday, behind the chit-chat of a dinner table.

> But really, in life people are not every minute shooting each other, hanging themselves, and making declarations of love. And they are not saying clever things every minute. For the most part, they eat, drink, hang about, and talk nonsense; and this must be seen on the stage. A play must be written in which people can come, go, dine, talk about the weather, and play cards, not because that's the way the author wants it, but because that's the way it happens in real life.
>
> Let everything on the stage be just as complex and at the same time just as simple as in life. People dine, merely dine, but at that moment their happiness is being made or their life is being smashed.[53]

This vision called for new acting and staging techniques, which were being pioneered by MAT. Rather than declaiming their lines, MAT actors were trained to sound like they were speaking in normal, conversational tones. Innovations in lighting and demanding respectful attention from the audience, which was not allowed entry and exit except between acts, made a performance's subtleties visible and audible. The MAT's adoption of the 'fourth wall' principle corresponded to Chekhov's portrayal, as both short story writer and dramatist, of unseen private life. Actors behaved and spoke as though unaware of the gazes directed at them from beyond the footlights, putting the audience into the position of voyeur.

To be sure, Chekhov found working with the MAT quite aggravating at times. He objected to the slow pace at which his plays were staged and was irritated by Stanislavsky's excessive and naturalistic sound effects. He responded instructively to one actor's naive explanation of the croaking frogs and howling dogs:

> 'It's realistic,' said the actor. 'Realistic,' A. P. repeated with a laugh. And then after a brief pause, he remarked: 'The stage is art. In one of [I. N.] Kramskoy's genre paintings he has some magnificently

drawn faces. What if we cut the painted nose from one of these faces and substituted a live one? The new nose would be "real," but the painting would be ruined.'[54]

To avoid these sound effects, he joked that he would write a play that began, 'How wonderful, how quiet! One can hear no birds, no dogs, no cuckoos, no owls, no nightingales, no clocks or bells, not so much as a cricket.'[55]

But Chekhov would never have entirely eschewed such sounds, sights and scents. Although his plays became increasingly symbolic and indirect in their meaning, they remained anchored in reality. As Laurence Senelick put it, 'Chekhov always overlays any symbolic inference with a patina of irreproachable reality.'[56] Moreover, as a play about the art, *Seagull* addresses the question of symbolism as a central theme, not least through the functioning of the seagull motif.

After returning to Melikhovo in early May 1898, Chekhov resumed the previous year's activities. In addition to doctoring peasants (and occasionally their animals), he helped organize and pay for livestock insurance, a huge boon to folks whose sustenance might depend on one horse and a few cows. Local peasant children were treated to berries and apples from his orchard; perhaps Chekhov remembered 'Because of Little Apples' ('Za iablochki', 1880), the most interesting of his first published stories, about a sadistic landowner who quite creatively punishes a young peasant couple he catches having stolen an apple in his anti-Edenic orchard.

Back at his own desk, in a very short period Chekhov managed to write three interconnected stories that have come to be known as the Little Trilogy: 'Man in a Case' ('Chelovek v futliare'), 'Gooseberries' ('Kryzhovnik') and 'About Love'. They came out in two issues of *Russian Thought*, with the second and third numbered to indicate their order in a series. A year later Chekhov told his publisher, Adolf Marks, that the three stories belonged to a cycle that was not yet finished, so their publication in his collected works would have to wait. He clearly envisioned growing the series – an unrealized intention – and he wanted all its parts published together. Unfortunately these three stories, among Chekhov's best known, are often anthologized separately.

Relevant entries in Chekhov's notebooks go back to 1895 and may well be connected with his attempt at a novel in the late 1880s, 'Stories from the Lives of My Friends'. The Trilogy certainly fits his description of that abandoned project, though the evidence is only circumstantial: back when Chekhov did set himself to writing a novel, as the literary world had been urging him to do, it was conceived as an interconnected cycle of stories; now, ten years later, Chekhov produced such a cycle, and he meant to make it longer.

The Trilogy is a frame tale depicting a trio of characters who in turn recount a number of tales. Both structure and setting recall Ivan Turgenev's mid-century cycle of stories *Notes of a Hunter* (*Zapiski okhotnika*); but whereas more than two-thirds of Turgenev's story-length works are frame tales, they are relatively rare in Chekhov.[57] The Little Trilogy features three chief characters: the veterinarian Chimsha-Himalaysky and the high-school teacher Burkin, out hunting; and the landowner Alyokhin, at whose estate they stop and with whom they continue an exchange of stories. The titles of the three stories refer to their lengthiest embedded narratives, but along the way a number of other anecdotes and micro-narratives are also told. Frame tales always represent a communication situation, and this makes telling, listening to, and making sense of stories a major theme; indeed, 'storytelling is the principal action' of the Trilogy.[58]

If the frame tale structure typically creates distance between the author and the narrator of the embedded tale, this cycle's most notable progressive narrative trajectory involves decreasing distance between story-teller and subject: Burkin tells a story about a colleague and neighbour who takes grotesque, caricaturish shape in his narrative (Belikov, the man in the case); Chimsha-Himalaysky tells a story about his brother, that is to say, about somebody very close to him but from whom he is eager to distinguish himself; and Alyokhin tells a story about himself. The story-teller's stance towards the other human beings about whom he is speaking thus becomes a meaningful structural component of the cycle.[59]

Each of the three main embedded stories, as well as the various anec-dotes peppering the cycle, represent affective dead-ends, unhappy traps for desire. The first two storytellers get started on the theme while chat-ting at night in a hut during their hunt. They begin with the story of a village headman's wife who, for ten years, has been afraid to leave her home except at night, and spends her days 'behind the stove' (*Stories*, p. 299). This takes them to Burkin's late colleague Belikov, a teacher of Greek who, as the man in the case, became Chekhov's most iconic character, a figure embedded in cultural consciousness to this day.

He was remarkable for always going out, even in the finest weather, in galoshes and with an umbrella, and unfailingly wearing a warm, padded coat. His umbrella had a cover, and his watch a cover of gray suede, and when he took out his penknife to sharpen a pencil, the penknife, too, had a little cover; and his face also seemed to have a cover over it, because he always hid it behind his turned-up collar. He wore dark glasses, a quilted jacket, stopped his ears with cotton, and whenever he took a cab, ordered the top put up. In short, the man showed a constant and insuperable impulse to envelop himself, to create a case for himself, so to speak, that would isolate him, protect him from outside influences. Reality irritated him, frightened him, kept him in constant anxiety, and, maybe in order to justify his timidity, his aversion to the present, he always praised the past and what had never been; the ancient languages he taught were for him essentially the same galoshes and umbrella, in which he hid from real life. (*Stories*, p. 300)

Belikov's obsessive worries about rules have turned him into an enforcer of petty norms and informer, which spreads his inhibitions among others. But when a new colleague in history arrives with his sister, the town busybodies conspire to make a match, and Belikov falls for the lively Ukrainian woman. This access of a desire, incompatible with his highly defended personality structure, provokes a crisis that eventually kills him. 'Now, lying in the coffin, his expression was meek, pleasant, even cheerful, as if he were glad that he had finally been put in a case he would never have to leave. Yes, he had attained his ideal!' (*Stories*, p. 309).

The image of the box or case concretizes the idea of the trap for desire, which is pursued further in the other two stories. In 'Gooseberries', the squalid estate that Chimsha-Himalaysky manages to purchase as the realization of his dream of regaining the lost estate of his childhood becomes another such trap. In 'About Love', paternal debt has trapped Alyokhin on his estate, 'like a squirrel in a wheel' (*S* x, p. 74), and a questionable morality has inhibited him from acting on his reciprocated love for the young wife of an older, wealthier, fatherly friend. Along the way there are anecdotes about a merchant and a cattle dealer who, at death's door, think only of money, and about Alyokhin's beautiful house servant Pelagaya, who unfathomably remains in an abusive relationship with Alyokhin's brutish cook. These anecdotes echo the story's main theme.

Chekhov's three case studies are remarkably reminiscent of the traps for desire that Freud was then conceiving as developmental stages from which remaining fixations may lie at the core of psychopathology. Freud would likely invoke castration complex and obsessional neurosis to describe the man in the case's excessive fear of spontaneity and self-exposure, his over-investment in the law, for which he presumes to speak, and his anxiety before it, which indeed lend themselves to grotesque and comic overtones.[60] The brother of Chimsha-Himalaysky has single-mindedly acquired the wealth necessary to buy an estate with gooseberry bushes; there his fantasy of reconstituting the lost family home and childhood memories of old-style landowner life achieves fulfilment in the tasting of his own fruits, however sour: an example of pathological narcissism. Alyokhin's trap is clearly Oedipal, with fear of transgression and paternal fealty cast in a mature, quietly tragic mode; his friend's wife Anna becomes linked with his own mother when her face reminds him of one seen 'in my childhood, in the album which lay on my mother's chest of drawers'.[61] Alyokhin both obeys the law and punishes himself for transgressive desires. Unlike Belikov and the lover of gooseberries he is not the least bit comic. This reflects the lack of distance between story-teller and the subject of his story (himself), and also Alyokhin's utter lack of pretention: he merely acquiesces to the law and suffers; indeed, his closing words cast himself as guilty of having broken an even higher one: 'I understood that when you love you must either, in your reasonings about that love, start from what is highest, from what is more important than happiness or unhappiness, sin or virtue in their accepted meaning'.[62] Even a declaration of erotic freedom can be twisted into a kind of moral masochism. There is no evidence that Chekhov ever knew of Freud, whose *Interpretation of Dreams* had not yet come out, but he seems to have been thinking along similar lines.

During this period Chekhov began collecting his early works, many of which he had forgotten. His productivity had declined sharply, and money worries troubled him: he was leading 'a bookkeeper's life', he wrote to Braz (2 July 1898). Now he was thinking of selling the rights to a comprehensive collection of his writings. Almost three years earlier he had asked A. A. Tikhonov for details regarding Adolf Marks's purchase of the rights to the poet Afanasy Fet's writings (29 March 1896), and now there were rumours that Marks 'wants to buy me', as he later put it in a letter to Gorbunov-Posadov (17 January 1899). He had 'grown tired of turning out collections every year and constantly giving them new titles', and it would be better for him to order and edit his collected works than leave it to heirs, he told Suvorin, in effect offering him the rights (24 August 1898; *Letters*, pp. 326–7). Suvorin's press was poorly organized, however, with little rhyme or reason applied to managing inventories in its bookselling operations, and its production quality was unreliable. There had been many accounting snafus with them over the years. In the end Chekhov would sign with Marks.

Late that summer Chekhov was invited to Yasnaya Polyana to celebrate Tolstoy's seventieth birthday, but declined: he could not be out at night in the cold, damp autumn weather. He also knew that Tolstoy dreaded the celebration; further, he could not stand the Tolstoyan Pyotr A. Sergeyenko, a schoolmate from Taganrog and 'the most tiresome man on earth [...] a hearse stood up on end' (24 August 1898; *Letters*, p. 327). For some reason, however, Chekhov would soon entrust this same Sergeyenko with a critical role in determining his financial future and his literary heritage: he would handle negotiations with Marks for the sale of the rights to all of Chekhov's narrative prose, past and future, and the publication of a full collection of his works. That 'hearse' would bear Chekhov's corpus! Perhaps it is an indication of how distasteful business dealings were to Chekhov that he put this most important one into the hands of an individual he disliked. Chekhov brokered all manner of deals and solicited contributions far and wide when it came to his philanthropic ventures, but advocating for himself was another story.

Chekhov had hoped to visit Mount Athos in Greece the next winter, finances permitting, and in spring, Paris, a city that made him feel 'as if he had broken out of prison' (*Letopis'* IV.2, pp. 682, 784); instead he arranged winter lodging in Yalta. On the way there in September he stopped in Moscow, where the weather had already turned nasty. He coordinated his stay with Suvorin, and he attended a rehearsal of *Seagull* at the Hunters Club. His life was about to undergo a series of decisive changes: the MAT would become all-important to him and he would fall in love with and eventually marry that theatre's leading lady; his father would die unexpectedly and Melikhovo would be abandoned as the central locus of the Chekhov clan; and his health would continue to decline.

Scene from Chekhov's *Seagull* staged by the Moscow Art Theatre,
1898, with Olga Knipper as Arkadina and Konstantin Stanislavsky
as Trigorin.

4

Yalta and the Moscow Art Theatre Years, Death in Badenweiler

C hekhov's life, already 'knocked off track' (*vybit iz kolei*), as he had been complaining about his health-determined travel, veered further in the last months of 1898 and by the end of 1899 was ordered entirely differently. Judging by photographs, as he approached his fortieth birthday he had begun to look like an old man.

Nemirovich-Danchenko first introduced Chekhov to Olga Knipper, his top female student, in a letter of early September 1898 that included casting plans for *Seagull*. He identified her as a 'very elegant, talented, and educated young woman, however, about twenty-eight years old', significantly younger than the character she was to play, Arkadina (*Letopis'* IV.2, p. 754). While in Moscow en route to Yalta, Chekhov saw her for himself. In addition to *Seagull*'s, Chekhov attended a rehearsal of A. K. Tolstoy's *Tsar Fyodor Ioannovich*, which would be the first play MAT staged. Afterwards Chekhov wrote to Suvorin that Knipper in her role as Irina in Tolstoy's play was 'best of them all', 'so fine that it even tickled the throat. [...] If I had stayed in Moscow, then I would have fallen in love with this Irina' (8 October 1898). Suvorin had travelled to Moscow to see the new theatre as well as Chekhov. The MAT cohort was flattered by his attention, and Nemirovich-Danchenko made a pitch for funding.

Chekhov also visited the Tretyakov Gallery to view the Braz portrait, accompanied by Shchepkina-Kupernik, Suvorin, the writer Nikolai Ezhov, and the artist Alexandra Khotiaintseva. Chekhov had grown quite friendly with Khotiaintseva, with whom he visited in both Nice and Paris, and over the years of their acquaintanceship she in turn produced a whole series of sketches, watercolours and silhouette caricatures of Chekhov – including a depiction of Chekhov viewing himself at the gallery – and later a memoir. Chekhov found Braz's framed portrait 'completely uninteresting', as he wrote to Sobolevsky (21 October 1898). With Khotiaintseva and Suvorin he also went to the circus, which Chekhov did enjoy (*Letopis'* IV.2, p. 763).

From the south he continued his philanthropic and civic engagement, allocating incoming theatrical honoraria to the Melikhovo school project and agreeing to his election to the board of trustees of the Yalta girls' gymnasium. Later in the autumn he would play a significant role in gathering contributions for children suffering from famine in the Samara region, publishing anonymously an article, 'Starving Children' ('Golodaiushchie deti'). Although Chekhov complained of isolation in Yalta, he found himself socializing with the great singer Feodor Chaliapin and the composer and pianist Sergei Rachmaninoff, among others. Rachmaninoff would give Chekhov a score of his Fantasy for Orchestra, 'The Rock' ('Utes'), with an inscription attributing the 'programme' of this composition to Chekhov's story 'On the Road' (1886; *Letopis'*, pp. 523, 529, 527). Yalta suited Chekhov at first, and this quickly resulted in some of his finest short stories.

Then, in mid-October, Chekhov learned from the Yalta bookseller I. A Sinani that Chekhov's father had died the day before in Moscow, after a surgical intervention for a strangulated hernia. His sister had wired Sinani to ask how Chekhov was taking the news, but neither she nor anyone else had actually *informed* Chekhov about it, and he would have remained in the dark had he not happened to stop by the store. A letter from Ivan (10 October 1898) telling him about the surgery and what looked to be a full recovery arrived only days later. Chekhov immediately sent Masha a brief telegram, and the following day he wrote a letter in which he proposed that his mother come to Yalta and, if she liked it, that the family settle there 'for good'; after the death of his father 'life won't be the same, as though the flow of Melikhovo life ended with his diary' (14 October 1898). Pavel Chekhov had maintained that daily record since moving to Melikhovo, and when he was away his children – especially Anton – would make entries, mimicking his laconic style and surprising juxtapositions. Now Masha wrote the final entry: '12 October P. E. Chekhov died in Moscow at 5 p.m.' (*Letopis'*, p. 523).[1]

The speed with which Chekhov conceived the plan to create a 'new nest' (*Letopis'*, p. 524) for the Chekhov family suggests that the notion likely preceded his father's death. It made sense: Chekhov had spent but a scant few months at Melikhovo in 1898 before foul weather chased him south, and he blamed his low productivity on the impossibility of settling down. As much as he loved Melikhovo, that period of his life was over. Meanwhile, something of a land rush was taking place in Yalta, and Chekhov took part. By the end of October he had bought (for 4,000 rubles, with a quarter down) a piece of land in Autka, then a Tatar village just outside Yalta. He soon engaged the architect Lev Shapovalov, a recent acquaintance, and within a few weeks excavation had started and building materials were being hauled to the site. At the start of 1899 they were laying the foundation for his new home. But his sister visited and persuaded him to hold on to Melikhovo (*Letopis'*, p. 527); Chekhov's assertion in letters that Maria and their mother would now wish to leave Melikhovo apparently reflected his own desires more than theirs. Now the plan was for his mother to remain at Melikhovo, to which she was accustomed, and for Chekhov to continue to summer there. But in late spring 1899 Chekhov would put Melikhovo up for sale. He would visit the estate for the last time in August, and at the beginning of September his mother would be brought to Yalta after all. Now, however, in December 1898 – not long after buying the land at Autka – he also bought a picturesque property with a small house overlooking the sea at Kuchuk-Koi, about 30 kilometres (18 mi.) towards Sevastopol from Yalta.

Chekhov was on a spending spree, using credit made possible by the increasingly real prospect of selling the rights to his collected works. He quickly assembled the first volume of his collected writings for Suvorin, but there was still no contract. Then, after the volume was finally in press – they were terribly slow – he signed with Marks, who had a reputation for well-turned-out books and good royalties, which Chekhov needed. For some reason Chekhov's earnings did not reflect his status as the leading Russian author of the day. Tellingly, when Goltsev of *Russian Thought* decided to raise Chekhov's pay from 250 to 300 rubles per printed sheet, generously taking his lowered output and fiscal pressures into account, they were at the same time paying the elderly has-been Grigorovich 500 rubles per sheet. Chekhov would occasionally gripe about what he earned, but he was incapable of asserting his status and negotiating for better – it was beneath his dignity.

Much about the Marks deal remains contradictory and confusing. While discussing the shape of Suvorin's edition of his works, Chekhov asked Suvorin for negotiating advice regarding the deal with Marks, as though Suvorin were a disinterested party. Was he seeking negotiating leverage with Suvorin, or perhaps offering a warning that their project might be aborted? Chekhov may have contemplated proceeding with both presses: the Suvorin edition was to be different from Marks's, not a full, chronologically ordered collection of his works but a numbered set of the volumes he had already published, maintaining their prior titles (*Letopis'*, p. 528; to Suvorin, 16 November 1898). But Marks insisted that Chekhov halt the Suvorin undertaking, as well as any republication of material that had first appeared in periodicals (with an exception for charitable purposes).

Chekhov agreed. The deal would extricate him from the disorder of Suvorin's press, he told Ivan (18 January 1899). He may also have wanted to detach his posthumous literary reputation from Suvorin. In addition to the Zola and Dreyfus affairs, another high-profile social and political issue soon divided the two. Police violence against University of St Petersburg students in early February 1899 led to widespread protests, the closure of universities and a ban on reporting the crisis in the press. Suvorin praised the government's handling of the matter, for which Chekhov took him sharply to task (4 March 1899). Still, when Suvorin was subjected to a court of honour organized by the Alliance of Russian Writers for Mutual Assistance, Chekhov offered his old friend support, albeit qualified. While listing many solid reasons for criticizing *New Times* and Suvorin himself, he wrote to Suvorin that the very notion of a court of honour for writers and critics is absurd 'in a backward country where there is no freedom of the press or of conscience, where the government and nine-tenths of society considers journalists their enemies, where life is so oppressive and foul and there is so little hope for better days ahead' (24 April 1899; *Letters*, pp. 353–5). The complicated and ambivalent letter ends by repeating a prior invitation for Suvorin to visit in Moscow. A few days later Chekhov wrote to Avilova denouncing the court of honour, and thus defending Suvorin, with much the same rhetoric he had used in defending Zola against Suvorin: 'Is it our business to be judges holding court? That's instead the business of the gendarmes, police, government officials especially designed for that fate. Our business is to write, and only write' (27 April 1899). Still, Chekhov was no aesthete who disdained activities other than artistic ones, as his medical and philanthropic work demonstrates. His study of Sakhalin meant that he had seen the violence and capriciousness of the legal system, and when colleagues in the literary world borrowed poses and practices from those of police, prosecutors, judges and wardens, he recoiled.

Questions of money and time weighed heavily on Chekhov. His explanation of the Marks deal to Mikhail includes a rare naming of his mortal illness: Suvorin's people 'were losing my manuscripts all the time, not answering my letters, and bringing me to despair with their slipshod attitude; I had tuberculosis, I had to think of how not to dump my writings on my heirs in the shape of a disordered mass of diminished worth' (29 January 1900). In revealing to Maria that negotiations were under way, he said that if the Marks deal came through there would be no need to sell Melikhovo; otherwise, he needed 15,000 rubles from a sale, and anything beyond that would be Maria's (9 January 1899). Chekhov's days were numbered, and it was time to put his literary estate in order. In a March letter to Avilova he referred to Sergeyenko, who brokered the deal with Marks, as a literary 'gravedigger' (23 March 1899), a metaphor that figures his collected works as a kind of cemetery. Soon thereafter he wrote to his sister of a plan to collect the published graphics of his late brother Nikolai and send them to the Taganrog library for safekeeping (29 March 1899). The parallel between this unrealized project and that of assembling his own life's work is striking.

In the run-up to buying Chekhov, Marks serialized his 'My Life' in the monthly literary supplement to his *Grainfield (Niva)*. This long, bleak story represents provincial life in the 1890s, an era of industrial expansion and lost illusions among the intelligentsia. Its first-person narrator, a young *intelligent* and nobleman, Misail, rebels against social convention and family expectations, though in a rather passive and masochistic way; as in 'Story of an Unknown Man', the main character's life choices involve submissiveness, humiliation and pain. For Freud he would have exemplified moral masochism: in rejecting the privileges and the behavioural conventions of his class and family background, the young nobleman takes on a self-punishing ethical code and style of life designed to assuage a guilty conscience. Thus the adult Misail submits to his father's beating (by hand and umbrella) as though he were still a child, even while he rejects paternal authority, renounces his inheritance, and leads a déclassé working man's life reprehensible to his father. The story's climax and turning point – the night when Misail's marriage ends in fact, if not yet on paper – involves a fall from this position of non-violence, with Misail drawn into a conflict between two 'vermin' connected with the degenerate former landowner who are fighting outside his home. Misail steps outside with a shotgun in response to screams and, losing control of himself, winds up repeatedly striking one of the drunken brawlers.

Although Misail lives so as not to hurt others (his guiding principle), he also fails to change them or to offer substantive help to those closest to him in critical moments. His sister Cleopatra is drawn into a damaging love affair with Dr Blagovo, a married physician with an academic research career in St Petersburg; intervening would involve conflict. By contrast, Misail's labour-gang boss, the contractor Radish, expresses a clear code of values and a vision of the world where conflict is inescapable in his repeated saying, 'Worm eats grass, rust eats iron, and lying eats the soul.' Radish pointedly condemns the doctor: 'Your Honor, there'll be no Kingdom of Heaven for you!' (*Novels*, pp. 460, 530).

Misail argues at one point with his sister's lover: 'Progress lies in works of love, in the fulfillment of the moral law. If you don't enslave anyone, are not a burden to anyone, what more progress do you want?' But it seems that the only way for Misail to avoid enslaving anyone else is to become something of a slave himself. The doctor, by contrast, has absolute faith in progress, 'that great X that awaits mankind in the distant future', and the insignificance of 'some insects' who play no part in getting to that future, as well as the ethical alibi of those, like himself, who do (*Novels*, pp. 467, 468). By the story's end this doctor has impregnated and abandoned Misail's tubercular sister.

Misail's non-violence and his non-resistance to that of others is often associated with Tolstoyanism, which Chekhov's story supposedly critiques. This simplifying view short-circuits the dualism and ambiguity of Chekhov's poetic world. As in such stories as 'Gusev' and 'Ward No. 6', the philosophical debates that occupy key characters function almost as musical counterpoint; moreover, ideological positions are functions of the personalities who hold them, and character psychology, rather than ideas in themselves or cursed questions of Russian cultural history, is the ground floor. Chekhov takes two prominent and rather extreme social and philosophical positions and sets them in play against one another, decisively affirming neither. In 'My Life' there is the further complication that all such discussions are filtered through the consciousness of the I-narrator. Misail's presentation is oddly flat and affectless: he reports even the positions with which he disagrees without evaluative commentary or irony.

The story's narrative world comprises cruel perpetrators and victims, but this opposition is vexed: perpetrators may be good-natured and well-meaning, like Dr Blagovo; the victims may be rigid replicators of a corrupt and abusive social order, like Misail's father, who does after all suffer. Perhaps the story's dominant opposition is between those who forget and those who remember. Perpetrators forget easily: so it is with the doctor in the citation above; the governor, who does not remember interrogating Misail when he encounters him at the story's end; and, most saliently, Misail's ex-wife, who writes to him that she has acquired a ring like King David's, with the inscription in Hebrew, 'Everything passes.' 'Forgive and forget your M.,' she tells him. Misail in contrast asserts, 'Nothing passes', and his narrative is itself a kind of masochistic probing of memory's wounds (*Novels*, pp. 537, 527–8, 536). But even this opposition breaks down. Why have a ring made for yourself with the motto 'Everything passes', if you are not troubled by memories?

Chekhov proposed the title 'In the Nineties' for this story, which implies a realistic or documentary thrust, and the provincial town he denounces owes much to Chekhov's native Taganrog. But the story's lasting power derives from undercurrents of meaning like that created by imagery involving memory and forgetting.

For example, the story is quite overdetermined in its familial structures. Anyuta Blagovo, the doctor's sister, is in love with the narrator and his sister's friend; she lurks in the background, sending Misail anonymous gifts. The story ends by describing encounters between the narrator, with his late sister's child, and Anyuta at his sister's gravesite. The child is now Misail's, and as this family portrait suggests, the mother position is occupied by a kind of amalgamation of the late sister and Anyuta Blagovo, herself a sister figure. Interestingly, the story opens with Misail's father expressing gratitude that Misail's mother is not alive to see what her son has become, and it closes at the grave of Misail's sister, a juxtaposition that also parallels mother and sister. A non-Freudian interpretation of the way erotic desire is superimposed on familial relations might see adequate motivation for these entanglements in the provincial setting, with its narrowness of choices; thus the engineer whose daughter Misail marries lives right across the street from Misail's family home. It is all suggestively close, and one might interpret this closeness as a kind of extension of familial ties, a realistic portrayal of provincial life, or both. Either way, broadening the field requires escaping the town for the great world, as do Misail's ex-wife and Dr Blagovo.

The involvement of virtually all of the story's characters in amateur theatre and musical performance makes this another major theme. Even the painting contractor Radish is enamoured of theatre and drops paying work to paint sets for the amateur stage at the Azhogin home. The star of this provincial circle is the engineer's daughter, who has studied singing at the St Petersburg Conservatory. The only other character with acting talent is Dr Blagovo, though his singing, piano-playing and comic mimicry of drunken workmen ('a real actor's performance') take place in the private salon of the engineer's daughter, with her and Misail as audience. These agile, liberated and self-indulgent performers see role-playing everywhere: the engineer's daughter taunts Misail early on, 'But confess, you don't quite feel comfortable in your new role [...] Your working costume hampers you, you feel awkward in it' (*Novels*, pp. 445, 476–7, 485). Misail and his sister, by contrast, can only be who they are. The sister catastrophically breaks down when she attempts to perform onstage; instead of playing a role she reveals her own true inner state, the spectacle of her utter despair: she is pregnant by Dr Blagovo, who has returned to his career and wife in Petersburg. It may seem intuitive to endow theatricality and authenticity with negative and positive valences, respectively, but then why do the most authentic and suffering characters love the theatre and aspire to artistic activity? As always in Chekhov, ambiguity reigns.

Meanwhile, the town's built environment has largely been designed by Misail's father, the town's only architect, whose 'giftlessness [...] became our style'. The father's design process, which 'could proceed and develop only from the reception room and drawing room', and continues in an ad hoc fashion, suggests a preoccupation with social convention – the rules of the drawing room – over art or utility; it is no surprise that he rejects Misail and Cleopatra for breaching small-town decorum. The verse from John is as it were reversed: in this Father's house there may be many rooms, but none for his children. In an even deeper irony, Misail hates the town's buildings, aesthetically repugnant manifestations of social inequity and injustice, but his occupation as a painter has him preserving what his father built.[2]

In November 1898 Chekhov suffered five days of blood spitting and, while himself still practising medicine when asked by poor residents of the area, consulted with Dr Altshuller of Yalta. At the beginning of the month Chekhov received his first letter from Maxim Gorky, who also sent a volume of stories. Chekhov responded warmly, though not without constructive criticism. Many of Chekhov's most striking writing tips are to be found in his letters to Gorky, who asked Chekhov to view him as a learner. Above all, Chekhov urged restraint in both rhetoric and authorial stance; he also advised Gorky to travel and gain more life experience, and to consider moving from Nizhny Novgorod to one of the capital cities so as to immerse himself in literary society (for example *Letopis'*, pp. 612–13; 3 February 1900). For his part Gorky praised Chekhov effusively. Two years later, when the two attended an MAT performance of *Seagull* together at the end of October 1900 and the audience made a greater fuss over Gorky's presence in the theatre than it did over Chekhov, Gorky rebuked his fans (*Letopis'*, p. 637). He was a perceptive reader of Chekhov and became a committed promoter and defender.

In mid-November 1898 Chekhov sent 'A Medical Case' (or 'A Doctor's Visit', 'Sluchai iz praktiki') to *Russian Thought*, and two weeks later he sent 'On Official Business' ('Po delam sluzhby') to *The Week*. Both are doctor stories in which the biomedical approach proves inadequate for understanding: in the first, a kind of anxiety disorder; in the second, the cause of suicide. 'A Medical Case', with its critical portrayal of the social consequences of industrialization, won approval from liberal critics.

On 17 December, the MAT premiered *Seagull*. Well after midnight, Nemirovich-Danchenko wired Chekhov that it had been a 'colossal success. We are mad with happiness.' Guests who had spent the evening with Chekhov found him very anxious until he received the uplifting news. Chekhov's grateful responding telegram lamented that he wasn't with them and compared himself, sitting in Yalta, to 'Dreyfus on Devil's Island' (*Letopis'*, pp. 537, 536). Although the next two performances had to be postponed when Knipper fell ill, the play soon continued its spectacular run.

Chekhov received a concrete proposal from Marks in a letter from Sergeyenko and responded positively on New Year's Day. Sergeyenko had told Maria that Chekhov should ask for 100,000 rubles, but Marks's first written offer was 50,000. Chekhov countered with 75,000, and Marks hastily agreed. There was provision for a generous but chimerical 5,000-ruble bonus for each additional volume (of a determined length) of new works; Chekhov jokingly promised not to live past eighty, frightening Marks and almost scotching the deal, which shrewdly counted on Chekhov's ill health.

The contract included extremely burdensome clauses. Chekhov would retain all royalties from productions of his plays, but he was selling the rights to all his writings – past and future – for the next twenty years. He could reject previously published works for inclusion in the edition – he deemed most early pseudonymous sketches unworthy, and only roughly a third of previously published titles would see print with Marks – but he still had to provide fair copies of every single one of them to Marks or else suffer penalties that would far outstrip his earnings.[3] Suvorin wondered if extreme financial need had compelled Chekhov to take this bad deal and offered an immediate loan of 20,000 rubles.

Interestingly, each of the parties boosted his position by reference to the anti-capitalist Leo Tolstoy. Chekhov averred that Tolstoy had prodded him to see to his collected works. Sergeyenko told Chekhov that Tolstoy had urged Marks to publish Chekhov's collected works, declaring them of greater interest than Turgenev's or Goncharov's. Suvorin told Chekhov that Tolstoy had said that Marks ought to pay 50,000 rubles for just one volume of Chekhov's works, to be published as a supplement to his journal *Grainfield* (*Letopis'*, p. 542). Over the next few years, friends urged Chekhov to break the agreement. In June 1901 Gorky assured Chekhov that Marks had already recouped more than he had spent on the agreement: Chekhov should cancel the contract, repay what Marks had given him, and sign with Znanie (Knowledge) publishers, in whose management Gorky was involved. Znanie could guarantee him 25,000 rubles in income per year (*Letopis'*, p. 668). But the money from Marks was all spent, Chekhov responded; he could not borrow such a sum, and he had no energy for conflict, 'nor the belief that this was really necessary' (24 July 1901). A year and a half later Gorky and others would still be trying. At that time Chekhov explained his poor judgement to Knipper with rare candour: 'You can't forget that when talk began about the sale to Marks of my writings, I didn't have a copper farthing, I was in debt to Suvorin, where I was being published most vilely, and the main thing, I was getting ready to die and wanted to put my affairs into at least some sort of order.' He rejected the idea of having a lawyer find a contract loophole: it would be 'somehow not literary to suddenly fasten on to a mistake or lapse by Marks and, taking advantage of that, reverse matters "legally"'. Last, Marks might happily sell the works back to Chekhov for what he paid: he had already published and sold them abundantly, so they were no longer worth 75,000 rubles (9 January 1903). At one point Chekhov thought Marks might at least allow him to give the Posrednik (Intermediary) publishing house his early comic works for low-cost publication oriented towards the peasantry, but Marks maintained a relentless grip on this cash cow (*Letopis'*, p. 741). When Chekhov took it up with him in person in Petersburg in May 1903, Marks presented to Chekhov a pile of expensively bound books and offered him 5,000 rubles towards his medical expenses – which Chekhov refused – but he gave no leeway on the contract. At the end of 1903 Gorky made a last effort. He and the writer Leonid Andreyev composed a letter requesting that the terms of the contract be changed; it would be signed by leading cultural and scientific figures and, to maximize pressure, presented during the upcoming jubilee celebration of Chekhov's literary activity. Chekhov got wind of the effort, however, and asked his friends not to proceed.

Once contracted, Chekhov halted publication with Suvorin and requested help from friends and colleagues in locating and copying his early pseudonymous works. He was now embarked on the project of rereading everything he had ever written to determine what should be preserved for his legacy, and what discarded. The former he edited, generally by cutting material and sometimes changing titles. In a letter soliciting assistance from Avilova he likened the process to the culminating image of Pushkin's elegiac masterpiece 'Recollection' ('Vospominanie', 1828) an unwinding scroll of memory on which 'to read with disgust my life...' (5 February 1899). Nothing could be left behind, and this made the project one of self-accounting.

What other major author reprised his or her career so systematically and thoroughly? While one might speculate on what the keenly analytic Chekhov learned about himself, and how that affected his last years, the impact on his creative productivity is beyond question: already constrained by declining health, the 'convict labour' he was putting into the Marks edition, as he described it in a letter to Nemirovich-Danchenko (24 November 1899), would mean that he had only a handful of new stories ahead of him, as well as his last two major plays.

Spring 1899 brought new literary friendships and further collaboration with the MAT. Alexander Kuprin turned up in Yalta and, over time, became a friend and protégé of Chekhov. Ivan Bunin visited as well, and his friendship with Chekhov deepened. Both would maintain close relations with Chekhov's sister after his death and enjoy stints as guests in the Yalta house; as an emigrant living in Paris after the Revolution, in 1933 Bunin would become the first Russian to win the Nobel Prize in Literature (Tolstoy had disdained it).

In mid-April Chekhov left Yalta for Moscow, where he took an apartment for the whole year. Only a few days later, against all expectations, the MAT had *Uncle Vanya* from Chekhov. He had published the play without concern for staging, and it then appeared on the provincial stage. The Maly Theatre in Moscow had asked Chekhov for performance rights, and Chekhov had promised them the play. But the Maly, a state theatre, needed approval from an official committee comprising professors who, apparently, were offended by Chekhov's treatment of the play's professor of literature. The committee demanded significant revisions, and this gave Chekhov an excuse to hand the play over to the MAT.

It was a busy and consequential month. Tolstoy and Chekhov visited one another. Chekhov called on Knipper and invited her to an art exhibition featuring Levitan. In May he attended (with Avilova, then in Moscow) a private performance of *Seagull*. He was not happy with the slow tempo of the play's fourth act and, in response to Stanislavsky's request for comments on his Trigorin, made one of his famously quizzical remarks: though he told others that Stanislavsky's spineless Trigorin spoke 'like a paralytic' and was nauseating to watch, to the actor he said that the character should be wearing shoes with holes in them and checked trousers (*Letopis'*, pp. 564, 566). The well-known photograph of Chekhov with the cast of *Seagull* and Nemirovich-Danchenko was taken that week.

Chekhov alternated between Moscow and Melikhovo, where he took pictures down from the walls and joined his mother in packing their belongings for shipping to Yalta. Potential buyers visited the estate. On a quick trip to St Petersburg for business with Marks he avoided Suvorin, not telling him he was coming or trying to see him. In mid-June Chekhov's correspondence with Knipper began; his second letter to her opens, 'Greetings, last page of my life, great actress of the Russian land' (17 June 1899). Knipper invited him to join her on holiday in the Caucasus, and

Chekhov and the MAT cast of *Seagull*, 7 May 1899.

Chekhov with his architect at the White Dacha, Yalta, 1899.

Chekhov leapt at this, proposing that they travel on together to Yalta (1 July 1899). A few weeks later, after a stop in Taganrog, he picked her up in Novorossiysk. In Yalta he stayed in a hotel, while Knipper lodged with the family of Chekhov's friend Dr Sredin. At the beginning of August they returned together to Moscow.

Melikhovo was sold to a lumber merchant who bought on credit. Chekhov received nothing up front or, unfortunately, afterwards, and in late 1903 the property came back from the insolvent buyer in deplorable condition, with the woods half logged. It was then resold to an acquaintance of Maria, who arranged a private mortgage that brought her income for years.[4] Towards the end of August Chekhov sent Marks his plays for volume seven of the collected works and left for Yalta, where he was able to inhabit a finished wing of his new house. Maria then brought their mother from Moscow to stay with him.

New philanthropic efforts began almost immediately. When the teacher from a village school about 40 kilometres (25 mi.) from Yalta came to seek his help in keeping the school from closing, Chekhov turned over all the cash he had on hand: 500 rubles (*Letopis'*, p. 578). He also continued to send books to the Taganrog library. During his years at the White Dacha, as the house at Autka has come to be called, Chekhov provided medical assistance to the area's poor, and he often helped individuals who, like himself, had come south for their health but lacked means to pay for room and board or an infirmary bed. The ill were arriving on their last legs, hoping for recovery but most often having travelled only to die. For many, especially literary associates, Chekhov's personal attention involved not doctoring, but visits by someone who cared. An organized, systematic approach to the problem was clearly needed. Although it upset Chekhov when a newspaper incited an avalanche of requests for help by incorrectly reporting his founding a sanitarium for indigent consumptives, before too long he had actually started raising funds for just such a venture. He asked such family and literary friends as Mikhail in Yaroslavl and Gorky in Nizhny Novgorod to get his solicitation for support published in newspapers. He donated 5,000 rubles of his own funds and attracted another 10,000 from others. These efforts led to the creation of a twenty-bed facility.

Towards the end of October, the MAT premiered *Uncle Vanya*. Congratulatory telegrams arrived via his new telephone after Chekhov had gone to bed; he answered the bell each time barefoot and shivering, and he rightly intuited less than resounding triumph. Knipper wrote to lament her own performance, which she attributed to a discrepancy between her understanding of the character of Yelena Andreyevna and that demanded by the directors. Chekhov soothed her: spoiled by the theatre's initial spectacular successes, she and her colleagues had unreal expectations. There would be ups and downs, but their task was to keep working and improving, correcting inevitable mistakes, and to 'let others worry about the standing ovations'. In any case, he told her, the play was already an old one and not worth the upset.[5]

Uncle Vanya is both the most revealing and the most mysterious of Chekhov's major plays. As a reworking of the unsuccessful but interesting *Wood Demon* (1889), it offers a rare opportunity to divine the creative process of a dramatist who usually destroyed drafts; still, much remains obscure about how and when *Uncle Vanya* emerged. Chekhov's letters are silent about the project, and the finished play's appearance alongside *Seagull* in an 1897 volume of his plays was a surprise: his first mention of it, in a letter to Suvorin complaining about the publishing house's slow progress on the volume, refers to the 'familiar to you *Seagull* and the unknown to anyone in the world *Uncle Vanya*' (2 December 1896). Given the qualitative leap *Uncle Vanya* represents over *Wood Demon*, and the former play's affinity to the poetics of Chekhov's last masterpieces, scholars who date its revision later rather than earlier seem most convincing.[6]

The chief characters of *Wood Demon* reappear in *Uncle Vanya*, though in a slimmer cast. The wood demon of the earlier play was a landowner, non-practising physician and pioneering environmentalist and farmer; in the eyes of most, something of a crackpot. In *Uncle Vanya* the conservationist figure is now an overworked *zemstvo* physician who experiments on a very small estate and, as a hobby, maps the district's environmental decline. When Chekhov left behind the title *Wood Demon*, he also largely abandoned a whole system of imagery tying values associated with nature conservancy to the realm of beneficently conceived woodland and water spirits of Russian folklore.

Plot too is streamlined in *Uncle Vanya*. Romantic intrigues proliferate in *Wood Demon*, and once the Voinitsky character is put out of the way by suicide at the end of Act Three, the play closes happily with multiple couples finding positive resolution. Romantic plot lines are fewer in the later play: both Vanya and the doctor are taken with the retired professor's young wife, Yelena; and both Yelena and her stepdaughter Sonya find the doctor captivating. This would more than suffice in plot tension for a well-made play, but *Uncle Vanya* eschews conventional plot structure, and all romantic tensions merely fizzle out.

There are similar innovations in *Uncle Vanya*'s handling of financial plot lines. In both plays the retired professor has moved to the estate of his late wife, which actually belongs to his daughter Sonya. She and her late mother's brother, Uncle Vanya, work the estate and provide for the professor. Crisis comes about by the professor's decision to sell the estate and instead invest in bonds, which would support him and his wife more comfortably; in both plays, the egocentric professor has not considered what this might mean for his daughter and his brother-in-law, who have been living and labouring on that estate. Whereas in *Wood Demon* the professor has already been selling woodlands (though we learn of it rather late), in *Uncle Vanya* the professor's proposal comes out of the blue, and it is not prolonged or intensified as a source of conflict. Again, plot development is unconventional: there has been no financial intrigue, properly speaking, and the proposal and resulting explosion are in immediate proximity. Further, the professor's joking, upbeat demeanour as he prepares to launch the plan suggests that, rather than plotting against the interests of others, he is thrilled to have found a solution to the unhappy financial circumstance that has forced them all to live together on the estate. Rather than malicious and calculating, he is ill and profoundly self-centred, and he simply cannot comprehend that a solution that makes him happy would not enthuse the others as well. Likewise, the offstage gunshot that ends the life of Voinitsky in *Wood Demon* is replaced in *Uncle Vanya* by the parody of a violent resolution, in which Vanya chases the professor with a revolver and theatrically shouts 'Bang' after shooting and missing at close range.[7] The vanishing and reappearance in Act Four of the Yelena character of *Wood Demon* is also done away with, as is the folkloric mill where she hid: the later play is more streamlined in its settings.

The titular hero of *Uncle Vanya* is no longer the doctor-environmentalist but Voinitsky: Uncle Vanya. As is often the case, Chekhov has devised talking names for this play, names whose semantics somehow resonate with the character to whom they apply. Of them, Vanya's is perhaps the most telling. In *Wood Demon* his was a distinctively heroic name: George Voinitsky, where the forename George evokes the militant, dragon-slaying saint and the family name Voinitsky derives from the Russian for 'war' or 'combatant'. George shoots himself at the end of Act Four, but nevertheless this name functions within a mytho-poetic dimension of the play involving the archetype of a hero's descent to the underworld to rescue a beloved. Enacted with heaps of irony in *Wood Demon*, the metaplot is there all the same, as becomes overt at the end of the play when Yelena (Helen) returns to her husband: 'I'm ready. [*To her husband.*] Come on then, carry me off like the statue of the Commendatore in *Don Giovanni* and let's go to hell together in your twenty-six gloomy rooms. That's all I'm good for.'[8]

In transforming *Wood Demon* into *Uncle Vanya*, 'George' has now become the utterly banal, unheroic 'Ivan', of which 'Vanya' is a diminutive (the equivalent of 'Johnny' in English). This is the backdrop to his outburst in Act Three: 'My life's gone to waste! I'm gifted, daring, intelligent... If I'd had a normal life, I could have been a Schopenhauer, a Dostoevsky...' (*Plays*, p. 101). What is more, his nomination in the play's title already displaces his character somewhat, it decentres the play's reference to him: this is not his name, strictly speaking, but how he is referred to by one other character in the play, his niece Sonya.

Vanya does attack the professor, but futilely. Much is made of 'Chekhov's gun', the putative rule that, if there is a gun hanging over the mantle in Act One, it must go off by the end of the play.[9] That dictum dates from around the time of *Wood Demon* (1889), and as we know from both *Wood Demon* and *Uncle Vanya*, even the most ardent ideologue can, in the course of time, come to refute 'what he defended seven years ago', which scandalizes Voinitsky's mother in both plays. In *Uncle Vanya* the gun comes from nowhere – there had been no mention or sighting of it – and it is fired at close distance only to miss, however impossibly. After more than fifteen years of resolving his full-length plays with gun-shots (counting from the time of *Fatherlessness*), *Uncle Vanya* finds a new, utterly undramatic way. 'Everything will be as before,' Vanya tells the professor when he and Yelena depart (*Plays*, pp. 69, 110).

Dr Astrov seeks respite from his grinding rural medical service as a guest of Uncle Vanya and Sonya and works there on his graphic depictions of the devolution of the local environment. Although the change of title from *Wood Demon* to *Uncle Vanya* shifts emphasis from the Astrov character to Voinitsky, Astrov arguably remains the play's most multifaceted, ethically ambiguous and interesting character. He loves trees; humans, not so much. As he tells Sonya in Act Two, 'I don't like people... and it's a long time since I've loved anyone.' Nevertheless, he serves them as a physician: 'I work harder than anyone in the district. You know that.' And he ago-nizes over his therapeutic failures. Unlike Khrushchev, Astrov has become a heavy drinker and a cynic. He makes remarkably crude advances towards Yelena, in whom he rightly suspects mutual attraction, but he is utterly insensitive to Sonya's feelings until Yelena rubs his nose in them. Among his acid comments in the play: 'A woman becomes "friends" with a man in a definite sequence: first she's an acquaintance, next a mistress – and only then his friend' (*Plays*, pp. 84, 83, 81). The contradictions in Astrov's character are attributed, in the first dialogue of *Uncle Vanya*, to overwork as a *zemstvo* physician. But reading *Wood Demon* reveals another cause of this turn in the character: in refashioning the earlier play into *Uncle Vanya*, the character Astrov incorporated not only Khrushchev, the wood demon, but features of the abandoned character Fyodor Orlovsky, a war veteran, heavy drinker, womanizer and son of a neighbouring landowner.

Nevertheless, Astrov's ecological hobby and physician's work ethic evoke admiration in other characters and viewers alike. He professes, 'when I walk past a peasant's trees I've saved from the axe, when I hear the rustle of young trees I've planted with my own hands, then I know I have at least some control over the climate, and if man is happy a thou-sand years from now I'll have played my little part' (*Plays*, p. 72). Chekhov's fellow doctors responded enthusiastically to Chekhov's por-trayal of one of their own. When the play was performed by the Moscow Art Theatre for the Eighth Pirogov Society Congress in January 1902, Chekhov's medical colleagues organized a kind of icon procession with a large photographic reproduction of the Braz portrait, so disliked by Chekhov, and donated it to the theatre. University professors and *zemstvo* doctors sent congratulatory telegrams, 'having seen in the performance of artists the work of a doctor-artist' (*Letopis'*, pp. 692–3). All by now knew of Chekhov's exceedingly poor physical condition and were responding less to the play than to the person of Chekhov, but they do seem to have seen themselves in Astrov.

Letters from Maria, Chekhov's stand-in amid a whirlwind of playgoing and socializing with the MAT, provoked complaints of lonesomeness: 'The piano and I – there's two objects in the house conducting their existence silently and bewildered: why were we put here, when there's nobody to play us?' (11 November 1899). It was feast or famine for Chekhov, who always opened his door when somebody knocked. Not only acquaintances but also utter strangers, including the deathly ill and penniless, might appear at his Yalta door.[10] When Levitan visited at the end of December and Chekhov expressed a longing for the landscape of central Russia, Levitan painted *Haystack* on a piece of cardboard cut to fit over the fireplace in Chekhov's study, where it still hangs today.

At the end of October 1899, Chekhov sent 'The Lady with the Little Dog' ('Dama s sobochkoi') to *Russian Thought*, where it appeared in December. In this short masterpiece, very often anthologized, an adulterous summer fling deepens into profound attachment, but one that only periodically defeats geographic distance and the constraints of marriage to unloved others. Relevant notebook entries precede Chekhov's romance with Knipper, and scholars have identified other prototypes for its heroine (including Tolstoy's Anna Karenina), but his deepening intimacy with Knipper surely found its way into the tale. Knipper seemed to think so, writing to Chekhov that it had given her lots to think about.[11] The story is set in Yalta, though Chekhov generally liked to be elsewhere than the setting of a work in progress, so that the material would be filtered by memory. At the end of the story, during one of their rare trysts in Moscow, the male hero spots his rapidly ageing self in a mirror and wonders that 'only now, when his head was gray, had he really fallen in love as one ought to – for the first time in his life' (*Stories*, p. 375). The coincidence of deep attachment and consciousness of life's rapid passing reflects Chekhov's biography, where love and marriage were simultaneous with bodily collapse: TB left him but a few years to live, and sent him directly from his wedding to a sanatorium. Was this mere bad luck,

Chekhov in his study at the White Dacha, with Levitan's *Haystack on a Moonlit Night* (1900) over the fireplace.

or might there have been a causal connection, with intimations of mortality actually making possible new and different sorts of relationships?

'Lady' in many respects picks up where Chekhov's Little Trilogy leaves off. Its handling of the adultery theme explores the moral to Alyokhin's story: 'I understood that when you love you must either, in your reasonings about that love, start from what is highest, from what is more important than happiness or unhappiness, sin or virtue in their accepted meaning, or you must not reason at all.'[12] Its heroine bears the same name as that of 'About Love', and she is encountered in the Crimea, to which the unhappy Anna of 'About Love' departs at that story's end to cure her worn nerves. Both women are unhappily married, but neither is jaded or takes her vows lightly. Among shared details: both stories involve meetings in the theatre at a critical moment in their romances; and both heroines wear lorgnettes that become freighted with erotic significance.

In the Little Trilogy, storytelling is implicated in the overarching theme of encasedness: the stories that are told are yet another kind of trap, a way of framing or closing off lived experience by assigning an ending; the person about whom the story is told is somehow finished, even if that person is one's former self, as in the case of Alyokhin. Life in the present progressive – the open horizon of living – escapes neat trajectory from beginning to ending. And so it is that 'Lady' deliberately eschews an ending. Its finale is figured as the beginning of something that is truly open-ended: 'And it seemed that, just a little more – and the solution would be found, and then a new, beautiful life would begin; and it was clear to both of them that the end was still far, far off, and that the most complicated and difficult part was just beginning' (*Stories*, p. 376). With the last two words of 'Lady with the Little Dog' being 'just beginning', it is no surprise that several critics who published articles on the story complained that it was unfinished, a sketch of sorts. And Chekhov violated the Victorian narrative tradition regarding the adultery plot, the most famous example of which in Russian literature also involves an Anna (Karenina): to demand an ending means insisting that transgressors get what's coming to them.[13] This bothered Tolstoy, who admired Chekhov's narrative art profoundly and often read Chekhov's stories aloud to friends and family, even assembling a volume of his favourites: 'Lady' he rejected as immoral (*Letopis'*, p. 607). (As regards Chekhov's drama: Tolstoy enjoyed the comic one-act plays, but he disliked Chekhov's dramatic masterpieces. Chekhov laughingly told the story of how Tolstoy had once told him, 'You know, I can't stand Shakespeare; but your plays are even worse...' [*Letopis'*, p. 642].) Still, the story may be Chekhov's most anthologized, and it has spawned many literary echoes and screen adaptations over the years.

By the end of 1899, volume one of his collected works with Marks had come out. For all the negative aspects of this bad deal, Chekhov's calculation that Marks would work quickly appeared validated. Marks was unhappy at how many of the early stories Chekhov was rejecting, but Chekhov insisted on the author's right to judge; and in any case, neither Chekhov nor Marks had quite realized just how much material their deal entailed. Chekhov now averred that he should have demanded 175,000 rubles rather than 75,000 (to Nemirovich-Danchenko, 24 November 1899).

In January 1900, Chekhov was made an honorary member of the Russian Academy of Sciences in the category of literature, Division of Russian Language and Literature; the honour was shared this year by Korolenko, with whom Chekhov had divided the Pushkin Prize twelve years earlier, and Tolstoy, who held such institutions in contempt. According to the table of ranks, in place (with modifications) since the time of Peter the Great, the title of academician corresponded to the rank of actual state councillor or, in the military, general;[14] unfortunately, the 'honorary' qualification meant that, unlike full-fledged academicians, Chekhov would receive no pension or other monetary reward.

That same month Chekhov acquired a third Crimean property, a waterfront dacha on the coast at Gurzuf, about the same distance from Yalta in the opposite direction as Kuchuk-Koi. This small house is now an auxiliary of the larger Chekhov house-museum at Autka. In the little cove it overlooks, fine for swimming, juts the so-called Pushkin scale, a massive rock to which Pushkin had himself swum during his own southern exile; this history appealed to Chekhov. Unfortunately, Chekhov suffered another bout of blood spitting around this time.

In March, Chekhov was informed that he had been awarded the Order of St Stanislav (third degree) for 'outstanding effort and special labours in his duties as a trustee of the Talezh school' (*Letopis'*, p. 617).[15] Chekhov's father had coveted medals, and Alexander reports him shamelessly requesting one for conducting the church choir in Taganrog. Neither parent ever showed interest in Chekhov's writings, though Pavel might demand the respect due to him as the father of famous sons; he would have relished awards now coming Chekhov's way far more than did Chekhov.

In April, Maria and Knipper arrived in Yalta together, to be followed a week later by the entire MAT, which had arranged for a Crimean tour. Chekhov took a hotel room in Sevastopol and attended several performances there. The first was *Uncle Vanya*, which he had not yet seen in any theatre. It was an enormous treat, but the physical strain was

Chekhov in Yalta, *c.* 1900.

considerable: Chekhov was ill and bleeding from the haemorrhoids that often tormented him. Stanislavsky's performance as Dr Astrov left him disappointed once again, and again Stanislavsky found Chekhov's corrections elliptical and enigmatic: 'He whistles, listen... whistles! Uncle Vanya cries, and Astrov whistles' (*Letopis'*, p. 619). Why couldn't Chekhov lay out his conception of this character more fully? Was holding back and arousing uncertainty in the directors' minds a tactic for maintaining the author's control over the play? Or are such remarks, which zero in on very concrete and often apparently insignificant details, utterly in keeping with Chekhov's metonymic artistic method, the way small parts stand for the whole, and apparently insignificant, contingent details are anything but insignificant?

Chekhov professed to liking the MAT's performance of Gerhart Hauptmann's *Lonely People* (*Einsame Menschen*, 1891) more than his own play: 'That's a real dramaturg! I'm no dramaturg; listen, I'm a doctor,' he told Stanislavsky (*Letopis'*, p. 619). The late nights and furious socializing continued in Yalta, where the troupe also staged *Seagull*. Gorky came at the invitation of Chekhov, who encouraged him to write for the MAT, and so too did authors Bunin, Kuprin and Dmitry Mamin-Sibiryak, among others. All visited Chekhov at his new home daily, and a jubilee-style celebration of the playwright was organized for the last performance of *Seagull* on 23 April.

In May Chekhov visited Moscow and a declining Levitan. The artist would die in July, having insisted that all his correspondence be burned. We thus surely lost many of Chekhov's most revealing and amusing missives; fortunately, Chekhov preserved his letters from Levitan.[16] On returning to Yalta he donated 1,000 rubles for a new school in the Tatar village of Mukhalatka (*Letopis'*, p. 625). In June he made a trip with Gorky, the artist Vaznetsov, and Drs Sredin and Aleksin to the Caucasus, where he rendezvoused with Knipper, who returned with him to Yalta and remained through July. The two apparently became intimate, or at least more comfortable with intimacy, in this period: a letter Knipper wrote to Chekhov after he had put her on the train at Sevastopol initiates their use of the informal, second-person form of address.[17] Privacy was tricky with others in the house, though the two got away to the Gurzuf dacha, or stayed in Autka while the rest of the family went to Gurzuf. When the Petersburg actress Vera Komissarzhevskaya showed up to see Chekhov in Yalta at the beginning of August – there had been a spark between them since her *Seagull* days, and she was asking Chekhov for his next play – Chekhov installed her at Gurzuf for a few days. Her letter to Chekhov afterwards shows that she was unaware that a jealous Knipper was lodged at Autka and had therefore been baffled by Chekhov's lack of attention. Chekhov in turn gave her two photographs of himself, one of which he apologetically inscribed: 'To Vera Fyodorovna Komissarzhevskaya the 3rd of August, on a stormy day, when the sea roared, from the quiet Anton Chekhov.' Although he did promise to send her *Three Sisters* (25 August 1900), the MAT would in the end obtain the rights to Petersburg performances of the play.

It was an awkward time: Chekhov was struggling to get *Three Sisters* written, and his larger family, including brothers Mikhail and Ivan with children, had descended on him, making it difficult for him to work. At the end of the summer he insisted that his mother depart for Moscow to winter with Maria.[18] Writing that play proved difficult – harder, Chekhov averred to Maria, than any of his others (9 September 1900), both due to the guests he could never turn away and because the stakes were higher. The MAT saw new material from Chekhov as fundamental to its survival and channelled pressure through Knipper. Chekhov conceived roles and wrote with this particular troupe of actors in mind. He warned that the play might have to wait until the following season: it needed time in his desk before rewriting, and in any case he ought to be present in Moscow during rehearsals. He did not trust Stanislavsky to handle four central female roles without his guidance (to Knipper, 15 September 1900, for example; *Letopis'*, p. 634).

Nevertheless, towards the end of October Chekhov arrived in Moscow with the new play. Its reception by befuddled members of the MAT was awkward. Knipper recalled:

> When Anton Pavlovich read *The Three Sisters* to us, the performers and directors who had long awaited a new play from our favorite writer, there was perplexity and silence. Anton Pavlovich gave a confused smile and paced up and down among us, coughing nervously. Then came individual attempts to pass some comment, and one could hear: 'It's not a play, just the outline.' 'It can't be performed, there aren't any roles, only the suggestion of them.'[19]

According to Nemirovich-Danchenko, an embarrassed Chekhov 'repeated several times: but I have written a vaudeville' (*S* XIII, p. 430). This confused them all, and still does, since the subtitle defines the genre of *Three Sisters* as a 'drama'.

That autumn Chekhov stayed at the Dresden hotel, but during the day he often worked at the apartment shared by Knipper and Maria. Gorky was in Moscow, too, and he accompanied Chekhov to MAT performances. The end of October brought a sad duty: Chekhov met Sinani, his Jewish bookseller friend from Yalta, at the train station and informed him of his son's death 'from melancholy', that is, suicide.[20] Chekhov often made his way to the sick and dying, not always to doctor but to attend. He was certainly stoic in facing his own mortal illness and death, and it is true that he had lost patience with the dying Nikolai. Many memoirists described him as cool, aloof and closed off to others. But there was a very special empathy, quite beyond his medical training, that frequently took him to the side of others just when they needed it most.

By mid-December, when Chekhov departed Moscow for the Pension Russe in Nice, *Three Sisters* had sunk in with Stanislavsky. He now called the play 'wonderful, [Chekhov's] most successful' (*Letopis'*, p. 642). Chekhov sent the MAT revised third and fourth acts and other alterations from abroad. Letters to Knipper include such acting instructions as, 'Don't make a sad face in any act [...] People who have long been carrying a grief within and are used to it just whistle and often lapse into thought' (2 January 1901). With Stanislavsky he pushed for understated treatments of scenes like the one in Act Three, where Natasha patrols the house at night putting out lights, and the death of Tuzenbakh at the play's end (2 and 15 January 1901). There was discussion of how loud the fire alarm bells ought to sound. As always, Chekhov pushed for subtlety: the noise should be quite distant, and instead of having Natasha look for thieves under the furniture, it would be enough for her to walk across the stage holding a candle, 'à la Lady Macbeth' (2 January 1901; *Letters*, p. 391). But Stanislavsky felicitously nixed Chekhov's idea of having Tuzenbakh's corpse carried across the stage after the duel; for once he was more Chekhovian than Chekhov, keeping the play's most dramatic moment offstage and quietly reflected in its effect on other characters, as had been the fire in Act Three. When Stanislavsky expressed concern over the similarity of this play's ending to that of *Uncle Vanya*, Chekhov stated the obvious: 'After all, *Uncle Vanya* is my play, not someone else's, and if your work reminds you of yourself, well, they say, that's as it has to be' (15 January 1901).

Indeed, if one catalogues dramatic features typically thought of as distinctively Chekhovian, then *Three Sisters* is arguably the most Chekhovian play of them all. Its temporal structure juxtaposes a progressive, linear chronology spanning some four years (or five, counting back to the father's death) with cyclical, calendric time, marked by seasons and holidays; thus the play's very first line, uttered by Olga: 'Father died exactly a year ago today, May the fifth. Your name day, Irina' (*Plays*, p. 110). Dialogue proceeds musically, as counterpoint and variations on a theme. More than any Chekhov play to date, *Three Sisters* lacks conventional soliloquy; characteristically, its first line integrates into disjointed dialogue information that might have been conveyed by soliloquy. Plot goes unresolved, if one can even speak of a single overriding plot line. An ensemble principle is already manifest in the title, and the cast of characters is greater than in any other of Chekhov's mature dramatic works. The play's surface offers a highly realistic representation of everyday life, but one cannot escape undercurrents of symbolic meaning, in part aroused by prolific repetitions and disjunctions in dialogue. Last on this short list might be its presentation of weak, ineffectual characters from the intelligentsia, with which one so associates Chekhov.

The play is set in an unnamed provincial city in the Urals, which in a letter to Gorky Chekhov likened to Perm (16 October 1900). But the setting, comprising a large house and garden, does not feel particularly urban or otherwise different from the country settings of all Chekhov's major dramatic efforts to date. The space of this play is highly ambiguous: a respite for the officers garrisoned there (Chebutykin plans to return when he retires), for the three sisters and their brother it is rather a kind of underworld in which they feel trapped. Brought there by their late father, an army general in service, they long to return to Moscow. Their sense of exile may reflect Chekhov's own, now that doctor's orders had him living in locales presumed to be healthful for consumptives:[21] the distance between Moscow and Perm (to the east) roughly equals that between Moscow and Yalta (to the south).

Other interesting connections with Chekhov's life include the motif of three sisters, one that recurs among paramours of the eldest three Chekhov brothers: most prominent were the Golden sisters, with whom Chekhov and his brothers had dallied in their student days, and one of whom (Natalya) Alexander married, fathering the future actor Mikhail Chekhov; but there were also the Markov sisters, the Yanov sisters, the Lintvarevs and the Shavrovs. Writes Rayfield, 'Chekhov must have felt "three sisters" to be the fairy-tale motif of his life.'[22] The duel at the end of *Three Sisters* echoes a similar event in Taganrog in the mid-1880s (*S* XIII, p. 423), and the conflagration of Act Three recalls a fire that nearly burned the Chekhovs out of Melikhovo. The depiction of military life in peacetime – Russian for the humdrum everyday is *byt* – has been connected to the artillery brigade garrisoned in Voskresensk, where the Chekhov family summered in the mid-1880s, and where Chekhov practised medicine in the summer of 1884.[23] Already in 1887, when Chekhov published 'The Kiss', critics found remarkable his grasp of the rhythms and feel of peacetime military life, of which he had no personal experience. In the Voskresensk summer of 1883 his sister Maria rejected a marriage proposition from a Lieutenant Yegorov, who took it badly;[24] although no duel ensued, this episode may stand behind the love triangle between Tuzenbakh, Solyony and Irina in *Three Sisters*.

Such interesting connections hardly help make sense of the play, however, whereas considering how the military theme fits into the larger whole might. The issue is less Chekhov's realistic portrayal of military life than how he reads that life and integrates it into *Three Sisters* as a perfect counterpart to that of the sisters. It is a life, largely composed of routines, in which individual will has no function: one follows orders. Thus the artillery brigade leaves the town at the end not because they wish to, as the three sisters have wished to, but because they are ordered to, just as the three sisters appear fated to remain where they are. What is more, garrison life involves an acute sense of the meaninglessness of day-to-day actions – divorced from any purpose the individual can divine – and also the peculiar loneliness of being compelled to live in close quarters and artificial communality with others. In this sense, the officers are perfect dance partners for the entrapped three sisters, who experience, as V. B. Kataev put it, 'the loneliness of a contemporary person within the family'.[25]

If the officers' existential situation in many respects doubles that of the sisters, then this likeness also foregrounds important differences. Chief among them would be gender, and also the fact that – as critics have remarked since the play's first performances – the sisters are in principle free to move to Moscow: they do not live under the same external constraints as the officers (at least until their brother gambles away their inheritance). Just as in 'The Kiss', the meaningless routine of military life serves as the backdrop for a sustained and developed fantasy that will be inevitably ruptured. The accurate portrayal of peacetime military *byt* matters less than the way military life helps construct a more universal (and rather existentialist) image of everyday life, one that resonates broadly with readers and viewers.

Further, in a play whose title declares it to be about sisters, military life becomes one way of defining masculinity. That term is provocatively absent in the play's title – why indeed no mention of the brother? – but all the more central in its very absence. The representation of masculinity ranges from the perfumed and posturing Solyony, to the lover and father Vershinin, to the useless Chebutykin, to the sisters' deceased father. Fatherhood is a particularly problematic dimension: Andrei becomes emasculated by the arrival of his children, at least one of whose paternity is questionable; Vershinin's family life is unhappy and entrapping; the betrayed Kulygin's kind concern for his child is mocked by his wife Masha. It was the father of the three sisters, the general, who brought them where they are and, in seeing to their education, made them what they are. The first two words of *Three Sisters* are 'Father died'; his departure a year earlier has rendered the continued presence of his daughters in this provincial city meaningless, and their education (in particular their mastery of foreign languages) useless. As was remarked earlier, all of Chekhov's large-scale plays might have taken the first's title, 'Fatherlessness'.

The general's death finds an opposing bookend with the killing of Tuzenbakh, Irina's fiancé, and the departure of the officers at the play's close. The action has made a full turn spiralling downwards. Chebutykin claims to have been in love with the sisters' mother, pretends to a paternal role and may have actually fathered Irina; but he becomes a negative presence, smashing the late mother's heirloom clock in the play's climax and passively overseeing the death of Tuzenbakh in the denouement of Act Four. Protopopov is another male defined by his absence. Likely the father of at least one of Andrei's children, and located inside the Prozorov house at the play's end – the sisters have left it for good – this proto-pop, or prototypical male, is the most important never-seen character in Chekhov's oeuvre. Exercising malign power nonetheless, by the end he has Andrei working for him as well. If *Three Sisters* has a villain, he is it; but Chekhov innovatively keeps this character, whose affair with Natasha may be the play's overarching complication, entirely off the stage.

In any case, the plot line involving Natasha, Andrei and Protopopov falls far short of delineating the overarching plot structure of the play. Rather, the play is composed of a set of orchestrated sub-plot lines, each of which is set up in the expository Act One, has its *zaviazka* or complication in Act Two, comes to crisis in Act Three and finds resolution in Act Four. Let us sketch this in brief.

Act Two: married and unhappy, Andrei has taken up gambling; the act ends with either a resumption or the continuance of the connection between his wife and Protopopov; Act Four: the play's denouement has Andrei thoroughly emasculated, working under Protopopov in the district council; his wife is now mistress of the Prozorov family home, where Protopopov visits while the the Prozorovs are all in effect exiled.

Act Two: Solyony declares his love for Irina and, rejected, vows to kill any successful rival; Act Four: there has been an offstage confrontation and challenge between Tuzenbakh and Solyony, and the play ends with Solyony killing Tuzenbakh offstage in a duel.

Act Two: Masha and Vershinin begin an adulterous affair, and the wife of Vershinin attempts to poison herself; Act Four: Vershinin and Masha are compelled to part.

There is also dramatic tension of sorts between the ideas of Vershinin and Tuzenbakh, expressed in their habitual philosophizing. Vershinin believes in progress and the meaningfulness of life; one need only live with an eye towards the future: 'In two or three hundred years, in a thousand years perhaps – time is not of the essence – a new and happy life will dawn [...] and therein lies the sole reason for our existence and, if you will, our happiness.' For the existentialist Tuzenbakh, one lives the senseless life one is in: 'life will be the same as always [...] Look, there's snow falling. What's the point of that?' (*Plays*, pp. 145, 146). The debate continues as a contrapuntal melodic line until the play ends. Nevertheless, the future-oriented Vershinin is trapped by his past, which takes the form of a wife and family hanging around his neck; and although Tuzenbakh adopts work as a supreme value, it is work as such, detached from any purpose or vision of progress to which it might lead: he will hire on at a brick factory – that is, to make the least technical material object one might make, thingness itself. Never mind that one builds things with bricks – there is no such goal, but only exhausting labour that masks the meaninglessness of life. Their positions are reiterated in the play's last lines by Irina, Olga and Chebutykin, as a kind of musical cadence bringing the production to a close. Indeed, music is the leitmotif of this scene: the regimental band is playing as the unit departs, and Masha declares, 'Oh, listen to the music.' Irina vows, following Tuzenbakh's position, 'I'll be working, working... '. Olga echoes Vershinin: 'it almost seems that any minute now we'll find out why we live, why we suffer... If only we knew.

if only we knew.' Chebutykin asserts, 'What difference does it make. What difference does it make', and Olga repeats, 'If only we knew, if only we knew!' (*Plays*, pp. 189–90). There has been no resolution to conflict on the plane of ideas; it is more like the ending of a musical piece.

And what of the aspiration to return to Moscow, so frequently declared? The plot function of this unresolved non-action has always troubled the play's readers and viewers. As the Prozorovs' stated intention from the start, it arouses the most overarching expectation; and yet 'going to Moscow' neither grows into a complication nor obtains a trajectory corresponding to conventional notions of plot construction, and by the play's ending has entirely fizzled out.

From the very start, critics objected: why can the Prozorovs not travel to Moscow? Why not just buy a train ticket? The project may lose financial viability due to Andrei's gambling debts, true, but another reason fits into the play's deeper meaning: perhaps Moscow is not actually a destination one might reach by road or train; perhaps they cannot return because the Moscow of their memories is not at all a place, but a time – and time is, after all, the first motif sounded in the play's dialogue. If longing for Moscow expresses a nostalgia for childhood, then returning would mean going back in time.[26] And though the motif of Moscow is absent at the play's end, it may be said to underlie it. The sisters have left their father's home. Masha declares, 'I'm never going into that house again, ever...' (*Plays*, p. 187); Olga and Irina echo her. In the logic of the play's action, and in the psyches of its main characters, leaving that house takes the place of either fulfilling or renouncing the desire to return to Moscow, and this may be what lies unsaid behind the ellipsis ending Masha's remark. In a sense, their going out into the world is nothing more than the normal order of things, just as was the death of their father a year before the opening of the play's action. It is an ending that anticipates the ending of Chekhov's next and last play, *Cherry Orchard*.

This winter's stay in Nice (December 1900 – January 1901) was shorter and quieter than that of two years ago. When Olga Valisyeva, a wealthy young heiress and translator of Chekhov, asked for advice on funding a public health venture with the proceeds from a house sale, Chekhov suggested a clinic devoted to skin diseases and began looking into the cost. He again contemplated a trip to Algiers with Kovalevsky, but that was not to be; instead the two travelled to Italy. From the Russian zoological research station at Villefranche, Chekhov sent Taganrog's museum a collection of sea creatures in jars of formaldehyde. During a night-time train ride in Italy, Chekhov told Kovalevsky that 'he can't make up his mind to work on some lengthy project, because, as a physician, he understands that his life will be short' (*Letopis'*, p. 651).

It was while Chekhov was travelling to Rome at the end of January that the MAT premiered *Three Sisters*. Nemirovich-Danchenko first errantly telegraphed news of the play's performance to Algiers, and then tried Naples before finally locating him. The initial audience reaction was less than spectacular; further, *Russian Thought* aggravatingly published a copy of the manuscript the MAT had been using in rehearsal rather than Chekhov's final version. But over time the play, as handled by the MAT, came to be considered Chekhov's greatest.[27] Unsurprisingly, the MAT began applying pressure for his next play, and the nagging only got worse as Chekhov's health declined.

By the middle of February, after a harrowing and insulting search by customs officials in Odessa, Chekhov was back home in Yalta. Knipper was performing *Uncle Vanya* and *Three Sisters* in St Petersburg with the MAT, but she arrived for two weeks in Yalta at the end of March and lobbied hard for marriage. Writing to her at the end of April, Chekhov relented:

> If you give me your word that not a soul in Moscow will know
> about our wedding until after it happens I will be willing to marry
> you on the very day of my arrival, if you like. For some reason
> I'm terrified of the wedding ceremony, the congratulations and
> the champagne which you have to hold in your hand with a
> vague smile. (26 April 1901; *Letters*, p. 388)

It is quintessential Chekhov to insist on maximum privacy for a fundamentally social ritual: the affirmation of their relationship by church, state and the broad public.

Once in Moscow, a medical examination found Chekhov's lungs considerably worsened, and he was ordered to embark immediately for a two-month koumiss cure in Ufa province (the fermented mare's milk consumed by natives there was thought to sometimes have a curative effect). This became the honeymoon plan for Chekhov and Knipper, who were married on 25 May. The wedding ceremony took place in secrecy, with only the minimally required number of witnesses. Knipper's familial sensibilities were in some measure respected, however: two of the four witnesses were her brother and her uncle, and Chekhov and Knipper went to visit her mother before departing for the koumiss resort of Aksyonovo. Among Chekhov's family only his brother Ivan knew of his plans, though he was not invited to the ceremony (which rather upset Knipper). His sister, who shared an apartment with Knipper, had written only the day before urging Chekhov not to marry, to avoid the 'additional excitement' of an 'odious' ceremony. 'If a certain person loves you, she would not leave you and there is no sacrifice entailed on her part. [...] There's always time to get hitched' (24 May 1901; *Letters*, p. 402). On learning they had wed she felt deceived and on the verge of losing the two people closest to her. Moreover, there had been multiple instances when she had herself received a proposal but, after consulting with Chekhov, had turned down the suitor. Now Maria suggested in letters that she too might marry, and she went so far as to ask Bunin, who had become close to the Chekhov family, to find her a mate.

Chekhov's response to Maria belittled the step he had just taken:

> I don't know if I've made a mistake or not, but I got married
> mainly because, first, I'm over forty; second, Olga comes from
> a highly moral family; and, third, if we have to separate, I'll do
> so without the least hesitation, as if I had never gotten married.
> After all, she is an independent person and self-supporting.
> Another important consideration is that my marriage has not
> in the least changed either my way of life or the way of life of
> those who lived and are living around me. Everything, absolutely
> everything will remain just as it was, and I'll go on living alone
> in Yalta as before. (4 June 1901; *Letters*, pp. 400–401)

A wedding had long been expected by friends and associates of the couple. In the event, Chekhov did not so much marry in secret as stage his privacy with great theatricality: he organized a banquet for friends on the day of the wedding that he and Knipper demonstratively skipped, instead departing from Moscow.

The long trip to Aksyonovo by train and river steamer began with a visit to Gorky, just out of prison and under house arrest in Nizhny Novgorod. The doctor who had organized their travel botched the tickets and connections, and Chekhov and Knipper spent a night on the floor of a peasant hut at the miserable river station 'Drunken Forest'. The resort itself proved quite primitive, and though Chekhov at first sent upbeat

Chekhov and Olga Knipper on their honeymoon in Aksyonovo, 1901.

letters praising the food, natural surroundings and fishing, he soon grew bored and unable to tolerate the discomfort and dietary regime; his weak gastrointestinal system was probably infected with tuberculosis. The couple left for Yalta earlier than planned, and at the end of the summer Knipper returned to Moscow, where Chekhov would join her in mid-September.

At home alone in Yalta, Chekhov fell ill: his weight was down, his cough awful, and the month in the health resort had benefited him less than travelling had harmed him. Chekhov now wrote a will in the form of a letter to his sister that he deposited with Knipper. This was not a legal document, but Chekhov's family considered it morally binding, and when Chekhov died, after the court made its decisions, the brothers and Knipper reallocated their inheritance according to these wishes.

Yalta

3 August 1901

Dear Masha,

I bequeath to you my house in Yalta for as long as you live, my money and the income from my dramatic works; and to my wife, Olga Leonardovna, my house in Gurzuf and five thousand rubles. You may sell my house if you so desire. Give my brother Alexander three thousand, Ivan five thousand, and Mikhail three thousand, Alexei Dolzhenko one thousand and Yelena Chekhova (Lyolya) – when she marries – one thousand rubles. After you and Mother die, all that remains except the income from the plays is to be put at the disposal of the Taganrog municipal administration for the purpose of aiding public education, while the income from the plays is to go to my brother Ivan and after his – Ivan's – death to the Taganrog municipal administration for the same educational purpose. I have promised one hundred rubles to the peasants of the village of Melikhovo to help pay for the highway. I have also promised Gavriil Alexeyevich Kharchenko (The Kharchenko House, Moskalevka, Kharkov) that I would pay for his older daughter's gymnasium education until she is released from tuition. Help the poor. Take care of Mother. Live in peace among yourselves.

Anton Chekhov

(*Letters*, p. 406)

The logic of who got what is fairly clear. Ivan would receive more than the other brothers because he struggled financially while serving as an educator. Knipper would receive less than Maria because Knipper could take care of herself, whereas Maria had been Chekhov's partner in managing his properties and finances and was unmarried with little earning capacity. Chekhov's lasting sense of debt to Taganrog repaid the city that had provided Chekhov's higher education and made him a physician, even if Chekhov had never earned a living as a doctor. And he may have had other Taganrog debts in mind: those of his father, who had cheated creditors and the buying public as a shopkeeper; his own, for courtesies and gestures of support, unknown to us, that kept Chekhov afloat when he was marooned there and finishing gymnasium after his family had fled to Moscow.

Chekhov stayed in Moscow for about five weeks in September and October. At a MAT performance of *Three Sisters* he took a bow onstage after the second act. But Alexander visited and wrote Mikhail, tersely, that their brother's condition was 'rather bad' (*Letopis'*, p. 678). After returning to the Crimea, Chekhov frequented Tolstoy, who was residing nearby at Gaspra (towards Sebastopol), and he hosted Gorky, who was exiled, under surveillance, prohibited from lodging within the city limits of Yalta, and looking for a suburban dacha. Chekhov also enjoyed the presence of Bunin that autumn. Both Bunin and Gorky left fascinating memoirs of this period, highlighting with particular vividness Tolstoy's affection for and admiration of Chekhov.[28] Tolstoy praised the dense economy of Chekhov's prose, and he also found in Chekhov a Russianness uncharacteristic of contemporary literature (*Letopis'*, p. 690).

As Chekhov's health declined he became ever more a public figure. The Yalta district school board made him a trustee of the Gurzuf *zemstvo* school. The St Petersburg Society of Don Cossacks decided that Chekhov, who hailed from the Don area, should be a member, and Chekhov later agreed to give them a story for a planned volume. January saw the special MAT performance of *Uncle Vanya* for the Pirogov Society, which turned into the celebration of Chekhov mentioned earlier. Chekhov asked Knipper to remove the large photographic reproduction of the Braz painting the doctors had presented to the MAT troupe from its frame and replace it with another (23 January 1902). That same month the Society of Russian Playwrights and Opera Composers awarded Chekhov the Griboyedov Prize for *Three Sisters*.

Chekhov and Tolstoy at Gaspra (Crimea), 1901.

Chekhov and Gorky, 1899 or 1900.

Meanwhile, Chekhov complained to Knipper about becoming winded on pruning just one rose and admitted to significant worsening over the winter (6 February 1902). In that condition, in February, he finished and sent off the story 'The Bishop' ('Arkhierei'), narrated from the perspective of a cleric dying of typhoid fever; he told Knipper that the idea went back fifteen years, which places its conception near the emergence of Chekhov's tuberculosis. Serving Mass during Passion week, the bishop has so outgrown his roots that he does not recognize his mother when he encounters her. She has come with a young niece to seek help from their exalted relation. The bishop dies on Easter eve, with this parting vision: 'And he could no longer say a word, he understood nothing, and imagined that he was now a simple, ordinary man, walking briskly, merrily across the fields, tapping his stick, and over him was the broad sky, flooded with sunlight, and he was free as a bird and could go wherever he liked!' (*Stories*, p. 435). Easter Sunday proceeds as always, including drunken celebration after services, and a month later the bishop is all but forgotten. Chekhov insisted that not a word be changed to appease censors.

In March a reluctant Chekhov was drawn into politics. Gorky (together with the dramatist Alexander Sukhovo-Kobylin) had been elected an honorary member of the Academy of Sciences, following in Chekhov's footsteps. Less than two weeks later, though, the government annulled the leftist Gorky's appointment. It would take Chekhov a few months to decide what to do. He tried to talk it over with Tolstoy, but Tolstoy had not acknowledged his own appointment as an academician and had no use for such institutions. Eventually Chekhov and Korolenko, who visited Yalta in May, agreed to resign from the academy in protest. Chekhov sent his letter towards the end of August. In this period, Chekhov also sent money to help support a group of 32 students who had been exiled to Irkutsk.

Chekhov mused in letters to Knipper about an arctic summer holiday 'to the North Pole, somewhere in Novaya Zemlya, or to Spitsbergen' (9 March 1902), but poor health scotched any such adventure. Knipper too fell seriously ill, following a miscarriage while the MAT was on tour in Petersburg that spring. She had surgery there – perhaps for an ectopic pregnancy[29] – and was brought to Yalta to convalesce, disembarking on a stretcher. At the end of May she and Chekhov travelled to Moscow, but she became acutely ill again with, as doctors finally concluded, peritonitis. Always proud of his diagnostic abilities, Chekhov had already figured this out and crowed in a letter to Nemirovich-Danchenko that he alone among the physicians attending Knipper had correctly ordered her not to eat solids (12 June 1902). After this frightening downturn Knipper recovered quickly, but now an utterly exhausted Chekhov needed recuperation. He accompanied Savva Morozov, a wealthy magnate who had been underwriting the MAT, to Morozov's estate in the Urals, near Perm. Though ill at ease and uninspired in the provincial empire of this 'Russian Rockefeller', as he called him, Chekhov nevertheless found ways to make his brief visit worthwhile: after touring a chemical factory owned by

Morozov, Chekhov persuaded his host to shorten the workers' twelve-hour workday (*Letopis'*, p. 712).

On returning to Moscow Chekhov was invited by Morozov to become a shareholder in the theatre. Knipper took a share, but the MAT lost the great actor and future director Vsevolod Meyerhold because he was not included.[30] Chekhov proposed investing between 3,000 and 10,000 rubles, but later backed out because he never received the money owed to him by Melikhovo's buyer.[31] He and Knipper continued their summer at the Alekseev (Stanislavsky) family estate of Liubimovka. For Chekhov it recalled the first Chekhov family holidays of the mid-1880s at the Kiselevs' Babkino, with its Moscow-region setting, a fine river, fishing and comfortable lodgings. In conceiving his last play he would draw on both Liubimovka and Babkino. Liubimovka was the property of a wealthy Moscow merchant family untouched by the kind of financial crisis depicted in *Cherry Orchard*, but Babkino and its gentry owners had long been declining. Lopakhin's proposal to divide riverfront property into sites for dachas for the ascendant middle class as a way of saving the estate originated in a plan by Kiselev to rescue Babkino.

In mid-August Chekhov returned to Yalta. There was painful correspondence with Knipper, who had blamed Chekhov's sister and mother for his early departure from Liubimovka, and who understood their request that he return as excluding her. Chekhov defused the situation as best he could, promising to return to Moscow in September and stay as long as weather permitted, after which he wished to winter in Nervi, Italy. And perhaps by way of reassuring Knipper, he asked if her doctor had said it would be alright for her to bear children. 'Now or later? Oh, my darling sweetheart, time is passing! By the time our child is eighteen months old I am sure to be bald, grey and toothless [...]' (10 September 1902).[32] Interestingly, Chekhov's last will and testament does not entertain the possibility of children, and Knipper's response of 14 September expresses surprise: 'You'd like to have a child? Then why were you against it before? Without a doubt, we'll have a child.'[33] When Chekhov became too unwell to travel, a new round of explanatory and reassuring letters proved necessary. In these letters Chekhov also deflected expectations from the MAT of a new play in time for the coming season: 'Nemirovich is demanding a play, but I'm not going to start writing it this year, although I've got a wonderful plot, by the way' (29 August 1902; see also 27 August).

In mid-September Chekhov wrote to Knipper that he was doing better and expected to come to Moscow soon, but he was profoundly saddened by news of the death of Zola, who had perished in his apartment of carbon monoxide poisoning. 'I didn't much like him as a writer, but as a person, however, these past few years, as the Dreyfus matter raged, I valued him very highly' (18 September 1902). A few days later, Dr Altshuller sounded his lungs – Chekhov had been avoiding it – and told him that he could travel to Moscow, but not before a hard frost. After a six-week stint in Moscow he returned to winter in Yalta (rather than Nervi).

Among Chekhov's 1902 accomplishments was penning a second, very successful press release soliciting funds for a sanatorium to house the tuberculars flocking to Yalta (*Letopis'*, pp. 726, 728). Chekhov had published a collectively signed appeal for support on behalf of the Yalta Philanthropic Society (Ialtiiskoe blagotvoritel'noee obshchestvo) back in 1899, helping to raise funds for a low-cost boarding house for the unwell that opened in August 1900. Now Chekhov was playing a central role in a successful bid to raise the funds needed to acquire land and construct the Society's own building for a sanatorium that might house forty to fifty people in need. Chekhov would be elected to the building committee in May 1903, and the resulting institution, named 'Yauzlar' (after a Crimean waterfall), was later renamed in memory of Chekhov (*S* XVIII, pp. 91–5, 301–2).

Looking forward, Chekhov proposed to Knipper summering in Switzerland (17 January 1903). Knipper agreed, but in the same breath asked: 'In the spring we'll be rehearsing *Cherry Orchard* – true?'[34] The MAT was applying considerable pressure. In retrospect, knowing how little time remained to Chekhov, and how poor his condition, the MAT's nagging seems remarkably unfeeling. How could they have not fathomed what loomed behind Chekhov's generally understated but frequent indications of physical discomforts and treatments (stomach problems, compresses, creosote, arsenic injections and so on)? Knipper tried to match Chekhov's complaints by lamenting her nervousness and self-loathing: 'I suddenly became ashamed that I call myself your wife. What sort of wife am I to you? You're alone, depressed, bored...'. Her expressions of guilt alternated with accounts of mad rounds of socializing and such delights as attending a concert of Jan Kubelik.[35]

True, Chekhov underplayed his condition, making it easy for others to imagine him in better shape than was the case. And Chekhov reassured Knipper: if she gave up the stage to stay with him, then he would be tormented by guilt.

I knew that I was marrying an actress, that is, when I married,
I realized clearly that you would be living in Moscow during
winters. I don't consider myself offended or abandoned by a
millionth: on the contrary, it seems to me that all goes well, or
as it must; and therefore: don't trouble me with your torments.
In March we'll start over again and again won't be feeling today's
loneliness. (20 January 1903)

For years he had tried to blame external circumstances for their lives apart:
'If we're not together now, then it's neither you nor I who is guilty for
that, but the demon who planted the bacillus in me and a love of art in
you' (27 September 1900). In fact, Chekhov's arrangement with Knipper
was just the sort envisioned in a letter to Suvorin eight years earlier: he
would marry, but 'everything must continue as it was before [...] give me
a wife who, like the moon, does not appear in my sky every day' (23 March
1895; *Letters*, pp. 272–3). Chekhov's health had been quite different then,
however; now he truly needed taking care of, which was not happening
at the White Dacha: providing a diet that his ruined guts could accom-
modate and keeping the house properly heated seemed beyond the staff
and Chekhov's mother. Chekhov had always been the one who saw to the
needs of others in the family, and nobody could quite face the reversal of
that situation, least of all Chekhov.

A bout of pleurisy and doctor's orders delayed Chekhov's return
to Moscow until the last week of April. There Dr Ostroumov, whose
clinic had treated Chekhov after his major haemorrhage six years earlier,
found that his right lung was shot, that he had emphysema and catarrh
of the intestines, 'and so on and so on'. So much for a summer abroad,
and wintering in Yalta was bad for him – he should stay in the Moscow
region. In the letter to his sister conveying the bad news, he told her that
they would have to sell the properties at Kuchuk-Koy and Gurzuf (24
May 1903). Masha urged him not to take a loss in a rushed sale or, for
that matter, a hasty purchase in the Moscow area: better to find a place
to rent for the coming winter, since even if he bought a place it would
not likely be habitable by this winter. She may have had her own interests in mind: would Chekhov pull out of Yalta altogether and sell the
White Dacha just when she was on the verge of becoming established
there as the director of a girls' school? But it was sound advice, given the
impulsivity with which Chekhov had been acquiring real estate and the
disastrous sale of Melikhovo. That this would turn out to be Chekhov's

last winter made her recommendation sage indeed. In any case, Chekhov had no thoughts of selling the White Dacha: he could still spend the dry autumn and spring seasons there.[36]

The day after Ostroumov's examination, Chekhov and Knipper left for two months at a dacha near Naro-Fominsk, southwest of Moscow. The fishing was good, and Chekhov visited old haunts from his first summer sojourns and early medical work in the Zvenigorod area while scouting properties to buy. *Cherry Orchard* was under way, but not without glitches: while Chekhov was out of the house some pages of his manuscript were blown out the window during a storm and ruined. When Chekhov revised he generally destroyed superseded drafts, so in such an instance there would be nothing written to fall back on. Much remains opaque about Chekhov's writing methods. Some have him thinking projects through in considerable detail before committing them to paper, but his close friend Potapenko asserted that Chekhov's creative work 'could not stand the eyes of another'; 'I don't know how he worked when he was alone. It seems that nobody knew that' (*Letopis'* IV.I, p. 88).

Before leaving Moscow, Chekhov had been invited to officially take over the fiction department of *Russian Thought*. He had already been helping there, especially with the manuscripts of novice writers. Now tightly connected with this venue, which published many of his finest post-Sakhalin stories, he was on '*ty*' terms – the familiar, second-person singular form of address – with its editors, Lavrov and Goltsev. Over the course of the summer they sent manuscripts and he rendered judgments, though he declined payment, at least until he could meet with them in person and be certain that he could do the job (6 October 1903; *Letopis'*, p. 765). Two months after the *Russian Thought* proposal he wrote to Sergei Diaghilev to turn down a similar invitation regarding his avant-garde St Petersburg journal *World of Art* (Mir iskusstva; 12 July 1903). Chekhov never fully assumed the position of *Russian Thought*'s fiction editor. He downplayed his role in a letter to his brother Alexander, who had enquired if he might publish with the journal: Chekhov had no real role or power at the journal, and his appointment was 'sort of honorary' (8 December 1903). But he did put much real work into it.

Why would Chekhov have entertained such positions at this stage of life? He had long been giving very sure-handed and authoritative advice to young authors who sent him their manuscripts, only some of whom were friends or acquaintances. Observers wondered at Chekhov's responsiveness to writers whose pieces would never merit publication;

after taking on the editorial role for *Russian Thought*, Chekhov still mentored beginners who approached him entirely without connection to the journal, and memoirists report him paying close attention to and writing comments on their manuscripts.[37] At some level, Chekhov must have liked editorial work and known he could do it well, and that it served the larger cultural scene. His venture with Marks also involved extensive editing of his own earlier works, so that in his last years Chekhov was actually working more as an editor than as a writer of drama and fiction. It is natural to lament Chekhov's declining productivity and to blame, in addition to ill health, the time lost to editing activities. But perhaps Chekhov was doing just what he wanted at this point in his life; or what he *could* do, at a time when creative work was torturous and slow. At the end of 1903, Chekhov was elected temporary chairman of the Society of Lovers of Russian Literature. He wrote to Alexei Veselovsky in Petersburg that he was greatly honoured but could not serve: his illness made running public meetings impossible, though maybe in a year or two he would be better. Meanwhile, perhaps he could help by providing editing services, proofreading, that sort of thing? (11 December 1903). To witness the leading Russian author of the day offer such grunt labour is stunning.

In July Chekhov and Knipper proceeded to Yalta, where Chekhov continued work on *Cherry Orchard*. Stanislavsky appeared to be in willful denial about Chekhov's condition, and in a letter to Knipper accused Dr Ostroumov of having made things up or erred with his diagnosis, ruining Chekhov's mood; 'and it's well known that his health depends on his inner tranquility.' He had gone too far, however, and begged Knipper not to think badly of him: 'We're grieving for Anton Pavlovich and those around him, and thinking about the play in entirely different minutes, when we're worrying about the fate of the theatre' (*Letopis'*, p. 759). The theatre was identified with Chekhov, and they needed both Chekhov and his play.

By the end of September, with Knipper back in Moscow, Chekhov was reporting the play finished, and he sent a fair copy to Moscow in mid-October. Nemirovich-Danchenko and Stanislavsky were elated: in stageability the play was greater than his previous ones, said Nemirovich-Danchenko, though the second act needed some cutting; Stanislavsky called it the best that Chekhov had written and famously asserted, *pace* Chekhov, that this was no comedy or farce, but a tragedy (*Letopis'*, pp. 768, 770). Much back and forth between Chekhov and the directors ensued regarding allocation of roles and stage decorations.

Chekhov followed the play to Moscow at the beginning of December, though his Yalta doctor asserted that Dr Ostroumov must have been drunk when he told Chekhov to winter in Moscow, as Chekhov wrote to Knipper (1 October 1903). But this was not inconsistent with medical thinking of the time, which often saw benefit in a change of environment. Chekhov's condition was deteriorating, so something different had to be done. Staying north fit the analogical therapeutic imagination that often governed ideas about what might harm or benefit consumptives: once a hard freeze had set in and the air grown dry, the Moscow winter would suit Chekhov's mucus-filled lungs. Or, Ostroumov may have seen the end approaching and thought Chekhov should spend his last months where he wished.[38] In Moscow, getting out and about proved difficult. Knipper and Maria had rented an upper-floor apartment in a building with no lift, and Chekhov climbed the stairs slowly, with frequent rests. Nevertheless, he attended rehearsals of the play almost daily and, more often than not, MAT performances in the evening.

On 17 January 1904, Chekhov's 44th birthday, *Cherry Orchard* premiered at the MAT. Continuing to avoid premieres of his plays, Chekhov had remained at home. Legend has it that he was unaware of the evening's planned celebration of his 25 years of literary activity (premature by a year, as Chekhov pointed out in a letter to F. D. Batiushkov [18 January 1904]). In honouring the playwright, Stanislavsky and Nemirovich-Danchenko had schemed also to guarantee the success of his play, about which they were unsure. After the second act Nemirovich-Danchenko sent Chekhov a note telling him that the play was going wonderfully, and though the audience had been informed that Chekhov was not in the theatre, the cast was asking if he might not visit during the intermission preceding Act Four. Nemirovich-Danchenko assured him that the audience, having learned of Chekhov's absence, would not again try summoning him to the stage. Once there, however, Chekhov found himself compelled to take the stage and remain standing at length, weak and coughing, to be celebrated. He was presented with such gifts as an antique laurel wreath, picked out by Stanislavsky and adorned with portraits of actors and students of the MAT. That theatre, Nemirovich-Danchenko declared in his speech, owed so much to Chekhov's 'talent', 'tender heart' and 'pure soul' that Chekhov should consider it his own (*Letopis'*, p. 788). Endless bombast arrived in telegrams from all over Russia. Chekhov, who had mocked such sententiousness all his writing life, could only submit to being its object. Later he rather gracelessly complained about the useless antique gifts, telling Stanislavsky that the valuable materials belonged in a museum; what he really needed, he said, was a mousetrap, and the best gifts he had received were fishing poles.[39]

During rehearsals, Chekhov had often clashed with Stanislavsky over his handling of the play. The MAT was a director's theatre, but this strength could translate into weakness if the director's vision for a particular work was lacking. Chekhov had been a lover of theatre since childhood and, however sketchy his stage directions, must have visualized very comprehensively how what he was writing might be embodied by actors on the stage. Losing control of that was always difficult for him. By now, however, a weakened and seething Chekhov regularly gave way.

Chief among Chekhov's many dissatisfactions was Stanislavsky's insistence on performing the play as tragedy. There were also casting disputes. As with *Three Sisters*, Chekhov wrote this play with specific actors and actresses in mind. It was particularly important to him that Stanislavsky play Lopakhin, the wealthy merchant (Stanislavsky's actual background), but Stanislavsky insisted on taking the wilted landowner, Gaev. Chekhov had originally conceived the role of Charlotte, the enchanting entertainer of German background, for Knipper, but she was assigned Ranevskaya. With this decision Chekhov ultimately agreed, especially as the significance of Charlotte, in many ways the play's most intriguing character, was further diminished when Stanislavsky cut her dialogue with Firs in the second act, again paining Chekhov. As if to make up for that, Stanislavsky stretched Act Four to forty minutes, when Chekhov claimed it should last about twelve.[40]

The slow tempo recast the emotional tenor of a play that Chekhov had conceived as vaudevillian. As the long writing process was finally concluding, Chekhov wrote to Stanislavsky's wife, the MAT actress Maria Lilina: 'What's emerged here is not a drama, but a comedy, and in places even a farce' (15 September 1903); to Knipper a few days later, he wrote, 'The last act will be gay, and indeed, the whole play will be gay and lightminded' (21 September 1903). Chekhov defined the play as a 'comedy' in its subtitle, but the MAT retarded its pace and amplified emotionality by way of staging it as a drama, which is also how they advertised the play, to Chekhov's great annoyance.

There is abundant documentation and study of Chekhov's differences with the MAT handling of *Cherry Orchard*.[41] The playwright never gets the last word, however, and in any case Chekhov's interpretive guidance regarding later plays was often enigmatic. Whatever sources one consults, interpreting *Cherry Orchard* remains a challenge, and the question of how its comic and tragic elements are modulated continues to be grist for literary-critical and theatrical mills. Just how can this play about a profligate gentry family that has gone far into arrears on a mortgage and loses its estate at a bank auction qualify as comedy? What sense might be made of Lopakhin's happy destruction of the orchard – 'Everybody come and watch Yermolai Lopakhin take an axe to the cherry orchard' – when he himself calls it 'the most beautiful place on earth!'? What is comic about the poignant ending, when the aged loyal former serf Firs, left behind in the locked house, lies down (most likely to die), worries whether his master was wearing a heavy coat and laments his own state: 'No strength left, nothing left, nothing... A real... numskull!...'? (*Plays*, pp. 238, 251). Calling *Cherry Orchard* 'a tragic play composed almost entirely of comic scenes' typifies attempts to make sense of the play's contradictions, for in spite of the author's indications, it is truly difficult to read this play as a comedy.[42]

To be sure, the play abounds in comic devices. First among them, perhaps, is self-repetition, as in Gaev's persistent imaginary billiard-shot calling. Localized chuckles are provoked by the miscommunication caused by Firs's deafness, Gaev's obtuseness, Lopakhin's mooing, the lackey Yasha's pretentions to cultural refinement, Epikhodov's mangled language, the circus-conjuring tricks of Charlotte, and such farcical moments as Vera's accidentally rapping Lopakhin on the head or the flustered Trofimov falling down the stairs after Ranevskaya takes his puritanism to task. As in Chekhov's early comic work, laughter is aroused, per Bergson, by the mechanical projected onto the human, which is to say, characters repeating themselves in words and behaviour. When Chekhov writes that 'the whole play will be gay and lightminded', he presumably has this dimension of it in mind.

There are other arguments for a comedic reading. On the one hand, the play deliberately eschews the resolving wedding of a bourgeois comedy; but on the other it does rely on that convention, leading the reader or viewer to expect a match between Lopakhin and Vera, which is only one of the play's many 'guns' – including the literal ones of Charlotte and Epikhodov – that fail to go off. As he was finishing the play, Chekhov wrote to Knipper, 'It seems to me that, however boring it may be, there's something new in my play. Not a single gunshot in the whole play, by the way' (25 September 1904). Its ending might also be called happy in a historical sense: the collapse of the estate means eradication of the material bases that had underlain serfdom and still supported terrible

social inequality. By far the dominant interpretation of the play continues to read it as representing the twilight of the gentry class in Russia,
which can be construed as a positive outcome. This socio-historical impli-
cation allows Lopakhin to celebrate both the beauty of the orchard and
its destruction. Losing the orchard should not trouble Anya, the eternal
student and revolutionary Trofimov tells her, because 'All Russia is our
orchard. [...] It's perfectly clear that to live in the present we've got to
expiate our past, make a clean break with it' (*Plays*, p. 225). A happy future
awaits, he tells her.

The cherry orchard's demise means different things for different characters. For Ranevskya, the orchard is above all a space for memory – thus
she hallucinates a vision of her mother among its blossoms – but these
memories are of loss. With the estate's sale, she has money in her pocket
(even if unscrupulously so: she is keeping the funds her aunt had sent
to help them buy the estate back at auction). She can follow her desires
and depart for France and the lover for whom she forsook home and
family in the first place, thus repeating herself. After the sale Gaev finds
a well-paying bank position in town and Epikhodov becomes estate manager for Lopakhin. Firs remains in the house where he served for many
decades, arguably a happy ending for this former house serf who has been
lamenting the end of serfdom for four decades, and probably better than
expiring in the hospital where he was to be sent. Anya and Trofimov
are free to embark on the life of their progressive dreams. Lopakhin has
redeemed his childhood and family history with a purchase that stands
to turn a tidy profit.

Varya and Charlotte are perhaps the play's grand losers. A match with
Lopakhin does not come off for Varya, though she ends up roughly where
she started, as a housekeeper for another gentry family. Homelessness
defines the artist-wanderer Charlotte: her situation at the play's end thoroughly reflects who she is.

Chekhov's hard-won social mobility was very much like Lopakhin's,
and he was sensitive to the socio-historical moment. Nevertheless, he
unlikely had the grand historical scheme foremost in mind when he
called the play a 'comedy' or 'vaudeville'. Rather, the dominant artistic
idea organizing not just the plot of the play but its whole texture, including its comic aspects, is that of repetition. It is indeed expressed at every
level of the play, including in otherwise peripheral and nonsensical verbal
details; as in Chekhov's early comic stories and plays, repetition is the
primary device of his humour.

Cherry Orchard is a play where, overwhelmingly, characters remain themselves. Situations do not change because characters are unable to; but when a situation does change, that too results from characters being unable to break established patterns. Lopakhin buffoonishly avoids the expected marriage proposal to Varya, just as he always has, and the marriage plot as a resolution of the play's overriding dramatic conflict comes to naught. Ranevskaya returns to her situation prior to the start of the play's action as an obsessed lover compelled to repeat. The estate is lost because neither Ranevskaya nor Gaev can envision the changes necessary to make it financially viable, per Lopakhin's proposal to subdivide land along the river for dachas for the new middle class. When Gaev tells Ranevskaya that he has the offer of a remunerative post at the bank, she answers, 'You? In a bank? Stay where you are...' (*Plays*, p. 219). Firs didn't want his freedom when the serfs were emancipated. Clumsy Epikhodov persists in amusing mutilation of both artefacts and language, with ridiculous verbal efforts to assuage a disappointed lover's damaged vanity. Trofimov the eternal student repeats revolutionary slogans and with them draws Anya into a life that purports to embrace change, though an emptiness lies behind those words. And Trofimov professes to be 'beyond such trivialities' as carnal love, which Ranevskaya finds preposterous (*Plays*, p. 231).

Repetition also plays out at the level of ostensibly insignificant detail, especially as regards numbers, where the numbers two and twenty-two predominate. Epikhodov is nicknamed 'Twenty-two disasters' (*Plays*, pp. 197, 215, 234, 236, 243). The estate is slated to be sold at auction on 22 August. Act One opens at 'nearly two' in the morning (*Plays*, p. 195). Ranevskaya has two rooms in the house, 'the white room and the purple room' (*Plays*, p. 197). Gaev's imaginary billiard shots are almost all doublets: 'double in the middle' (*Plays*, p. 201), 'double bank into the middle' (*Plays*, pp. 211, 222), 'double into the corner' (*Plays*, p. 218), 'Double off the yellow into the middle' (*Plays*, p. 249). The cherry orchard yields every second year, and Firs answers Ranevskaya's remark that she is 'so glad you're still alive' with a disjunctive, 'The day before yesterday' – that is, two days ago (*Plays*, p. 202). The list could be expanded, but what does it mean? Repetition: two is the basic number signifying repetition; the number twenty-two is a numerical icon of repetition repeated.

Repetition is implicated in clearly non-comic aspects of the play as well, most notably in the twice-occurring breaking string, on whose note *Cherry Orchard* ends. An utterly realistic detail, the sound was actually heard by Chekhov once in the steppe. He features the sound of a bucket breaking loose in a mine shaft in the 1887 story 'Happiness', and in 'Tumbleweed' (from the same year) the converted Jew who tells his life story to the narrator relates his horrifying experience of a cable break while being lowered into a mine shaft. In *Cherry Orchard* the explanation for the sound and its resonance are in keeping with the play's fictional world: Lopakhin suggests that 'a bucket must have snapped loose somewhere off in the mines. But a long way off' (*Plays*, p. 223); this mining activity becomes the deus ex machina that restores the neighbour Pishchik's finances in Act Four.

Still, many symbolic readings of this sound and its repetition at the play's very end have been put forward. Valency's fine book on Chekhov takes the breaking string for its title and controlling metaphor in summarizing Chekhov's distinctive achievements: Chekhov represented a 'world in transition', when 'snapped' the 'golden string that connected man with his father on earth and his father in heaven, the age-old bond that tied the present to the past'.[43] The image of invisible subterranean action evoked by a mining accident – a space where much is happening beyond the direct apprehension of the play's characters and its viewers – also stands nicely for Chekhov's indirect mode of presentation. It opens up a space for the undercurrents of meaning that have long been appreciated in Chekhov, for a symbolic dimension to his work. To the characters onstage the uncanny sound augurs nothing good. 'There was something disagreeable about it,' Ranevskaya shudders (*Plays*, p. 223). Their reaction of dread, and the thud of the axe against a cherry tree that follows when it is repeated at the end of Act Four, put one in mind of Atropos cutting off the string of a man's life. This interpretation accentuates the tragedy of life ending on this estate, and also the imminent end of Chekhov's own life.

But above all that sound relates to the commanding constructive principle and theme of repetition. As a sound effect in the play – one that a thorough analysis would want to consider in the context of the play's many other sound effects – the breaking string occurs twice: first in Act Two, where it breaks up the evening outdoors stroll of the main characters, and then again at the highly marked position of the play's ending. The sound thereby becomes a figure for repetition. What is more, if we follow Freud's understanding of the uncanny, which always already involves a repetition (of repressed, unconscious ideas or visions), then the characters' response to the sound's first occurrence may also evoke repetition.

When the twang resounds at the end of the play its connection with repetition becomes overt. And the sound's second occurrence has no witnesses other than the play's audience. There are no reactions onstage to provide cues regarding its significance; what it means is the effect it has not on characters, but on the play's viewers. And what is that effect? First and foremost, to cause the viewer to remember the prior snapping of the string, to provoke the process of memory in the viewer on the field of the play's fictional world. Chekhov thereby not only foregrounds the theme of repetition in his play, he compels the play's viewer to experience it, and this happens at the very end, when the play is over, when the loss of the cherry orchard (the axe thud) is replicated in the viewer's world by the 'loss' of the play, now ended. In this way Chekhov enacts in the play's viewers a touch of nostalgia, the same sense that one has lost something irretrievable that pervades the world of the play's characters (especially Ranevskaya). In its attempt to reach out and touch the playgoer, in its shifting of the emotions from stage to viewer, the ending of *Cherry Orchard* has its predecessor in the freeze-scene ending of Gogol's *Government Inspector* (Revizor, 1836).

In mid-February 1904 Chekhov left for Yalta. The day before departing, he visited the southern Moscow suburb of Tsaritsyno to see a winter dacha for sale, as he and Knipper now envisioned both summering and wintering near Moscow. Knipper, in Petersburg with the MAT, urged Chekhov to make an offer, and when he was unenthusiastic blamed Maria, who she supposed had dissuaded him from the purchase. Chekhov deflected the hostility, responding that he had not discussed the matter with Masha, and that Knipper should decide about this dacha as he was no good in such matters.[44] After that Knipper more or less dropped the idea of buying and proposed a rental instead. From Yalta Chekhov complained of shortness of breath and digestive distress. He continued to evaluate manuscripts for *Russian Thought*, and he had a visit from his brother Alexander, who came with his family and, Chekhov reported to Knipper, was sober and good company (8 March 1904). In attending to reviews of *Cherry Orchard* in various theatres around the country, what he read left him less than entirely happy with Stanislavsky's acting or dilatory directing.[45]

Chekhov also followed the outbreak of hostilities between Japan and Russia at Port Arthur (now Lüshunkou, China). In April he wrote to his old comrade from the days of *Alarm Clock*, Alexander Amfiteatrov, 'If I'm healthy, then in July or August I'll go to the Far East not as a correspondent, but as a physician. I think that a doctor will see more than a correspondent' (13 April 1904). Did Chekhov actually anticipate such dramatic improvement of his condition? Back in February, too, he had written to Veselovsky that he would be able to take up his duties as chair of the Society of Lovers of Russian Literature the following year, as he expected to winter in Moscow (2 February 1904).

On 1 May Chekhov left Yalta for Moscow. He arrived so ill that he could not leave the apartment or, most days, even his bed. Sleeplessness and pains in his extremities complemented a cold, pleurisy and digestive distress. His new physician, Dr Taube, ordered him to the Black Forest resort town of Badenweiler for his 'emphysema', and 1 June became the target for departure. Meanwhile, Chekhov asked Goltsev to send manuscripts to him for evaluation, since he did not expect to make it to the office of *Russian Thought* (10 May 1904). He seemed happy to have visitors, but before he could leave there was one last, highly embarrassing problem with his publisher Marks. Chekhov had promised Gorky that the Znanie press could publish *Cherry Orchard*, and Znanie had already paid Chekhov handsomely (4,500 rubles), in essence financing his trip abroad. Because the contract with Marks allowed Chekhov to publish new works elsewhere only in journals or in volumes with a philanthropic purpose, Znanie also undertook to donate a significant portion of the proceeds from this publication to charity. But Chekhov made the mistake of providing Marks with his text before the Znanie publication could come out, and Marks, violating Chekhov's wishes, rushed the play into print in a self-standing volume not part of the collected works, thus undercutting Znanie. Among Chekhov's last letters from Badenweiler is an apology to Konstantin Piatnitsky of Znanie, promising to repay the funds he had received for the rights to publish the play; they could settle the matter privately, he says, but he would prefer that Znanie sue him for restitution, which 'won't change our fine relations', so that he, Chekhov, might in turn bring a legal case against Marks, by whom he admits to having been 'rather pettily and stupidly deceived' (19 June 1904). Now in his last weeks of life, Chekhov also arranged for another shipment of books to Taganrog.

Chekhov was not well enough to dress and leave his apartment until the end of May. On 3 June he and Knipper departed for Germany. The day before, the author Nikolay Teleshov had visited and was shocked by Chekhov's condition; Chekhov told him that he was leaving 'to die', using a harsh euphemism (*Letopis'*, p. 809). Nevertheless, Chekhov put on a brave and positive face about this journey and its therapeutic prospects. He and Knipper stopped in Berlin for a useless consultation with a gastric specialist referred by Taube; there they were kindly attended by the Berlin correspondent of *Russian Gazette*, Grigory Yollis, whose employer Sobolevsky had asked to help. Afterwards Yollis reported to Sobolevsky that 'Chekhov's days were numbered', that he 'had thinned horribly, coughed and struggled for breath with the slightest movement, and his temperature was always high' (*Letopis'*, p. 811).

As much as Chekhov loved travel, this voyage can only have hastened his death. Under the strain of barely functioning lungs, his heart was now failing as well. At first he felt better in Badenweiler and thought of proceeding to Italy and returning to Yalta via Constantinople. But within a few days of settling into the upmarket Römerbaden hotel, the couple was asked to leave: other guests were disturbed by Chekhov's coughing and did not care to lodge so close to a dying man. After about ten days in the smaller and less comfortable Villa Frederika, they moved again, this time to the Hotel Sommer. Chekhov had been writing upbeat letters about the improvement in his health; already in Berlin he praised the food, and especially the bread, saying that he hadn't 'eaten so well and with such an appetite in a long time. [...] And so you can tell Mother and anyone else who's interested that I'm on my way to recovery or even that I've already recovered' (6 June 1904; *Letters*, p. 472). In his last letter to Maria, however, he admits that he cannot eat or even move about: 'Apparently my stomach is ruined beyond hope. About the only remedy for it is to fast, in other words, to refrain entirely from eating, and that's that. And the only medicine for being short-winded is to keep perfectly still.' Having complained in previous letters about Germany's order, tranquillity and lack of talent (16, 21 June), he concluded this one with the remark, 'There's not a single well-dressed German woman; their lack of taste is depressing' (28 June 1904; *Letters*, p. 474).

Once settled in Badenweiler, Knipper warned Maria to expect the worst, but to say nothing to Chekhov or his mother: 'I beg you, Masha, don't lose control, don't cry, there is nothing dangerous, but it is very grave. Both of us knew we could hardly expect complete recovery.' She promised to bring Chekhov home as soon as he had gained a bit of strength, adding: 'If Taube had hinted that something could happen to his heart, or that the process was not stopping, I'd never have decided to go abroad.'[46] On the one hand, Chekhov continued to plan ahead, making arrangements to return to Russia by sea and having a new suit made for the hot weather by sending Knipper to a tailor in Freiburg with a recently acquired suit as model. On the other, when arranging for funds to be sent for the voyage home, Chekhov told Knipper to have them sent not in his name but hers, 'just in case' (*Letopis'*, p. 475).

In the early hours of 2 July 1904 – it was 15 July by Western calendars – Chekhov awoke gasping for breath. One of a helpful pair of Russian students lodging in the hotel went for the doctor. In the meantime, Knipper applied ice to Chekhov's heart, at which Chekhov, who had not been fully conscious, smiled: 'You don't put ice on an empty heart' (*Letopis'*, p. 817). Was the remark literal, reflecting Chekhov's understanding of the physiological process under way in him? Or should it be read as metaphorical and pertaining to Chekhov's emotional state? This image of an inner void has echoes elsewhere in the late Chekhov's self-characterizations and in his art; most strikingly, perhaps, with the empty bookcase Gaev eulogizes in *Cherry Orchard* and the vacated house that ends the play.[47]

Shortly before his death, Chekhov had thought up a humorous, Chekhonte-style plot that, in retrospect, invites reading as a farce on his own soon-to-be absence. Feeling a bit better, he had insisted that Knipper leave for a walk; when she returned hungry, they found they had missed the gong summoning guests to supper. This led to imagining a resort hotel, filled with wealthy, red-cheeked Europeans and Americans spending the day in all manner of outdoor and spa activities, who bring robust

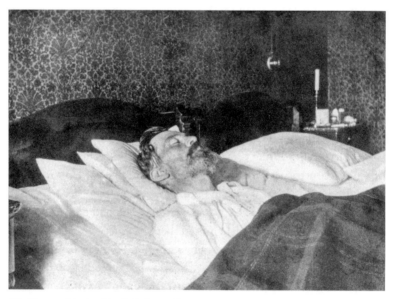

Chekhov on his deathbed, Badenweiler, 1904.

appetites to the dining room only to learn that the chef has run away: there will be no supper, a brutal insult to their bellies (*Letopis'*, p. 816). Chekhov's tale gave Knipper the last laugh of their life together, but the image of a void located where the desires of all others are pointed grows sobering in view of Chekhov's death a few hours later. The scenario recalls Chekhov's practical joke of organizing a wedding banquet at which the bride and groom did not appear.

Chekhov's last words, and certain details of his posthumous journey back to Moscow, have become legendary. Dr Schwörer arrived at around 2 a.m., injected camphor to stimulate the heart, and ordered oxygen and the customary champagne for a dying colleague.[48] Chekhov announced his own prognosis, 'Ich sterbe' (I'm dying), addressing the resort physician in the latter's own language and affirming his own keen medical eye with nearly his last breath. He took the goblet, said to Knipper (in Russian), 'I haven't drunk champagne for a long time', then lay on his left side and died.

It took a week to convey Chekhov's corpse to Moscow, via St Petersburg, for burial in the Novodevichy Monastery cemetery, site also of his father's grave. That story involves ironic disjunctions and miscommunications of a sort that none can resist calling Chekhovian.[49] Yollis of the *Russian Gazette* came from Berlin immediately to help: it was no trivial matter to arrange for a wagon carrying the coffin to be attached to a passenger train in which Knipper could travel, and to get them to and across the Russian frontier. News of Chekhov's demise spread rapidly in Germany and, after a short delay, in Russia, but information about his transport was sketchy and hundreds of mourners wishing to pay respects gathered at the wrong train station in Berlin. Small crowds brought flowers and wreaths to German and Polish stations as the train passed. At the frontier, in Verzhbolovo (Virbalis in Lithuanian), the coffin and flowers and wreaths were transferred to a different wagon, since Russia's railway gauge was wider than Europe's; this is where Chekhov's corpse was famously placed in a refrigerated wagon labelled 'For Oysters', probably made available due to a typhoid-caused collapse of the market for fresh oysters. In St Petersburg the time of Chekhov's arrival was not known in time to organize a fitting reception, and Knipper was surprised to be met at the station only by a few journalists unknown to her. As word got out, though, others came, wreaths were sent (including by Marks) and prayers for the dead were held. Suvorin and other notables paid respects and then many (including Kuprin, Tikhonov, Vasily Rozanov and Diaghilev)

Chekhov's funeral procession, Moscow, 1904.

proceeded to Moscow by fast train for the funeral, while Chekhov's body
travelled on a different track.

In Moscow there was further confusion: the fast train was also carrying a number of high government officials and the body of a general staff
officer who had died in France. The detachment sent to greet that body,
including a military band, met Chekhov's wagon by mistake. But also
present were at least 3,000 mourners for Chekhov, who blocked transfer
of his coffin to the hearse, instead carrying it by hand across Moscow
from the Nikolaevsky Station to Novodevichy Cemetery. Gorky and
Chaliapin had turns at shouldering Chekhov's remains, and Knipper,
Nemirovich-Danchenko and Goltsev followed right behind. Among
stops were the entrance to the MAT building, where wreaths were presented while Chopin sounded from within; the building that housed
Russian Thought; and finally, the statue of the great surgeon Nikolai
Pirogov, which stood across from the clinic where Chekhov had recovered
from his haemorrhage. Maria, Mikhail and Ivan brought their mother,
who had been told about Chekhov's death at the last possible moment;
they had to guess where they might intersect with the procession and
made their way through the crowd with difficulty.

In the days leading up to the funeral, *Russian Thought* announced
it would pay funeral expenses in Moscow; Suvorin had wished to do

the same. Goltsev picked out a gravesite next to that of the liberal, Dostoevsky-era poet Pleshcheyev, who had been so helpful to Chekhov in his transition from 'small-press' workman to major literary figure. As he was leaving the cemetery, however, he ran into Chekhov's brother Alexander and old friend and fellow writer Vladimir Giliarovsky, who had come to arrange for burial next to Chekhov's real father (rather than a literary one), per Chekhov's wishes; plans were revised. Telegrams were crossing every which way and information was belated: Alexander was on his way to meet the coffin in St Petersburg when it was already travelling from there to Moscow and so missed his brother's funeral.

It was a funeral without speeches, which been forbidden by the police. After the service had ended, however, small groups came and went and offered all manner of proclamations. There were two requiem services at the monastery the next day, and the actors of the MAT organized the traditional fortieth-day requiem service. Many of Chekhov's friends and associates were away for summer holidays and could attend only 'in thought', as Stanislavsky's message to Knipper put it. Tolstoy telegraphed, 'I am sincerely grieved by the death of kind Anton Pavlovich Chekhov and by the irreplaceable loss to Russian literature.' To a correspondent of the newspaper *Rus'* he praised Chekhov's universality – a feature hitherto most famously applied to Pushkin in Dostoevsky's famous celebratory speech of 1880 – and said that Chekhov was an 'incomparable artist', that though his 'unusual language' might seem 'awkward' at first, it captivates and reveals unusual and otherwise inaccessible images. Chekhov 'created new forms, and, discarding any false modesty, I assert that in technique he, Chekhov, is far superior to me', and that, 'like Dickens and Pushkin and a few like them, he can be reread many times' with profit.[50]

Fine last words.

REFERENCES

Introduction

1 As Vasily Grossman has a fictional character assert in *Life and Fate* [*Zhizn'i sud'ba*], trans. Robert Chandler (New York, 1987), p. 282.

2 For example Walter Horace Bruford, *Chekhov and His Russia: A Sociological Study* (New York, 1947); Kirin Narayan, *Alive in the Writing: Crafting Ethnography in the Company of Chekhov* (Chicago, IL, 2012).

3 A perspective announced in Savely Senderovich and Munir Sendich, eds, *Anton Chekhov Rediscovered: A Collection of New Studies with a Comprehensive Bibliography* (East Lansing, MI, 1987); see the programmatic foreword by Senderovich, 'Towards Chekhov's Deeper Reaches', pp. 1–8. A recent study that offers a systematic and penetrating approach to Chekhov's poetic features is Radislav Lapushin, *'Dew on the Grass': The Poetics of Inbetweenness in Chekhov* (New York, 2010).

4 Vladimir Nemirovitch-Dantchenko, *My Life in the Russian Theatre*, trans. John Cournos [1936] (New York, 1968), pp. 154, 188.

5 Vsevolod Meyerhold, 'Naturalistic Theater and Theater of Mood', trans. Joyce C. Vining, in *Chekhov: A Collection of Critical Essays*, ed. Robert Louis Jackson (Englewood Cliffs, NJ, 1967), p. 67.

6 Vladimir Nabokov, *Lectures on Russian Literature* (New York, 1981), p. 251.

7 See for instance Anton Chekhov, Maria Fornes et al., *Orchards: Seven Stories by Anton Chekhov and Seven Plays They Have Inspired* (New York, 1986).

8 See Carol Apollonio's remarks in 'Forum on Translation', in *Chekhov the Immigrant: Translating a Cultural Icon*, ed. Michael C. Finke and Julie De Sherbinin (Bloomington, IN, 2007), p. 30; Donald Rayfield, *Anton Chekhov: A Life* (Evanston, IL, 2000), p. 513; I. A. Bunin, 'Chekhov', trans. Cynthia Carlile, in *Anton Chekhov and His Times*, ed. Andrei Turkov (Fayetteville, AR, 1995), pp. 172–3.

9 Cited in 'Forum on Translation', *Chekhov the Immigrant*, p. 34, and vigorously disputed by the forum's participants.

10 For examples, see Janet Malcolm, *Reading Chekhov: A Critical Journey* (New York, 2002); Rosamund Bartlett, *Chekhov: Scenes from a Life*

(London, 2004). There are also Chekhov museums in Alexandrovsk-Sakhalinsky and Yuzhno-Sakhalinsk (both on Sakhalin); at the former Lintvarev estate in Sumy, Ukraine; and in Badenweiler, Germany, where Chekhov died. See V. B. Kataev, 'Muzei' ('Museums'), in *A. P. Chekhov: entsiklopediia* [A. P. Chekhov: Encyclopaedia], ed. V. B. Kataev (Moscow, 2011), pp. 662–74.

11 Emphasis added. Cited from Genadii Shaliugin, 'Chekhov v krugu kolleg' [Chekhov Among His Colleagues], *Brega Tavridy* [The Tauric Shore], 5–6 (1999), p. 276.

12 Grossman, *Life and Fate*, p. 283.

13 Ernest Simmons, *Chekhov: A Biography* (Chicago, IL, 1970), p. 107.

14 Ibid., p. 304; Mikhail Gromov, *Chekhov* (Moscow, 1993), p. 156. See also Evgenii B. Meve, *Meditsina v tvorchestve i zhizni A. P. Chekhova* [Medicine in the Art and Life of A. P. Chekhov] (Kiev, 1961), p. 132.

15 For examples of physician-authored studies of Chekhov, see Robert Coles, 'The Wry Dr Chekhov', in *Times of Surrender: Selected Essays* (Iowa City, IA, 1988), pp. 49–56; William Ober, 'Chekhov among the Doctors: The Doctor's Dilemma', in *Boswell's Clap and Other Essays: Medical Analyses of Literary Men's Afflictions* (Carbondale, IL, 1971), pp. 193–205; Meve, *Meditsina*; John Coope, *Doctor Chekhov: A Study in Literature and Medicine* (Chale, Isle of Wight, 1997). A collection of Chekhov's stories oriented towards courses in the medical humanities is Jack Coulehan, ed., *Chekhov's Doctors: A Collection of Chekhov's Medical Tales* (Kent, OH, 2003). See also the entries for Chekhov in the Literature Arts Medicine Database (LITMED), New York University, http://medhum.med.nyu.edu.

16 See the discussion in Michael Finke, *Seeing Chekhov: Life and Art* (Ithaca, NY, 2005), p. 3.

17 For an overview of Chekhov's literary production that includes model attempts at categorizing and periodizing his work, see 'The Shape of Chekhov's Work', appendix to Ronald Hingley, *A Life of Anton Chekhov* (Oxford, 1989), pp. 320–29.

1 Family Background and Early Years

1 Savely Senderovich, 'Anton Chekhov and St George the Dragonslayer (An Introduction to the Theme)', in *Anton Chekhov Rediscovered: A Collection of New Studies with a Comprehensive Bibliography*, ed. Savely Senderovich and Munir Sendich (East Lansing, MI, 1987), pp. 167–87.

2 A. P. Chudakov, 'Chekhov v Taganroge' [Chekhov in Taganrog], in *Chetyrezhdyi Chekhov* [Chekhov Times Four], ed. Igor' Klekh (Moscow, 2004), pp. 18, 21.

3 Ibid., p. 32.

4 Donald Rayfield, *Anton Chekhov: A Life* (Evanston, IL, 2000), p. 52.

5 V. B. Kataev, ed., *A. P. Chekhov: entsiklopediia* [A. P. Chekhov: Encyclopaedia] (Moscow, 2011), p. 10. Chekhov's brother Mikhail cites this remark and also the influence of their uncle Mitrofan's

literary talents, as well the superb storytelling of their mother and
maternal grandmother; see Mikhail Chekhov, *Anton Chekhov:
A Brother's Memoir*, trans. Eugene Alper (New York, 2010), pp. 23, 2,
11; originally published as *Vokrug Chekhova: vstrechi i vpechatleniia*
[Around Chekhov: Encounters and Impressions] (Moscow, 1933).

6 The positive impact of Chekhov's *gymnasium*, which treated all students
respectfully and where few classmates suffered maltreatment at home, is
cited in Rayfield, *Anton Chekhov*, esp. pp. 15–20.

7 One rich source of information is the painstakingly researched and
beautifully illustrated A. P. Kuzicheva, *Chekhovy: Biografiia sem'i*
[The Chekhovs: A Biography of the Family] (Moscow, 2004).

8 As pointed out in Chudakov, 'Chekhov v Taganroge', p. 34.

9 Cited from Simmons, *Chekhov*, p. 6. Eventually Mikhail revised his
view and used that same formula about his own childhood. In fact, both
were repeating a phrase of their father's: 'I had no childhood in my own
childhood' (Rayfield, *Anton Chekhov*, p. 21).

10 Kuzicheva, *Chekhovy*, pp. 105, 110.

2 From Novice to Fame

1 In Anton Chekhov, *Twelve Plays*, trans. Ronald Hingley (Oxford,
1992), pp. 215–366.

2 The editors of the academy edition of Chekhov's works see these plays
as one and the same (*S* XI, pp. 394, 396–8), as does Chekhov authority
V. B. Kataev, 'Tvorcheskii put' A. P. Chekhova' [The Creative Path
of A. P. Chekhov], in *A. P. Chekhov: entsiklopediia* [A. P. Chekhov:
Encyclopedia], ed. V. B. Kataev (Moscow, 2011), p. 36. Donald Rayfield
argues that *Platonov* was written after Chekhov came to Moscow,
in the otherwise fallow spring of 1881; see his *Anton Chekhov: A Life*
(Evanston, IL, 2000), pp. 59, 80, 606 n. 44.

3 See Peter Brooks, *The Melodramatic Imagination: Balzac, Henry James,
Melodrama, and the Mode of Excess* (New Haven, CT, 1995).

4 Chekhov, *Twelve Plays*, p. 364.

5 Ibid., p. 301.

6 See the discussion in Michael C. Finke, *Seeing Chekhov: Life and Art*
(Ithaca, NY, 2005), pp. 139–71.

7 M. Smolkin, 'Shekspir v zhizni i tvorchestve Chekhova' [Shakespeare
in the Life and Works of Chekhov], in *Shekspirovskii sbornik*
[A Shakespeare Collection], ed. A. Anikst (Moscow, 1967), p. 80.
See also Eleanor Rowe, *Hamlet: A Window on Russia* (New York,
1976), pp. 107–13.

8 On *Seagull* see James M. Curtis, 'Ephebes and Precursors in Chekhov's
The Seagull', *Slavic Review*, XLIV/3 (Autumn 1985), pp. 415–37. For the
example of Chekhov's 'At Sea', see Finke, *Seeing Chekhov*, pp. 38–50.

9 See Julie W. De Sherbinin, *Chekhov and Russian Religious Culture:
The Poetics of the Marian Paradigm* (Evanston, IL, 1997).

10 'Forum on Translation', in *Chekhov the Immigrant: Translating
a Cultural Icon*, ed. Michael C. Finke and Julie De Sherbinin
(Bloomington, IN, 2007), p. 46.

11 Commentary in *S* 1, p. 557.

12 'Elements Most Often Found in Novels, Short Stories, Etc.', trans. Peter Constantine, in *Anton Chekhov's Selected Stories: Texts of the Stories, Comparison of Translations, Life and Letters, Criticism*, ed. Cathy Popkin (New York, 2014), pp. 3, 4.

13 See the discussion in Finke, *Seeing Chekhov*, p. 31.

14 Ieronim Iasinskii, *Roman moei zhizni. Kniga vospominanii* [The Novel of My Life: A Book of Memoirs] (Moscow, 1926), p. 265.

15 For a fuller discussion of the pseudonym issue, see Finke, *Seeing Chekhov*, esp. pp. 31–8.

16 For all Chekhov's Moscow residences, see D. M. Evseev, 'Moskovskie adresa Chekhova' [The Moscow Addresses of Chekhov], in *A. P. Chekhov. Entsiklopediia*, ed. Kataev, pp. 337–44.

17 See for example Chekhov's letter of 20 February 1883.

18 Chekhov placed this piece in *Nature and Hunting* (*Priroda i okhota*), a journal that did not typically publish fiction and offered no payment. Chekhov enjoyed a free subscription, however, and he eschewed pseudonyms in publishing there.

19 See 'The Shape of Chekhov's Work', appendix to Ronald Hingley, *A Life of Anton Chekhov* (Oxford, 1989), pp. 320–29, esp. p. 322.

20 On the significance of Chekhov's signing 'At Sea' and other works with his proper name, see Finke, *Seeing Chekhov*, esp. pp. 18–50; and Marena Senderovich, 'Chekhov's Name Drama', in *Reading Chekhov's Text*, ed. R. L. Jackson (Evanston, IL, 1993), pp. 31–48.

21 In Simon's 1973 *The Good Doctor*, as adapted for the PBS television anthology series *Great Performances* in 1978, 'The Sneeze' features Ed Asner and Richard Chamberlain. Set in Russia, it nevertheless reflects values and sensibilities of the 1970s United States, and the sneeze occurs during a performance of Chekhov's *Cherry Orchard*.

22 Henri Bergson, 'Laughter', in *Comedy: 'An Essay on Comedy' by George Meredith / 'Laughter' by Henri Bergson*, ed. Wylie Sypher (Garden City, NY, 1956), p. 79.

23 See Vsevolod Meyerhold, 'Naturalistic Theater and Theater of Mood', trans. Joyce C. Vining, in *Chekhov: A Collection of Critical Essays*, ed. Robert Louis Jackson (Englewood Cliffs, NJ, 1967), pp. 62–8.

24 As argued in Finke, *Seeing Chekhov*.

25 On this episode as something of a self-propagated myth, see L. E. Bushkanets, 'Mify o Chekhove, sprovotsirovannye im samim' [Myths about Chekhov, Instigated by He Himself], in *Problemy pisatel'skoi biografii: k 150-letiiu A. P. Chekhova* [Problems of the Author's Biography: For the 150th Anniversary of A. P. Chekhov], ed. I. E. Gitovich (Moscow, 2013), pp. 94–114.

26 Mikhail Chekhov, *Anton Chekhov: A Brother's Memoir*, trans. Eugene Alper (New York, 2010), p. 98. The original Russian title was *Around Chekhov* (*Vokrug Chekhova*).

27 See Finke, *Seeing Chekhov*, pp. 86–98.

28 A complete list of sources can be found in *S* XVI, pp. 538–45.

29 Decades later, during the Nazi occupation of Paris, Efros, who had emigrated from Russia after the Revolution, was taken from an old-age

home and shipped to the concentration camp at Treblinka, where she perished; see *Letters*, p. 48, and Elena Tolstaia, *Poetika razdrazheniia: Chekhov v kontse 1880-kh – nachalo 1890-kh godov* [A Poetics of Irritation: Chekhov at the End of the 1880s – Beginning of the 1890s] (Moscow, 1994), pp. 54–5.

30 See Donald Rayfield, 'What Did Jews Mean to Chekhov?', *European Judaism*, VIII (Winter 1974), pp. 30–36, as well as his treatment of the topic over the course of *Anton Chekhov*. See also Gabriella Safran, *Rewriting the Jew: Assimilation Narratives in the Russian Empire* (Stanford, CA, 2000), pp. 147–89.

31 See the discussion in Tolstaia, *Poetika razdrazheniia*, pp. 50–51, and her discussion of the biographical context involving Efros, pp. 15–55; in English, see Helena Tolstoy, 'From Susanna to Sarra: Chekhov in 1886–1887', *Slavic Review*, L/3 (Autumn 1991), pp. 590–600. For a reading of the story's Judaeophobic and gynophobic implications nuanced through attention to its biblical allusions, see Savely Senderovich, 'O chekhovskoi glubine, ili iudofobskii rasskaz Chekhova v svete iudaisticheskoi ekzegezy' [On Chekhov's Depths; or, Chekhov's Judeophobic Story in the Light of Judaistic Exegesis], in *Avtor i tekst: sbornik statei* [Author and Text: A Collection of Articles], ed. V. M. Markovich and Vol'f Shmid (St Petersburg, 1996), pp. 306–40; see also Safran, *Rewriting the Jew*, pp. 160–67.

32 Rayfield, *Anton Chekhov*, p. 157.

33 Retitled 'The Wolf' (*'Volk'*) in Chekhov's collected works.

34 E. M. Gushanskaia and I. S. Kuz'michev, eds, *Aleksandr i Anton Chekhovy. Vospominaniia, perepiska* [Alexander and Anton Chekhov: Memoirs, Correspondence] (Moscow, 2012), p. 410.

35 See 'Petr G. Kravtsov', https://en.wikipedia.org, accessed 11 August 2021.

36 The play was actually staged nine days earlier in Saratov, causing Chekhov to rush to join the Society of Dramatic Writers – he had lacked the needed fifteen rubles, but stood to lose any royalties from provincial performances of the play if he was not a member of the professional organization (*Letopis'* I, p. 348).

37 Anton Chekhov, *Anton Chekhov's Selected Plays*, trans. and ed. Laurence Senelick (New York, 2005), p. 50.

38 Ibid., p. 71, with modification to the translation. The harsh original here was 'Zamolchi, zhidovka!', with the latter word's ending indicating a female referent.

39 Cited in Chekhov, *Selected Plays*, p. 380.

40 Ibid., p. 65.

41 *New York Times*, 1 May 1966, cited in *Letters*, p. 70.

42 Chekhov, *Selected Plays*, p. 32.

43 Tolstaia, *Poetika razdrazheniia*, p. 49.

44 See Chekhov's letters to Suvorin of 30 December 1888 and 7 January 1889.

45 For a fascinating treatment of this story, see Marena Senderovich, 'Chekhov's "Kashtanka": Metamorphoses of Memory in the Labyrinth of Time (A Structural-phenomenological Essay)', in *Anton Chekhov*

Rediscovered: A Collection of New Studies with a Comprehensive Bibliography, ed. Savely Senderovich and Munir Sendich (East Lansing, MI, 1987), pp. 63–75.

46 M. Chekhov, *Anton Chekhov*, pp. 105–6.

47 For examples of the journey metaphor and the food/intellect association in Spencer, see Herbert Spencer, *Education: Intellectual, Moral, and Physical* (New York, 1914), pp. 118–19, 108, respectively. On the story as depicting a rite of initiation, see Giuseppe Ghini, 'La *Steppa* di Čechov come viaggio iniziatico. Una lettura *mitologica*', *Russica Romana*, VIII (2001), pp. 121–34.

48 See for instance David Maxwell, 'A System of Symbolic Gesture in Čexov's "Step'", *Slavic and East European Journal*, XVII/3 (Summer 1973), pp. 146–54.

49 See Robert Louis Jackson, 'Space and the Journey: A Metaphor for All Times', *Russian Literature*, XXIX (1991), pp. 427–38.

50 See Nils Åke Nilsson, *Studies in Čechov's Narrative Technique: 'The Steppe' and 'The Bishop'* (Stockholm, 1968).

51 For a number of connections with the visit to see his grandfather at the age of eleven, see Rayfield, *Anton Chekhov*, p. 25.

52 M. Chekhov, *Anton Chekhov*, p. 30. See also Rayfield, *Anton Chekhov*, pp. 33–4.

53 See Michael C. Finke, 'Chekhov's "The Steppe": A Metapoetic Journey', in his *Metapoesis: The Russian Tradition from Pushkin to Chekhov* (Durham, NC, 1995), pp. 134–66.

54 For a biographical approach to this article, see M. S. Voloshina, 'Zagadka "Nikolaia i Mashi"' [The Riddle of 'Nikolai and Masha'], in *Chekhovskie chteniia v Ialte: Chekhov i XX vek. Sbornik nauchnykh trudov* [Chekhov Readings in Yalta: Chekhov and the 20th Century – A Collection of Scholarly Works], ed. V. A. Bogdanov (Moscow, 1997), pp. 267–76.

55 On this unrealized project, see Chekhov's letter to Suvorin of 11 March 1889; see also remarks in letters to Leikin and Tikhonov from 22 and 31 May 1889, and Hingley, *A Life of Anton Chekhov*, pp. 121–2.

56 See for instance his letters to Alexander and Suvorin of 8 and 14 May 1889, respectively.

57 Rayfield, *Anton Chekhov*, p. 199.

58 Senderovich, 'Chekhov's Name Drama', pp. 31–48. See also Finke, *Seeing Chekhov*, pp. 25–38.

59 See the commentary in *S* VII, pp. 675–8.

60 The professor was partly modelled on one under whom Chekhov had studied, Alexander I. Babukhin (1835–91; *S* VII, p. 670).

3 Explorer and Homebody: Sakhalin Island to Melikhovo

1 Mikhail claims that Chekhov looked over his notes in Mikhail Chekhov, *Anton Chekhov: A Brother's Memoir*, trans. Eugene Alper (New York, 2010), p. 163; originally published as *Vokrug Chekhova: vstrechi i vpechatleniia* [Around Chekhov: Encounters and Impressions] (Moscow, 1933).

2 As Chekhov explains, what he calls the northern part of the island is, geographically speaking, the middle section; he did not explore the uncolonized northern section.

3 See Cathy Popkin, 'Chekhov as Ethnographer: Epistemological Crisis on Sakhalin Island', *Slavic Review*, LI/1 (Spring 1992), pp. 36–51.

4 Anton Chekhov, *Sakhalin Island*, trans. Brian Reeve (Richmond, UK, 2007), p. 65.

5 See Conevery Bolton Valenčius, 'Chekhov's *Sakhalin Island* as a Medical Geography', in *Chekhov the Immigrant: Translating a Cultural Icon*, ed. Michael C. Finke and Julie De Sherbinin (Bloomington, IN, 2007), pp. 299–314.

6 Chekhov, *Sakhalin Island*, pp. 214–15.

7 Ibid., p. 322.

8 Ibid., pp. 97–102.

9 Ernest J. Simmons, *Chekhov: A Biography* (Chicago, IL, 1970), p. 347.

10 See the discussion in Michael C. Finke, *Seeing Chekhov: Life and Art* (Ithaca, NY, 2005), pp. 155–71.

11 M. Chekhov, *Anton Chekhov*, pp. 172–3. See the discussion in Finke, *Seeing Chekhov*, esp. pp. 99–138.

12 See the discussions in Finke, *Seeing Chekhov*, pp. 99–138; John Tulloch, *Chekhov: A Structuralist Study* (Totowa, NJ, 1980); and Petr Dolzhenkov, *Chekhov i pozitivizm* [Chekhov and Positivism] (Moscow, 1998).

13 On duelling, see Irina Reyfman, *Ritualized Violence Russian Style: The Duel in Russian Culture and Literature* (Stanford, CA, 1999).

14 As pointed out by Vladimir Nabokov in Aleksandr Pushkin, *Eugene Onegin*, trans. and commentary Vladimir Nabokov, 2 vols (Princeton, NJ, 1981, repr. 1990), vol. II, p. 17.

15 See his letter to A. I. Smagin, who was trying to help him buy a place in the Ukraine (16 December 1891).

16 On critical reaction to the story, see the editors' commentary in *S* VIII, pp. 456–63.

17 Janet Malcolm, *Reading Chekhov: A Critical Journey* (New York, 2002), p. 193.

18 See the discussion in Finke, *Seeing Chekhov*, pp. 104–6.

19 Ieronim Iasinskii, *Roman moei zhizni. Kniga vospominanii* [The Novel of My Life: A Book of Memoirs] (Moscow and Leningrad, 1926), p. 278.

20 M. Chekhov, *Anton Chekhov*, pp. 189–91.

21 See Robert Louis Jackson, '"If I Forget Thee, O Jerusalem": An Essay on Chekhov's "Rothschild's Fiddle"', in *Anton Chekhov Rediscovered: A Collection of New Studies with a Comprehensive Bibliography*, ed. Savely Senderovich and Munir Sendich (East Lansing, MI, 1987), pp. 35–49.

22 Most notably in A. P. Chudakov, *Chekhov's Poetics*, trans. Edwina Cruise and Donald Dragt (Ann Arbor, MI, 1983); and Nils Åke Nilsson, *Studies in Čechov's Narrative Technique: 'The Steppe' and 'The Bishop'* (Stockholm, 1968).

23 See Wolf Schmid, '"A Vicious Circle": Equivalence and Repetition in "The Student"', excerpt translated by Cathy Popkin, in *Anton Chekhov's*

Selected Stories: Texts of the Stories, Comparison of Translations, Life and Letters, Criticism, ed. Cathy Popkin (New York, 2014), pp. 646–9.

24 *Letopis'* IV.1: 11; N. I. Gitovich, ed., *A. P. Chekhov v vospominaniiakh sovremennikov* [Chekhov in the Memoirs of Contemporaries] (Moscow, 1986), pp. 249–50.

25 According to the diary of F. F. Fidler (*Letopis'* IV.1: 61). On Avilova, see *A. P. Chekhov: entsiklopediia* [A. P. Chekhov: Encylopaedia], ed. V. B. Kataev (Moscow, 2011), pp. 370–71.

26 See Donald Rayfield, *Anton Chekhov: A Life* (Evanston, IL, 2000), esp. pp. 301–4. See also the commentary in *Letters*, pp. 266–7.

27 Especially in Rayfield's 1997 biography of Chekhov, where every ambiguous remark in letters to or from Chekhov is interpreted as evidence of a liaison.

28 I. A. Bunin, 'Chekhov', in *A. P. Chekhov v vospominaniiakh*, ed. Gitovich, p. 492. See also *Letters*, pp. 267–8.

29 See for instance the letter to Suvorin of 27 March 1894.

30 Some of Chekhov's contemporaries, among whom an affair between Yavorskaya and Chekhov was rumoured, saw her in the female character; one even speculated that Yavorskaya, ever seeking publicity, had prompted that reading (*Letopis'* IV.1: 294).

31 See Serge Gregory, *Antosha and Levitasha: The Shared Lives and Art of Anton Chekhov and Isaac Levitan* (Dekalb, IL, 2015), pp. 144–51; and *Letopis'* IV.1: 168.

32 Rosamund Bartlett, ed., *Anton Chekhov: A Life in Letters*, trans. Rosamund Bartlett and Anthony Phillips (London, 2004), p. 339.

33 See the discussion in M. O. Goriacheva, 'A. P. Chekhov i teatr' [A. P. Chekhov and the Theatre], in *A. P. Chekhov: entsiklopediia*, pp. 529–34.

34 See for instance Chekhov's letters to V. V. Bilibin and Ye. M. Shavrova of 1 November 1896.

35 Mariia P. Chekhova, *Iz dalekogo proshlogo* [From the Distant Past] (Moscow, 1960), p. 164; Mikhail P. Chekhov, *Anton Chekhov i ego siuzhety* [Anton Chekhov and His Plots] (Moscow, 1923), p. 126.

36 A succinct list of such echoes may be found in Rayfield, *Anton Chekhov*, pp. 352–3.

37 For a very detailed analysis of the medallion scene in *Seagull*, see Harai Golomb, 'Referential Reflections around a Medallion: Reciprocal Art/Life Embeddings in Chekhov's *The Seagull*', *Poetics Today*, XXI/4 (2000), pp. 681–709.

38 Lydia Avilov, *Chekhov in My Life*, trans. and introd. David Magarshack (New York, 1950). Chekhov further played with this motif in giving Nemirovich-Danchenko a medallion straightforwardly inscribed, 'You have brought my *Seagull* to life. Thank you!' (*'The Seagull' Produced by Stanislavsky: 'The Seagull' by Anton Chekhov, Production Score for the Moscow Art Theatre by K. S. Stanislavsky*, ed. and introd. S. D. Balukhaty, trans. David Magarshack (New York, 1952), p. 82.) For a succinct debunking of Avilova's tale, see Karlinsky's commentary in *Letters*, pp. 266–7.

39 M. Chekhov, *Anton Chekhov*, p. 116; Rayfield, *Anton Chekhov*, pp. 350–51. For a summary of the play's echoes of both the

Lika–Potapenko affair and Levitan's dramatic entanglements, see also Gregory, *Antosha and Levitasha*, pp. 144–51. He associates the character Arkadina with Lidiya Yavorskaya.

40 See the discussion in Finke, *Seeing Chekhov*, esp. ch. 1.

41 Cited in Iurii Sobolev, *Chekhov. Stat'i. Materialy. Bibliografiia* [Chekhov. Articles. Materials. Bibliography] (Moscow, 1930), p. 89. For additional such remarks by Chekhov, see also the memoir of I. L. Leont'ev-Shcheglov, 'Iz vospominanii ob Antone Chekhove' [From Reminiscences about Anton Chekhov], in *A. P. Chekhov v vospominaniiakh*, ed. Gitovich, pp. 59–70, esp. p. 59.

42 I. N. Potapenko, 'Neskol'ko let s A. P. Chekhovym' [Several Years with A. P. Chekhov], in *A. P. Chekhov v vospominaniiakh*, ed. Gitovich, p. 331.

43 Ibid., p. 332.

44 As Robert Louis Jackson points out in '*The Seagull*: The Empty Well, the Dry Lake, and the Cold Cave', in *Chekhov: A Collection of Critical Essays*, ed. R. L. Jackson (Englewood Cliffs, NJ, 1967), p. 102.

45 Nabokov considered this a defect in Chekhov's poetics. The 'fixed labels', 'some special gag which a character repeats throughout the play at the most unexpected or rather expected moments', were adduced as a sign that he was inadequately schooled in the dramatic form; see Vladimir Nabokov, *Lectures on Russian Literature* (New York, 1981), p. 291.

46 Anton Chekhov, 'Peasants', trans. Avrahm Yarmolinsky, in *The Portable Chekhov*, ed. Avrahm Yarmolinsky (New York, 1947; repr. 1968), p. 312.

47 Ibid., p. 351.

48 See the discussion in Finke, *Seeing Chekhov*, pp. 158–9, 163.

49 Robert Coles and Michael Finke, 'A Conversation with Dr Robert Coles: Annton Chekhov and William Carlos Williams', in *Chekhov the Immigrant*, ed. Finke and De Sherbinin, pp. 277–8.

50 See the discussion in Julie De Sherbinin, 'American Iconography of Chekhov', in *Chekhov the Immigrant*, ed. Finke and De Sherbinin, pp. 113–20.

51 See *Letopis'* IV.2: 749, and the discussion in *Letters*, p. 320.

52 As argued in: Savely Senderovich, *Chekhov – s glazu no glaz: istoriia odnoi oderzhimosti A. P. Chekhova. Opyt fenomennologii tvorchestva* [Chekhov Eye to Eye: The Story of an Obsession of A. P. Chekhov – A Study in the Phenomenology of Art] (St Petersburg, 1994); Julie De Sherbinin, *Chekhov and Russian Religious Culture: The Poetics of the Marian Paradigm* (Evanston, IL, 1997); and Vera Zubarev, *A Systems Approach to Literature: Mythopoetics of Chekhov's Four Major Plays* (Westport, CT, 1997).

53 Cited from A. Skaftymov, 'Principles of Structure in Chekhov's Plays', trans. George McCracken Young, in *Chekhov*, ed. Jackson, p. 73.

54 Vsevolod Meyerhold, 'Naturalistic Theater and Theater of Mood', trans. Joyce C. Vining, in *Chekhov*, ed. Jackson, p. 66.

55 K. S. Stanislavsky, 'A. P. Chekhov at the Arts Theater', trans. Cynthia Carlile, in *Anton Chekhov and His Times*, ed. Andrei Turkov (Fayetteville, AR, 1995), p. 126.

56 Introduction to *Cherry Orchard* in *Anton Chekhov's Selected Plays*, trans. and ed. Laurence Senelick (New York, 2005), p. 320.

57 See Thomas Eekman, 'The "Frame Story" in Russian Literature and A. P. Čexov', *Signs of Friendship to Honor A. G. F. van Holk, Slavist, Linguist, Semiotician*, ed. J. J. van Baak (Amsterdam, 1984), pp. 401–17.

58 Charles Isenberg, *Telling Silence: Russian Frame Narratives of Renunciation* (Evanston, IL, 1993), p. 119.

59 As was noted by Zinovii Papernyi, *Zapisnye knizhki Chekhova* [Chekhov's Notebooks] (Moscow, 1976), pp. 286–7. See also John Freedman, 'Narrative Technique and the Art of Story-telling in Anton Chekhov's "Little Trilogy"', in *Critical Essays on Anton Chekhov*, ed. Thomas A. Eekman (Boston, MA, 1989), pp. 102–17; repr. *South Atlantic Review*, LIII/1 (January 1988), pp. 1–18; and Isenberg, *Telling Silence*, p. 112.

60 See Isenberg, *Telling Silence*, p. 124.

61 Anton Chekhov, 'About Love', trans. Constance Garnett, in *Anton Chekhov's Selected Stories*, ed. Popkin, p. 373. See Freedman, 'Narrative Technique', pp. 110–12, and Isenberg's brilliant reading of the cycle, *Telling Silence*, esp. p. 118.

62 Chekhov, 'About Love', p. 378.

4 Yalta and the Moscow Art Theatre Years, Death in Badenweiler

1 For the diary, see A. P. Kuzicheva and E. M. Sakharova, *Melikhovskii letopisets: Dnevnik Pavla Egorovicha Chekhova* [The Melikhov Chronicler: The Diary of Pavel Yegorovich Chekhov] (Moscow, 1995).

2 *Novels*, pp. 442, 440. Vladimir Nabokov praises Chekhov's subtlety in handling this irony in his *Lectures on Russian Literature* (New York, 1981), p. 250.

3 See the editors' commentary in *S* X, pp. 339, 340. For a full treatment of Marks and Chekhov, see I. P. Viduetskaia, *A. P. Chekhov i ego izdatel' A. F. Marks* [A. P. Chekhov and His Publisher A. F. Marks] (Moscow, 1973).

4 *Letopis'*, pp. 575, 778; Donald Rayfield, *Anton Chekhov: A Life* (Evanston, IL, 2000), p. 584.

5 Z. P. Udal'tsova, ed., *Perepiska A. P. Chekhova i O. L. Knipper* [The Correspondence of A. P. Chekhov and O. L. Knipper], 2 vols (Moscow, 2004), vol. I, pp. 46–8; Chekhov's letters of 27 October, 30 October, 1 November 1899; *Letopis'*, p. 588.

6 See the discussion in *Letters*, pp. 280–81, 290; the commentary in *S* XIII, pp. 388–92; and Donald Rayfield, *Chekhov's 'Uncle Vania' and 'The Wood Demon'* (London, 1995), or his *Understanding Chekhov: A Critical Study of Chekhov's Prose and Drama* (Madison, WI, 1999), pp. 165–82.

7 See the reading of this metadramatic scene in Gary Saul Morson, 'Prosaic Chekhov: Metadrama, the Intelligentsia, and *Uncle Vanya*', *Triquarterly*, 80 (Winter 1990/91), pp. 118–59, esp. pp. 153–5.

8 Anton Chekhov, *Twelve Plays*, trans. and ed. Ronald Hingley (Oxford, 1992), p. 210.

9   As stated in a letter to Alexander Lazarev (Gruzinsky) of 1 November
     1889, and also cited from conversations with Chekhov by memoirists
     (see *P* III, pp. 273, 464).

10 See for instance Chekhov's letter to Vladimir Nemirovich-Danchenko
     of 24 November 1899.

11 Udal'tsova, ed., *Perepiska*, vol. I, p. 57.

12 Anton Chekhov, 'About Love', trans. Constance Garnett, in
     *Anton Chekhov's Selected Stories: Texts of the Stories, Comparison of
     Translations, Life and Letters, Criticism*, ed. Cathy Popkin (New York,
     2014), p. 378.

13 See the discussion in Caryl Emerson, 'Chekhov and the Annas', in *Life
     and Text: Essays in Honour of Geir Kjetsaa on the Occasion of His 60th
     Birthday*, ed. E. Egeboerg, A. J. Mørch and O. M. Selberg (Oslo, 1997),
     pp. 121–32. The critical reaction is summarized in the commentary in
     S X, pp. 425–30.

14 M. B. Mirskii, *Doktor Chekhov* [Doctor Chekhov] (Moscow, 2003), p. 35.

15 Rayfield reports that half the Taganrog gymnasium teachers received
     this award: Rayfield, *Anton Chekhov*, p. 507.

16 See ibid., p. 513.

17 Udal'tsova, ed., *Perepiska*, vol. I, p. 67.

18 See the treatment of this period in Rayfield, *Anton Chekhov*, pp. 513–17.

19 O. L. Knipper-Chekhova, 'About A. P. Chekhov', trans. Cynthia
     Carlile, in *Anton Chekhov and His Times*, ed. Andrei Turkov
     (Fayetteville, AR, 1995), p. 207. See also commentary in *S* XIII, p. 429.

20 Rayfield, *Anton Chekhov*, pp. 518–19.

21 As asserts David Magarshack, *Chekhov the Dramatist* (New York,
     1960), p. 253.

22 Rayfield, *Anton Chekhov*, p. 515.

23 V. B. Kataev, 'Tri sestry' [Three Sisters], in *A. P. Chekhov. Entsiklopediia*
     [A. P. Chekhov: Encyclopaedia], ed. V. B. Kataev (Moscow, 2011), p. 237.

24 Rayfield, *Anton Chekhov*, pp. 98–9.

25 Kataev, 'Tri sestry', p. 238.

26 Thus Saul Morson says that 'the wish for an essentially different
     temporality is expressed as the heroines desire to "go to Moscow," which
     is less a specific place than a different temporal dimension'; see his
     Narrative and Freedom: The Shadows of Time (New Haven, CT, 1994),
     pp. 215, 217. See also the remarks of Magarshack on time (*Chekhov
     the Dramatist*, pp. 259–60), and the meticulous analysis of the play's
     temporal structure in C.J.G. Turner, 'Time in *Tri sestry*', *Canadian
     Slavonic Papers / Revue Canadienne des Slavistes*, XXVIII/1 (March
     1986), pp. 64–79.

27 See the commentary, *S* XIII, p. 347. Karlinsky calls it 'one of the three
     conceivable contenders for the title of the greatest play ever written in
     Russian' (*Letters*, p. 386).

28 See Ivan Bunin, *Memories and Portraits*, trans. Vera Traill and
     Robin Chancellor (London, 1951); Ivan Bunin, *About Chekhov: The
     Unfinished Symphony*, trans. Thomas Gaiton Marullo (Evanston, IL,
     2007); Maksim Gorky, *Reminiscences of Tolstoy, Chekhov and Andreyev*
     (New York, 1959).

29 This is Rayfield's forensic diagnosis. He also makes a strong case that Knipper must have been impregnated while she and Chekhov were apart, and that Dr Chekhov would have been aware of this: *Anton Chekhov*, pp. 556–7.

30 Ibid., p. 553.

31 See letters to Savva Morozov (2 February 1902) and Knipper (10 September 1902).

32 Cited from Anton Chekhov, *A Life in Letters*, ed. Rosamund Bartlett, trans. Rosamund Bartlett and Anthony Phillips (London, 2004), p. 502.

33 Udal'tsova, ed., *Perepiska*, vol. II, p. 39.

34 Ibid., p. 133.

35 Ibid., pp. 125, 130.

36 See *P* XI, pp. 527–8; Rayfield, *Anton Chekhov*, pp. 577–8.

37 Such as the journalist Mikhail Pervukhin (*Letopis'*, p. 780).

38 See Chekhov's discussion of Professor Ostroumov's orders in his letter to Suvorin of 17 June 1903.

39 K. S. Stanislavskii, 'A. P. Chekhov v khudozhestvennom teatre. (Vospominaniia)' [A. P. Chekhov in the Art Theatre (Recollections)], in *A. P. Chekhov v vospominaniiakh sovremennikov* [A. P. Chekhov in the Memoirs of Contemporaries], ed. N. I. Gitovich (Moscow, 1986), p. 412. On Chekhov's jubilee, the social institution of literary jubilees in Russia, and Chekhov's treatment of the jubilee in his fiction and drama, see Anna Muza, 'Chekhov's Jubilee and the Jubilee in Chekhov', *Bulletin of the North America Chekhov Society*, XVII/2 (Fall 2010), www.chekhbul.com.

40 For an excellent recent translation of *Cherry Orchard* that includes both variants of Chekhov's text, see Anton Chekhov, *The Cherry Orchard: A Comedy in Four Acts*, trans. Richard Nelson, Richard Pevear and Larissa Volokhonsky (New York, 2015). The volume also offers a concise summary of the changes Stanislavsky wrought and their implications for performance by Nelson (pp. xv–xxi). A persuasive reading of the play that emphasizes Chekhov's original conception of the roles of Charlotte and Lopakhin is Savely Senderovich, 'The Cherry Orchard: Čechov's Last Testament', *Russian Literature*, XXXV (1994), pp. 223–42.

41 See for example Galina Iu. Brodskaia, *Alekseev-Stanislavskii, Chekhov i drugie. Vishnevosadskaia epopeia* [Alekseyev-Stanislavsy, Chekhov and Others: The Cherry Orchard Epopee], 2 vols (Moscow, 2000), esp. vol. II.

42 Maurice Valency, *The Breaking String: The Plays of Anton Chekhov* (London, 1966), p. 284.

43 Ibid., pp. 289–90.

44 Udal'tsova, ed., *Perepiska*, vol. II, pp. 364, 370.

45 See his letter to Knipper of 29 March 1903.

46 Cited from Rayfield, *Anton Chekhov*, p. 594.

47 For speculation on the psychological dynamic that might have culminated in this sense of an empty self, see Finke, *Seeing Chekhov*, esp. pp. 194–200.

48 See Maia Sheikina, '"Davno ia ne pil shampanskogo" ['It's a Long Time since I Drank Champagne'], in *Tselebnoe tvorchestvo A. P. Chekhova*

(Razmyshliaiut mediki i filolologi) [The Healing Art of A. P. Chekhov (Reflections of Physicians and Literary Scholars)], ed. M. E. Burno and B. A. Voskresenskii (Moscow, 1996), pp. 42–5.

49 What follows largely relies on *Letopis'*, pp. 815–17; M. Dolinskii and S. Chertok, 'Poslednii put' Chekhov' [Chekhov's Final Voyage], *Russkaia literatura* [Russian Literature], 2 (1962), pp. 190–201; Rayfield, *Anton Chekhov*, pp. 597–9; and Galina S. Rylkova, 'Oyster Fever: Chekhov and Turgenev', *Bulletin of the North American Chekhov Society*, XXV/1 (Fall 2007), pp. 1–6.

50 Dolinsky and Chertok, 'Poslednii put'', pp. 198–9.

SELECT BIBLIOGRAPHY

The following list of materials available in English, though far from comprehensive, promises a strong start towards a deeper understanding of the life and writings of Anton Chekhov.

1 Select Translations of Chekhov's Writings

The two most useful volumes for a reader who wishes to get to know Chekhov, his writings and the secondary literature on both, are the latest Norton Critical Editions of his stories and plays:

Popkin, Cathy, ed., *Anton Chekhov's Selected Stories: Texts of the Stories, Comparison of Translations, Life and Letters, Criticism* (New York, 2014)
Senelick, Laurence, ed. and trans., *Anton Chekhov's Selected Plays* (New York, 2005)

The broadest selections of stories and plays are to be found in the early twentieth-century translations of Constance Garnett (and others, all out of copyright and very widely republished), and also in Ronald Hingley's translations in the multi-volume *The Oxford Chekhov*, ed. and trans. Ronald Hingley (London, 1965–80), which are annotated and have been republished in accessible paperback editions by Oxford University Press. Nevertheless, I generally prefer the translations of Ann Dunnigan and the team of Richard Pevear and Larissa Volokhonsky, which are far more faithful to Chekhov's lexicon and stylistics. The following recommendations probably reflect a bias towards American English and a reader's perspective on Chekhov's plays rather than one with a view for performance.

Chekhov's Drama
The Cherry Orchard, trans. Richard Nelson, Richard Pevear and Larissa Volokhonsky (New York, 2015)
The Complete Plays, ed. and trans. Laurence Senelick (New York, 2006)
The Essential Plays, trans. Michael Henry Heim (New York, 2003)
The Major Plays, trans. Ann Dunnigan (New York, 1964)

Chekhov's Fiction

Chekhov: The Early Stories, 1883–1888, trans. Harvey Pitcher and Patrick
  Miles (New York, 1982; repr. Oxford, 1994)
The Complete Short Novels, trans. Richard Pevear and Larissa Volokhonsky
  (New York, 2004)
Fifty-two Stories, trans. Richard Pevear and Larissa Volokhonsky
  (New York, 2020)
Selected Stories, trans. Ann Dunnigan (New York, 1960)
The Shooting Party, ed. Julian Symons., trans. A. E. Chamot, revd Symons
  (London, 1986; repr. Chicago, IL, 1987)
Stories, trans. Richard Pevear and Larissa Volokhonsky (New York, 2000)
The Undiscovered Chekhov: Fifty-one New Stories, trans. Peter Constantine
  (London, 2001)
Ward Six and Other Stories, trans. Ann Dunnigan (New York, 1965)

Chekhov's Letters

Bartlett, Rosamund, ed., *Anton Chekhov: A Life in Letters*, trans.
  Rosamund Bartlett and Anthony Phillips (London, 2004)
Heim, Michael Henry, and Simon Karlinsky, trans., *Anton Chekhov's
  Life and Thought: Selected Letters and Commentary*, ed. and
  commentary Simon Karlinsky (Berkeley, CA, 1973, repr. 1975,
  repr. Evanston, IL, 1997)

Chekhov's Non-Fiction

Sakhalin Island, trans. Brian Reeve (Richmond, 2007); includes travel sketches,
  From Siberia, extensive notes, a biographical outline and a selection of
  pertinent letters

II On Chekhov's Life

Bartlett, Rosamund, *Chekhov: Scenes from a Life* (London, 2004)
Hingley, Ronald, *A Life of Anton Chekhov* (Oxford, 1989)
Malcolm, Janet, *Reading Chekhov: A Critical Journey* (New York, 2002)
Rayfield, Donald, *Anton Chekhov: A Life* (Evanston, IL, 2000)
Sekirin, Peter, ed. and trans., *Memories of Chekhov: Accounts of the Writer
  from His Family, Friends and Contemporaries* (Jefferson, NC, 2011)
Simmons, Ernest, *Chekhov: A Biography* (Chicago, IL, 1970)
Turkov, Andrei, ed., *Anton Chekhov and His Times*, trans. Cynthia Carlile
  and Sharon McKee (Fayetteville, AR, 1995)

III On Chekhov's Writings

Apollonio, Carol, and Radislav Lapushin, eds, *Chekhov's Letters: Biography,
  Context, Poetics* (Lanham, MD, 2018)
Barricelli, Jean-Pierre, ed., *Chekhov's Great Plays: A Critical Anthology*
  (New York, 1981)

Bitsilli, Peter, *Chekhov's Art: A Stylistic Analysis*, trans. Toby W. Clyman and
     Edwina Cruise (Ann Arbor, MI, 1983)
Chudakov, Aleksandr P., *Chekhov's Poetics*, trans. Edwina Cruise and Donald
     Dragt (Ann Arbor, MI, 1983)
Finke, Michael C., *Seeing Chekhov: Life and Art* (Ithaca, NY, 2005)
—, and Julie De Sherbinin, eds, *Chekhov the Immigrant: Translating a
     Cultural Icon* (Bloomington, IN, 2007)
Gottlieb, Vera, *Chekhov and the Vaudeville: A Study of Chekhov's One-act Plays*
     (Cambridge, 1982)
—, and Paul Allain, eds, *The Cambridge Companion to Chekhov*
     (Cambridge, 2000)
Jackson, Robert Louis, ed., *Chekhov: A Collection of Critical Essays*
     (Englewood Cliffs, NJ, 1967)
Kataev, Vladimir, *If Only We Could Know! An Interpretation of Chekhov*,
     trans. Harvey Pitcher (Chicago, IL, 2003)
Kramer, Karl, *The Chameleon and the Dream: The Image of Reality in Čexov's
     Stories* (The Hague, 1970)
Lantz, K. A., *Anton Chekhov: A Reference Guide to Literature* (Boston, MA,
     1985)
Lapushin, Radislav, *'Dew on the Grass': The Poetics of Inbetweenness in Chekhov*
     (New York, 2010)
McConkey, James, ed., *Chekhov and Our Age: Responses to Chekhov by
     American Writers and Scholars* (Ithaca, NY, 1984)
Magarshack, David, *Chekhov the Dramatist* (New York, 1960)
Meister, Charles, *Chekhov Criticism, 1880 through 1986* (Jefferson, NC, 1988)
Pitcher, Harvey, *The Chekhov Play: A New Interpretation* [1973]
     (Berkeley, CA, 1985)
—, *Responding to Chekhov: The Journey of a Lifetime* (Cromer, 2010)
Popkin, Cathy, *The Pragmatics of Insignificance: Chekhov, Zoshchenko, Gogol*
     (Stanford, CA, 1993)
Senderovich, Savely, and Munir Sendich, eds, *Anton Chekhov Rediscovered:
     A Collection of New Studies with a Comprehensive Bibliography*
     (East Lansing, MI, 1987)
Senelick, Laurence, *Anton Chekhov*, Macmillan Modern Dramatists
     (London, 1985)
—, *The Chekhov Theatre: A Century of the Plays in Performance*
     (Cambridge, 1997)
De Sherbinin, Julie, *Chekhov and Russian Religious Culture: The Poetics
     of the Marian Paradigm* (Evanston, IL, 1997)
Wellek, René, and Nonna D. Wellek, eds, *Chekhov: New Perspectives*
     (Englewood Cliffs, NJ, 1984)
Winner, Thomas, *Chekhov and His Prose* (New York, 1966)

ACKNOWLEDGEMENTS

Completion of this small book about a big life, during which occurred all manner of personal, professional and global health disruptions, took far longer than it ought to have, and would not have been reached without the positive attitude and patience of Michael Leaman of Reaktion Books, together with editor Phoebe Colley, who helped to get the manuscript in its final shape, and picture editor Alex Ciobanu. I am also grateful for research support from the College of Arts and Sciences at the University of Illinois, Urbana-Champaign. Writer and Chekhov fan Marc Grigorov read a rough, long, early version of the book and, at a critical moment, offered very helpful advice; without it, this book might never have seen light of day. Savely Senderovich, under whose aegis I first published on Chekhov some 35 years ago, offered several valuable corrections. My greatest debt is to my friend and *chekhoved* colleague Radislav Lapushin, who encouraged me to keep at this project and backed up words with all manner of practical help: he answered or pointed me towards answers to many questions, and he read the manuscript, spotting slips and offering useful suggestions. It should go without saying that all remaining faults are mine alone.

PHOTO ACKNOWLEDGEMENTS

The author and publishers wish to express their thanks to the below sources of illustrative material and/or permission to reproduce it. Some locations of artworks are also given below, in the interest of brevity:

Collection of the author: pp. 86, 123, 162; from *Fragments* (*Осколки*), no. 43 (26 October 1896): p. 128; map courtesy John F. Oyler: p. 81; SPUTNIK/Alamy Stock Photo: p. 150; The State Tretyakov Gallery, Moscow: pp. 45, 138.

INDEX

Page numbers in *italics* indicate illustrations